D1534783

THE ISLANDS SERIES

STAFFA

THE ISLANDS SERIES

* Published in the United States by Stackpole
† Published in the United States by David & Charles Inc.

The series is distributed in Australia by Wren Publishing Pty Ltd, Melbourne

STAFFA

by *DONALD B. MacCULLOCH*

DAVID & CHARLES

NEWTON ABBOT LONDON NORTH POMFRET (VT) VANCOUVER

ISBN 0 7153 7101 0
Library of Congress Catalog Card Number 75–26360

© Alastair de Watteville 1975

This fourth revised edition has been included in the Islands series
since it naturally fits the Islands concept; it differs typographically
as it is reproduced by photolithography from the original text. The
first edition (1927) was titled *The Isle of Staffa*. The second (1934)
and third (1957) editions were titled *The Wondrous Isle of Staffa*.

Set in 10 on 12 Baskerville
and printed in Great Britain
by REDWOOD BURN LIMITED, Trowbridge & Esher
for DAVID & CHARLES (HOLDINGS) LIMITED

South Devon House, Newton Abbot, Devon

Published in the United States of America
by DAVID & CHARLES INC.
North Pomfret, Vermont 05053, USA

Published in Canada
by DOUGLAS, DAVID & CHARLES LIMITED
132 Philip Avenue, North Vancouver, BC

CONTENTS

ILLUSTRATIONS

Between pages 156 and 157
A western headland
King George V off Staffa (*David Webster of Oban*)
Arms of Alastair de Watteville of Staffa (*A. E. L. de Watteville*)
The Great Face with MacKinnon's Cave (*Daily Mail*)

IN TEXT

(*Photographs not otherwise acknowledged are from the author's collection*)

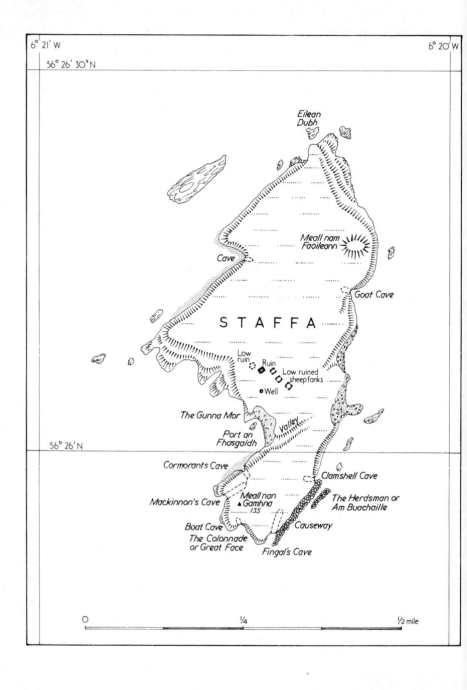

6° 21' W

6° 20' W

56° 26' 30" N

Eilean Dubh

Meall nam Faoileann

Cave

Goat Cave

S T A F F A

Low ruin

Ruin

Low ruined sheep fanks

Well

The Gunna Mor

Port an Fhasgaidh

Valley

56° 26' N

Cormorants Cave

Clamshell Cave

Mackinnon's Cave

Meall nan Gamhna
135

The Herdsman or Am Buachaille

Boat Cave

Causeway

The Colonnade or Great Face

Fingal's Cave

O

¼

½ mile

OWNER'S INTRODUCTION

I became the owner of Staffa largely by luck. Browsing one day at an estate agent's window, amongst the particulars of rather unremarkable flats and houses offered for sale I saw " The Island of Staffa, Argyll." The notice seemed so out of place that for a moment I could not believe that it meant what it said. Then, gradually, I saw the opportunity for what it was, an invitation to bid for that fantastic, legendary island. This was a time for action—not for cool, detached appraisal! Two days later Staffa was mine.

Whatever instinct had taken me to that agent's window yielded a further prize. About a year later I discovered that an ancestor of mine, Colin MacDonald of Boisdale, had owned Staffa from 1785 to 1800. After six generations, but only two real changes of ownership, the island had come back into the family.

Staffa is uninhabited and wholly unspoilt. Declared a Site of Special Scientific Interest by the Nature Conservancy Council, it is right that it should remain so. Preserving its present character, however, need be no bar to making it more accessible. Many of the people who visit Scotland on holiday would like to see Fingal's Cave and other examples of Staffa's amazing structure. At present they can only do so with difficulty. My ambition is to make the island a safer and easier place to reach, whilst not disfiguring it in any way.

Since I approached the author, Mr Donald MacCulloch, in 1974, to suggest that his book on Staffa might be republished he has painstakingly revised the previous edition. In particular he has rewritten most of pages 48 to 51 which refer to the geological history of Staffa, bringing it into line with current informed opinion. I am sincerely grateful to him for all the trouble he has taken, for his enthusiastic support for this new edition, and for the copyright in the work which he has assigned to me so that I could arrange with Messrs David & Charles

for the book to be added to the other titles in their Islands
series.

ALASTAIR DE WATTEVILLE

Kellan Mill,
Aros,
ISLE OF MULL,
ARGYLL
March 1975

The illustration below sets out the succession of owners of Staffa
since records were first kept, and shows how the present owner
is descended from a previous one. Harriet was a daughter by
Colin MacDonald's first marriage; Ranald, later Sir Reginald,
was the eldest son of his second marriage.

OWNERSHIP   DESCENT

OWNERSHIP		DESCENT
Mac Quarries of Ulva	1777	
Captain Dugald Campbell of Auchnabaw	1780	
Colonel Charles Campbell of Barbreck	1785	
Colin MacDonald of Boisdale	1800	
Ranald MacDonald of Boisdale	1816	Alexander MacDonald of Aird and Valley = Harriet
Claude Russell (trustee)	1821	Alexander MacDonald = Flora Macrae
The Forman family of Edinburgh	1968	Rev Kenneth A Mackenzie = Mary Isabella
Rev Gerald Newell	1972	Dr F R W de Watteville = Mary Flora
Alastair de Watteville		Kenneth de Watteville

FOREWORD TO THE THIRD EDITION

by

SIR EDWARD B. BAILEY

F.R.S.

Formerly Director of
the Geological Survey of Great Britain

It so happens that Scotland possesses in Staffa and Glen
Roy the two most eloquent natural monuments found anywhere in the British Isles. In the following pages Mr MacCulloch has set out practically all that is known regarding Staffa.
His unrivalled first-hand acquaintance with this " wondrous
isle " has been supplemented by tireless research into docu-
mentary evidence, both published and unpublished. He has,
moreover, a happy knack of communicating interest in his pursuit of knowledge. Much of his book is a veritable detective
story, and in reading it one shares the author's pleasure in the
successful pursuit of one clue after another.

It is a commentary on the medieval outlook on Nature that,
in spite of the age-old proximity of culture in Iona, local Gaels
and Norsemen seem to have taken Staffa for granted. Still,
there are indications of their thoughts on the subject afforded
by the names of Staffa itself and of Fingal's Cave. The island
was actually inhabited in desultory fashion until early in the
nineteenth century. Mr MacCulloch's treatment of this dour
human struggle supplies one of the most arresting features of
his narrative.

Staffa was " discovered " for the outer world in 1772. Immediately the island leapt into fame, and from 1773 onwards
it has continued to be an object of pilgrimage—truly remarkable
under the early conditions of transport that are well described
by the author. There were at the start two main reasons for
its appeal, since towards the end of the eighteenth century there
had emerged a new appreciation of the charm alike of science
and of scenery. The foundations of geology were just being
laid, and the idea of extinct volcanoes in countries such as

France and Scotland was for many years to become hotly debated. The geologist drew much of interest from Staffa, while it inspired the poet, painter and composer. It may be mentioned here that Jules Verne in his novel *The Green Ray*, which culminated on Staffa, supplies the first known reference to the much debated phenomenon named in its title. It is now accepted that the green ray is a genuine product of refraction and not a mere optical delusion.

To-day probably most visitors will definitely wish to learn the story of Staffa as a lava which long since poured out over volcanic ash and, dissected by shrinkage cracks in the act of cooling, has eventually come under the attack of the Atlantic Ocean. This information the author furnishes, taking into consideration the adjacent Isle of Mull. " To deal with the geology of Staffa," he justly remarks, " without mentioning that of Mull would be like describing a twig without mentioning the tree from which it grew." His statements on the geology of these two islands are based upon the most modern evidence.

Finally, I cannot think of a more appropriate name than MacCulloch for the author of an up to date account of Staffa, since it conjures up in imagination Dr John MacCulloch, the great pioneer in West Highland geology.

E. B. BAILEY

February 1957

PREFACE TO THE FIRST EDITION

THIS BOOK owes its origin to a fortnight spent on the Island of Staffa during the month of June, 1922, along with my father and Mr Dan Cameron, a native of Tobermory, who were inspecting and repairing the appliances for the safety of tourists, fitted by Messrs MacBrayne, Ltd, the West Highland Steamship Co.

During our sojourn, I photographed the most interesting features of the island, and some time afterwards was asked to publish these photographs with a description of each place of interest, but on searching for reliable information discovered that it was very scarce, and difficult to obtain. A few books contain a brief reference to the subject, but no single book has been found devoted wholly to Staffa, with the exception of a series of nine coloured aquatint views of the island drawn by William Daniell, A.R.A., which, along with a brief description, were bound together and published in 1818 at the price of £2 os. od. per volume. Copies of this publication are now very scarce.

The sources from which the information has been obtained are many and varied, whilst fourteen years having been spent sailing on the "Staffa and Iona" route by my father has enabled me to obtain a considerable amount of oral testimony, added to what has come under my personal observation.

The written and oral information obtained having reached beyond the bounds of a single article, I have taken it upon myself to embody it in book form, trusting that such information, along with the illustrations, may prove useful to anyone having an interest in this remarkable island, which ranks amongst the foremost of the world's natural wonders.

In compiling this book every care has been taken to procure trustworthy information.

Under these circumstances I must beg the indulgence of the reader for any shortcomings on my part.

Finally, I wish to offer my thanks to Professor J. W. Gregory, F.R.S., who occupies the Chair of Geology in the University of Glasgow, for examining the geological sections, and to Mr

John McCormick, F.S.A. SCOT., author of *The Island of Mull*, etc., for examining the topographical and other parts of this book.

DONALD B. MacCULLOCH

GLASGOW,

January, 1927.

PREFACE TO THE SECOND EDITION

Since the first edition of this book appeared I have paid several brief visits to Staffa and have continued my search for interesting information regarding the island. The result has been the accumulation of so much additional material that this edition may be regarded as a new book. It has been re-written entirely and enlarged to about three times its original size. It also contains eight additional illustrations—seven reproductions of rare old prints of Staffa and one aerial view of the island. I have modified the title slightly: the previous title was *The Island of Staffa*. The present title suggested itself by reason that the island inspires wonder and wondering admiration.

One of my most valuable "finds" since the first edition appeared has been that of a *very* rare publication in folio form (eighteen inches by twelve inches) written in French, entitled *L'Ile de Staffa et sa grotte basaltique*, by C. L. F. Panckoucke. The copy which I had the privilege to peruse is believed by librarians to be the only one in Britain; there is no copy in the British Museum. Panckoucke was a Chevalier of the Legion of Honour and a Correspondent of the Academy of Archaeology of Rome. His folio on Staffa forms one of six parts describing a tour of the Hebrides, which were published in Paris in 1831. He visited Staffa on the *Maid of Morven* from Glasgow and must have had a busy time during his stay, for, in addition to thirty-two pages of letterpress, his folio contains ten full-page plates showing views of the island, "sketched on the spot by C. L. F. Panckoucke," and two full-page plates of diagrams. These drawings are quaint and interesting. His description of the island and his geological conclusions and suggestions are also very interesting. He quotes the works of the Continental geologists who had visited Staffa before him, but apparently he was not aware of the detailed geological descriptions and dimensions of Staffa given by Dr John MacCulloch in his *Western Islands of Scotland* (1819) and *Highlands and Western Islands of Scotland* (1824), as he does not mention them.

Until recently I was unaware that my family connection with Staffa dates back for about eighty years. From 1854 to 1857, inclusive, my paternal grandfather served as Chief Officer on the paddle steamer *Maid of Lorn*, later re-named *Plover*, which plied on the Glasgow-to-Inverness weekly route at that time, and included an extended sail from Oban to Staffa and Iona in her voyage, during the summer months. On one occasion she broke a paddle shaft when off Treshnish Point but managed to reach Tobermory under sail. In addition, my maternal grandmother was born and brought up in a small and very isolated clachan, called Baliacrach, on the north-west coast of Mull, north of Staffa. Indeed, this region holds me with close ties of friendship in addition to its scenic attractions.

In most books which mention Staffa, the reference to the island is so brief that the quotations from these sources given herein contain the substance, if not the whole, of the reference. I have therefore thought it unnecessary to include a bibliography. The title of book, or other source of reference, is attached to each quotation, and where any book has appeared worthy of perusal by the reader I have indicated so.

I have found so many willing helpers in my continued search for information regarding Staffa that I regret lack of space does not permit of individual mention, and can only hope that this little book will repay them to some extent for their goodness. I feel in duty bound, however, to acknowledge my indebtedness to Mr G. E. Troup, of Edinburgh, for granting me free access to his unique library of books relating primarily to St Columba and Iona, within which are many interesting references to Staffa. This collection is probably the finest in existence dealing with these subjects, containing, as it does, many rare and valuable works, including the folio of Panckoucke already mentioned.

To the late Professor J. W. Gregory, F.R.S., who kindly assisted me in connection with the first edition, I also owe a special debt of gratitude for valuable assistance and advice while revising and enlarging the sections of this book dealing with the geology of Staffa. His tragic death by drowning in June 1932, when his canoe capsized in the rapids of the Urubamba River (which flows past the famed Machu Picchu, lost city of the Incas), Northern Peru, while leading a geological expedition to examine and study the volcanic centres of the Andes, occurred while I was engaged on this work. He was a generous-hearted man of science of world-wide repute who also won fame as an intrepid explorer. To me, his encouragement, his guiding suggestions and his candid but kindly criticisms will always remain cherished memories.

I am also deeply indebted to Professor E. B. Bailey, F.R.S., who succeeded Professor Gregory in the Chair of Geology in the University of Glasgow, for favouring me with a considerable amount of valuable information and explaining points on which I was not clear regarding the very complex geology of Mull, which includes that of Staffa. He also read over the revised and enlarged geology sections of this book, in typescript, on which he made valuable criticisms and suggestions. Professor Bailey played a major part during the Geological Survey of Mull and Staffa and compiled the Geological *Memoirs* of these islands.

My special thanks are also due to Mr Alastair Grant, a literary Gael and an old school companion, for very helpful advice on many points, and to Mr Dugald MacArthur, a native of Iona, for assistance in my search for early references to Staffa, some of which were very difficult to locate.

DONALD B. MacCULLOCH

GLASGOW,
April, 1934.

PREFACE TO THE THIRD EDITION

More than twenty years have elapsed since the last edition of this book was published, excluding a small, popular edition, and it has been a very eventful period in human history. Violence and change seem to have been the ruling factors. Previously-held ideals and values, which were thought to be immutable, have dissolved in the clash of conflicting beliefs and with them have faded many of the old standards of faith, respect and reverence. National frontiers and national names have changed with such bewildering frequency in the turbulence of warfare and power politics that national geography has become a real quandary. So far, there does not appear to be any sign of abatement in this state of flux in things mental and material.

Amid all this tumult of wars of arms and wars of ideals there is at least one retreat of solace for the perplexed who, though not dismayed by the present and future, seek intervals of relaxation free from human distractions, and this is in exploring and pondering the wonders, the grandeur and the beauties of Nature:

> Happy the man whose lot it is to know
> The secrets of earth. He hastens not
> To work his fellows' hurt by unjust deeds,
> But with rapt admiration contemplates
> Immortal Nature's ageless harmony,
> And how and when her order came to be.

Fortunately, there still are many persons who are attracted by this philosophy and adventure, and pilgrims continue to find their way to the shrines of Nature like the wonderful little Island of Staffa with its amazing natural colonnades and its awesome caves. Indeed, during the past few years there has been so many visitors to Staffa that a demand has arisen for a complete history of the island dealing with its varied aspects.

This new edition of my book on Staffa is completely revised and enlarged and includes new photographs. A considerable amount of new material has been introduced, including a new chapter dealing with early transport to Staffa and the island's ownership.

Since the previous edition was published, I have visited the island frequently to refresh my memory and explore some parts more minutely, but mainly for the pleasure of roaming over the island and viewing the surrounding scenery. More often have I viewed it from the north end of Iona, rising sheer from the deep blue sea in a tabular mass of vivid bronze against a pale azure sky in the amber glow of a westering sun. Also, from the same viewpoint, in times of storm when the mist and rain had cleared sufficiently to reveal it in its element of mighty billows crashing white on its dark cliffs and scud racing across a leaden sky.

Where any statement in this edition differs from the corresponding statement in previous editions, the present one should be regarded as being more correct.

When preparing this new edition I had the privilege, once again, of access to some new and rare sources of information about Staffa in the unrivalled library of books dealing with Iona, Staffa, and cognate subjects, belonging to the late Mr G. E. Troup, c.b.e., of Edinburgh. He also advised me at intervals of interesting items relating to Staffa which he located during his researches into the history of Iona. His death occurred when I was completing this work. Our long friendship and his goodness in laying open to me invaluable sources of reference are memories which I shall always cherish.

I must also express a deep debt of gratitude to Sir Edward B. Bailey, f.r.s., formerly Director of Geological Survey of Great Britain, who assisted me when writing the geological sections of the last edition, for his goodness in reading over and making valuable suggestions on the revised parts of this edition dealing with that subject, thus bringing up-to-date these parts of this book. He is one of the highest authorities on the geology of Mull and Staffa.

Another good friend, Mr Robert W. Munro, of Edinburgh, kindly led me to new and valuable sources of information regarding Staffa which he located in his diligent research into old manuscripts and documents on various subjects relating to the West Highlands and Islands.

PREFACE TO THE FOURTH EDITION

It is with pleasure that I have agreed with Mr Alastair de Watteville, the present owner of the Island of Staffa, to have a new and up-to-date edition of this book published, the only book ever published wholly devoted to Staffa. The third edition went out of print in 1967 and copies are now very difficult to obtain.

Mr de Watteville is showing considerable enthusiasm and energy in bringing to the notice of the public, especially visitors to Scotland, this famous little island which ranks among the principal natural wonders of the world.   It is good to learn that he intends to leave Staffa in its natural state and accessible to visitors.

This publicity for Staffa is now more than ever necessary because Caledonian-MacBrayne, the shipping company, have decided to withdraw and not replace their now aged turbine steamer *King George V* which, as successor to previous pleasure steamers, plied during the summer months since 1936 on the Staffa and Iona route.   Thus Staffa is now more isolated than it has been for more than one hundred years.

I wish Mr de Watteville every success in his worthy endeavour to make the wonderful island of Staffa a place of pilgrimage for all persons who admire the outstanding works of nature.

DONALD B. MACCULLOCH

" *Staffa,*"
    6 Arnwood Drive,
        GLASGOW G12 OXY.
        1975

CHAPTER I

INTRODUCTORY

OFF THE WEST COAST OF SCOTLAND lies a lonely little island which has probably won more world-wide renown than any other natural feature of Britain. This famed islet is Staffa. Foam-girt by stormy Hebridean seas, it rises serene, presenting colonnaded cliffs and caves, amazing not only in size but in form and symmetry. Since the island was "discovered," in 1772, its most imposing rock structure, Fingal's Cave, has ranked among the foremost of the natural wonders of the world. Even so, the island has other very interesting geological formations which would have gained distinction were it not for this minster of the sea.

My first acquaintance with Staffa was made at the tender age of about three months. On that occasion I viewed it from the paddle steamer *Grenadier*, which plied on this route for many years, while on my way to spend a holiday on the neighbouring island of Iona. Naturally, I have to accept the evidence of others regarding that visit, and I do not remember if the wonderful formation of Staffa had any effect upon my very youthful mind. I like to believe that, unconsciously, I absorbed impressions which were to be engraved more deeply later in life.

That early acquaintance with Staffa was the first of my many brief visits to the island by steamer from Oban and by "lugsail" and motor boat from Iona, landing on some occasions and being prevented from landing at other times by the heavy surge breaking on its rocky coast. Although I viewed its principal features and explored it to some extent during those brief visits, I was unable to explore the island thoroughly and at leisure until the sojourn which suggested this book, namely, a fortnight's stay on Staffa, in a temporary shelter, during the month of June 1922, along with my father and a friend. My eagerness to land on Staffa on that occasion, for a prolonged stay, was whetted by our inability to effect a landing at our first attempt, owing to the heavy Atlantic swell which could be seen crashing at the foot of the cliffs and sending white spray high into the air. On our second venture, however, two days later, we were favoured with an ideal day and landed safely with our gear from the paddle steamer *Fusilier* on to this lonely little Hebridean isle.

Staffa is a small uninhabited member of the Inner Hebrides, lying approximately north and south, about seven miles west of the nearest point of the Island of Mull, and about six miles north by east of the Island of Iona. The nearest inhabited island is Gometra, which lies about four miles to the north-east.

Although it has won so much renown, Staffa is only about three quarters of a mile long by about one quarter of a mile broad at its broadest part, and one and a half miles in circumference. Its superficial area is about seventy-one acres and its shape is that of an irregular oval. Its highest elevation, of about one hundred and thirty-five[1] feet above sea level at mean tide, is at the precipitous south end, from which point it slopes down gradually towards the north, except for a small eminence, Meall nam Faoileann, at the north-east. At the extreme north end it contracts to a low and comparatively flat point. The greater part of the coastline is formed of columnar cliffs, but the formation is most striking at the south and south-east.

It is now generally agreed that the name "Staffa" is derived from the Old Norse words *stafr*, meaning "pillar" or "post" (the old Norse buildings were of wood), and *ey*, meaning " island," hence " pillar island." The word *stafr* also means "staff" or "stick." Several far-fetched derivations of the name "Staffa" have been suggested, but there is little reason to doubt the one given above, as Norse place-names are numerous throughout the Hebrides. Indeed, most of the islands in the neighbourhood of Staffa have Norse names.

[1] The Ordnance Survey gives the height as one hundred and thirty-five feet, while the Admiralty charts give it as one hundred and twenty-nine feet. This difference in height really occurs between the different datum-lines used. The Ordnance Survey datum is mean sea level, while the Admiralty datum is high water spring tides. As spring tides here range about twelve feet, the difference between the two datum lines is six feet, which makes the two heights given for the island equal.

The earliest reliable account of the Western Isles, or Hebrides, is Donald Monro's *Description of the Western Isles of Scotland, called Hybrides*, and in none of the published editions of that book is there any mention of Staffa, although he mentions several of the neighbouring islands. Donald Monro held the office of High Dean of the Western Islands and his book is an account of his pastoral round made in 1549. There is also no mention of Staffa in Bishop Leslie's *History of Scotland* (1578), although he mentions the Treshnish Isles which are only about five miles from Staffa. "Carneborg," one of the Treshnish Isles, is also mentioned by John of Fordun, in 1380, but he does not mention Staffa.

The earliest reference to Staffa in print would seem to be a brief mention in George Buchanan's *History of Scotland*, first published in 1582. In describing the Hebrides, Buchanan says: "Four miles from Gometra on the south stands Stafa." There is no evidence that Buchanan ever was near Staffa himself, and he tells us that he derived his information concerning the Hebrides from Dean Monro, whom he describes as " a pious and diligent person." Thus it may seem rather surprising at first sight that the Dean does not mention Staffa in his book. This apparent anomaly was resolved by my good friend, Mr Robert W. Munro, Edinburgh, who discovered a hitherto unpublished manuscript of Monro's *Description of the Western Isles*, in which there occurs this mention of Staffa:

Narrest this Gometra be four mile of sea to ye south lyis ane Ile callit Stafay half mile lang, abundant of girsing of ye mekle vine, gude heavin for hieland galayis, utter fyne for storme and symmer and wynter scheling also.

Dean Monro's *Description* was not printed and published until 1774, and Buchanan must have had access to a manuscript containing the above account of Staffa. It is rather surprising that his account of Staffa does not appear in any published edition of Dean Monro's book. The only criticism I have to make of it is that the island has no good sheltered haven: but the Dean would probably have visited it when the weather was calm and he may therefore be referring to the bay in the south-west of Staffa, called Port an Fhasgaidh ("shelter bay"), but which is really exposed to the prevailing winds of this region.

The earliest map showing Staffa which I have been able to locate is Blaeu's map of Scotland in his Atlas published in 1654. On it the name is spelt "Stafa." On the first printed map of the Western Isles, by Abraham Ortelius (1570), appear the names Iona, Carndeburg (Cairnburg), Ulway (Ulva), but not Staffa. These islands mentioned are all in the vicinity of Staffa.

Sacheverell, Governor of the Isle of Man, who visited Mull and Iona in 1688, describes the view from the top of Dun I, the highest hill on Iona, as a " prospect of several islands of different form, some of them high and craggy." Anyone who has viewed the surrounding scenery from the top of Dun-I will recall that Staffa is the island which merits most the latter part of this description. Yet there is no indication in Sacheverell's account of his tour in this region that he had heard of the name or significance of Staffa. It is also surprising that Martin Martin, the Skye doctor, who toured the Hebrides *circa* 1695, does not mention Staffa when describing the surrounding islands in his *Description of the Western Isles of Scotland*, published in 1703. His book is certainly one of the most valuable of contemporary accounts of these islands.

Another early traveller in Scotland, who has left an account of his visit to Mull and Iona, was Richard Pococke, Bishop of Ossory, Ireland, who came during the month of June 1760— but here again there is no mention of Staffa. Although Pococke's tours in Britain were made between the years 1743 and 1761, his manuscripts were not published until the latter part of the nineteenth century. This delay in publication has allowed Pennant to be regarded as the first systematic explorer of comparatively unknown regions of Great Britain, whereas Pococke is more worthy of the credit: his sketch of Iona Cathedral is believed to be the earliest of this subject in existence. Apparently Pennant knew of, and consulted, Pococke's manuscripts when preparing for his first tour through Scotland, in 1769.

Staffa's remarkable geological formation would surely have aroused the enthusiasm of this Irish prelate, had he seen it or heard of it, for he had visited the Giant's Causeway, Ireland, in 1747 and again in 1752, and found it so interesting that he not only communicated descriptions of it to the Royal Society but suggested a theory (resembling crystallisation) to account for its formation.

The inhabitants of Iona and western Mull were surely aware of the peculiar structure of Staffa, but apparently did not regard it as of any importance, or they would have mentioned it to Pococke. In all his travels he was very curious regarding all features of interest, both the works of man and nature. He was a keen antiquarian and possessed a valuable collection of fossils and minerals. He mentions that when nearing Bunessan, in Mull, on his way to Iona Ferry, he noticed " several hills about Ardscrinish which resembled the Giant's Causeway, in irregular pillars," and reflected sufficiently to remark, " it would be curious to know if there is anything of the kind in Ila which is directly opposite the Causeway." So we can assume that Staffa was not regarded as of importance by the neighbouring islanders at the time of Pococke's visit to Iona in 1760.

That the inhabitants of the adjacent islands were acquainted with Staffa previous to 1772 is evident from the statement of Sir Joseph Banks, who "discovered" the island in that year. He says that on asking his local guides for the name of its greatest cavern, it was readily given to him, which indicates that the cave, and therefore the island, was well-known to them. Dr Johnson, the great lexicographer, in *A Journey to the Western Islands of Scotland* (1773), says:

When the islanders [of Ulva] were reproached with their ignorance or insensibility of the wonders of Staffa they had not much to reply. They had indeed considered it little, because they had always seen it; and none but philosophers, nor they always, are struck with wonders otherwise than by novelty.

Being in close proximity to Iona, the wonderful formation of Staffa could hardly remain unknown to some of the many voyagers bound for the sacred isle, as for many centuries Iona has been an important place to those of Christian faith. Even St Columba, who lived during the sixth century, and his zealous apostles, were surely familiar with Staffa, as it is distinctly visible from Iona. It also lies directly on the route which these hardy pioneering servants of the Master would follow when sailing northward on their venturesome voyages in frail coracles to spread the Gospel and civilisation throughout the then heathen Hebrides and mainland of Scotland. It is surprising, therefore, that Adamnan does not mention any island which can be identified as Staffa in his famous *Life of Saint Columba*.

There is some evidence, however, for believing that the monks of Iona not only knew of Staffa but regarded it with some affection. According to Panckoucke, a French visitor to Staffa in 1830, the townships of Stäfa and Jona, on the shores of Lake Zurich, Switzerland, were given their names by Iona monks who founded two settlements there. (In early descriptions of Staffa, the name is usually spelt with one *f*, and in those early writings the letter *j* is often substituted for the letter *i*). This theory regarding the origin of the names of these two Swiss towns is quite reasonable, as the monks of Iona spread to many parts of Europe, especially when they were being persecuted by Danish and Norwegian pirates, during the eighth and ninth centuries, and later, when they were expelled from Iona by the zealots of the Reformation. It must have been Iona monks of an early period, probably some of those who fled from the Norsemen, or Northmen, who gave the Swiss towns of Stäfa and Jona their names, because the records of these Swiss towns go back for about nine centuries. It is worthy of note that the earliest manuscript of Adamnan's *Life of St Columba* is in the public library of Schauffhausen, Switzerland, about thirty miles north of Jona.

Although unrecorded in literature previous to the time of Dean Monro, the Norse name of the little island of columns—Staffa—indicates that its remarkable formation, as well as its actual existence, was known as far back as the time of the Norse possession and settlement of the Western Isles of Scotland, which lasted from about 890 until 1266. The Western Isles were thus under Norse rule for about four hundred years; and this rule ended nearly seven hundred years ago. Even previous to that time Staffa was probably known to, and may have been a rendezvous of, those piratical Vikings, both Danes and Norwegians, who preceded the actual settlers. Those pagan sons of Odin and Thor swept the western seas of Scotland periodically in their dreaded dragon ships (thirty or forty men

in each clinker-built boat), always leaving behind them a trail
of death and destruction. Their names are significant,
Thorfinn the Skull-cleaver, Eric the Bloody-axe, Einar the
Despoiler.

> The blade of the bloody Norse
> Has strewn the shores of the Gael
> With many a floating corse
> And with many a woman's wail.

Staffa was surely known locally during those early times, yet
the first authentic record we have of its remarkable formation
exciting the interest of any one is not until the year 1772, when
a Mr Leach, an English gentleman, while on a visit to Drimnin,
in Morvern, happened to go near it on one of his fishing ex-
cursions. Being struck with the singularity of its appearance,
he landed on it, and examined it particularly. A few days
after Mr Leach's visit, Sir Joseph Banks landed at Drimnin,
while on his way northward on a Natural History expedition
to Iceland, when Mr Leach told him of what he had seen; and
it was that famous man of science who, on his return to London,
first brought the wonders of the island to the notice of the public.
He is usually referred to as the discoverer of Staffa.

When one views Staffa from a distance, even of one mile,
nothing remarkable may be noticed except, perhaps, the dark
openings of its huge caves. From the south-east it appears like
a dismantled giant warship lying at anchor, heading south-west.
On coming closer, however, its peculiar formation appears.
It is seen to be of a threefold character. From a basement of
tuff, or rock composed of volcanic debris, rise colonnades of
basaltic rock, which form the faces of the cliffs and the entrances
to the most important caves. These colonnades, in turn, are
overlaid with a mass of amorphous basalt.

As lofty cliffs form the greater part of the coastline, there are
only a few places where visitors may land with safety. There
is no sandy beach on Staffa, the coast consisting of rugged black
and brown weathered basaltic rock and a few small patches of
coarse black shingle in the creeks. The usual landing place is
at Clamshell Cave, in the south-east of the island, but even here
fairly calm weather is necessary. The dull movement of the
Atlantic swell causes the sea level to rise and fall on this rocky

coast at all times and is liable to damage a boat if precautions are not taken.   Incidentally, it is extremely difficult to convey an effective impression of the unbroken swell of the sea by means of a photograph; the undulations are so smooth that the outlines blend into one another and there is not sufficient contrast of highlight and shadow to indicate height or depth.   On some of the photographs in this book the sea appears to be comparatively calm, though actually the swell was deep and heavy. Unless during rough weather, it does not break on the rocks, but boils up quickly, though quietly, to a considerable height, sluicing over the rock surfaces and then falling back with tremendous suction, or undertow.

During the summer months tourists are landed on Staffa daily by motor boats from the pleasure steamer for about one hour, weather permitting, but in this brief period only a glimpse of the island can be obtained.   These daily visitors are not allowed to climb to the summit plateau of the island or view the magnificent cliff scenery of its western coast, as time does not permit.   To explore Staffa thoroughly one requires to camp on the island or else reside with some of the neighbouring islanders and sail across when the weather is favourable.   Apart from these brief visitations during summer, Staffa is left entirely to the shaggy sheep and cattle, the seabirds and the stormy Hebridean seas.

The surface of the island is composed of an irregular grassy plateau which forms a good pasturage for sheep and cattle belonging to the neighbouring islanders.   The highest eminence at the north end, or rather north-east, is called Meall nam Faoileann (Gaelic for "the rounded hill of the seagulls"). It is merely what Dr Johnson might have called an inconsiderable protuberance.   The highest part of the southern end of the island, near Fingal's Cave, is called Meall nan Gamhna ("the rounded hill of the stirks").   As this latter point is the highest on the island, it is surmounted by the usual cairn of stones.

There is one small spring well on Staffa, which I have indicated on the map of the island, as it may prove useful to anyone landing without a supply of fresh water.   Abraham Mills, a vulcanist, who visited Staffa in 1788, says: " On the island are two springs of excellent fresh water"; but I failed to locate a second well, which apparently was at the north end of the island. The water in the one which I found and utilised is rather insipid, owing to the thin soil through which the water percolates.

All those who admire the work of Nature will be amply repaid for their exertions by exploring Staffa at leisure. Indeed, to appreciate fully the solemnity of a place like Fingal's Cave, one must visit it alone and muse upon it, as it is a wonder and not a novelty. Should any visitor feel disappointed with Staffa on his first visit, however, and fail to understand why it has received so many glowing tributes from eminent personalities in every walk of life, let him consider whether or not this disappointment is due to his own defective perception rather than to any lack of splendour in the scene: " it is only as men seek that they truly find." A lady once said to Turner, the famous artist: " I never see sunsets the way you see them, according to your pictures." Turner replied, "Quite possible, madam, but don't you wish you could?"

The natural grandeur, the wonderful structures and the significance of the whole island of Staffa are too diversified to be appreciated fully in one hasty visit, and anyone who has the opportunity should return there as often as possible, as the fascination of the scene grows rather than diminishes with each succeeding visit. When viewing a scene like Staffa we should not only look at it but look into it and ponder on the mighty forces that formed it. Although the man of science may try to estimate the age of Staffa in eras, epochs, or even years, to the layman with his limitations of human history it appears as a solemn sanctuary where time stands still.

When viewed from the sea, the southern part of the island seems to possess an indefinable brooding, or awesome, atmosphere, which cannot be conveyed by any photograph, and the few artists who have made Staffa the subject of a picture do not appear to have had much success in capturing this impression. The reason may be that the scene is grand and austere rather than beautiful.

Some readers may think that if Staffa is so obviously impressive the detailed descriptions given in this book are unnecessary, in the sense that " good wine needs no bush." This opinion, however, is a superficial conception of the subject. Those who wish to know and appreciate its full significance will, I hope, find interest in learning something about its origin, the prodigious forces and aeons of time that have gone to its shaping, its unusual aspects and how it has appealed to persons qualified to judge.

CHAPTER II

DISCOVERY OF STAFFA BY SIR JOSEPH BANKS

As mentioned in the previous chapter, the merit of Staffa's discovery as an object of scientific interest and picturesque grandeur was due to Sir Joseph Banks, who landed on the island in August 1772, while on a Natural History expedition to Iceland; he was really Mr Banks at that time and only twenty-nine years of age.

Previous to that voyage, Banks had accompanied Captain Cook, as chief of the scientific department on board the *Endeavour*, during Cook's first voyage round the world. Banks is described in *Cook's Voyages* as a naturalist, which in his case is a very appropriate term, as he was one of those early men of science who took an interest in all natural phenomena, though his special subject was botany. Botany Bay, in Australia, was so named by Cook when Banks told him that all the plants he found there were new to science; Cook's actual words are: " The great quantity of plants Mr Banks and Dr Solander found in this place occasioned my giving it the name of Botany Bay." One of the headlands forming the entrance to Botany Bay is called Cape Banks, and his name occurs also in the title of several other islands, straits, etc., in Australia and the Pacific. His name is associated with the Hebrides in the northern hemisphere—Staffa—and also with the Hebrides in the southern hemisphere—Banks Islands, a small group, also of volcanic origin, situated close to the New Hebrides, in the South Pacific.

That first round-the-world expedition of Cook's, which lasted from 1768 to 1771, was organised by the Royal Society and sent to the Pacific with the task of observing the transit of Venus as its main object. The expedition undertook a considerable amount of other scientific work, however, and with such satisfactory results that a second expedition was undertaken immediately. Banks was asked to organise the scientific section of the second expedition, but neither he nor his assistants

accompanied Cook on his second voyage. He had a disagreement with the Admiralty regarding accommodation for his
staff and their equipment, and also aroused the jealousy of
certain naval officers. Fortunately, his labours were not in
vain, for he planned and carried out a Natural History expedition to Iceland and made use of the staff and equipment which
he had intended for Cook's second voyage. It was while
northward-bound for Iceland at that time that he "discovered"
Staffa. Contrary wind and tide caused him to sail into the
Sound of Mull on the night of 12th August 1772. He anchored opposite Drimnin, in Morvern, and in the morning he
and his fellow-scientists were invited ashore to breakfast with
the local laird. It was during the conversation on that occasion
that Banks was told about Staffa, and his eagerness to see it
caused him to set off in the laird's boat by one o'clock of the
same day.

Sir Joseph Banks was one of the leading men of science of his
day, and is one of the great men in the history of botany. His
work was acknowledged by his election as President of the Royal
Society in 1778—the highest honour in the British realm of
science—and he retained that office until his death in 1820.
In 1781 he was knighted. It was Banks who organised the
expedition of Bligh in the *Bounty* which was really a botanical
expedition, and it was through his influence that Bligh was
appointed to command it. Although Bligh was a martinet, or
even a tyrant, he was really a very capable and intelligent officer.

Banks's description of his discovery and exploration of Staffa
was first presented to the public along with six drawings in a
book, in the first of two volumes of Pennant's *Tour in Scotland
and a Voyage to the Hebrides in 1772*, published in Chester in
1774-5 and dedicated to Sir Joseph Banks. Pennant's *Tour*,
including Banks's account of Staffa, can also be found in
Pinkerton's *Voyages*, VOL. III, published in 1809.

The first published reference to Banks's discovery of Staffa,
including information supplied by himself, really appeared in
The Scots Magazine (the leading news publication in Scotland at
that time), VOL. XXXIV (1772), p. 637, as follows:

On the 29th of October arrived at Edinburgh from Iceland, and other
places in the north seas, where they had been on a voyage for discoveries, Mr

Staffa from the south east showing, on extreme right, the mouth of Fingal's Cave, with the islands of Gometra (left) and Ulva behind and, in the far distance, the north-west promontory of Mull

(*Above*) Fingal's Cave according to Sir Joseph Banks, who discovered it in 1772; here printed the right way round, the original (reversed in printing) is a mirror image; (*below*) a nineteenth-century engraving of the mouth of Fingal's Cave; the figure with the cockade is thought to be Sir Reginald MacDonald of Staffa

Banks, Dr Solander and Dr Lind, after having visited the Northern isles of Scotland, and particularly that of Staffa, which is reckoned one of the greatest natural curiosities in the world: it is surrounded by many pillars of different shapes, such as pentagons, octagons, etc. They are about 55 feet high, and near five feet in diameter, supporting a solid rock of a mile in length, and about 6o feet above the pillars. There is a cave in this island which the natives call the Cave of Fingal: its length is 371 feet, about 115 feet in height, and 51 feet wide; the whole sides are solid rock, and the bottom is covered with water 12 feet deep. The Giant's Causeway in Ireland, or Stonehenge in England are but trifles when compared to this island, elegant drawings of which were taken on the spot.

A similar notice (almost word for word) to that given above appeared in the English publication, *The Gentleman's Magazine*, VOL. XLII (1772), p. 540, dated Thursday, 19th November 1772. A brief description of Banks's discovery of Staffa and Fingal's Cave was also published in 1773 in Swedish newspapers, in a letter contributed by Dr Uno von Troil, a Swede, who had been one of Banks's companions when he visited the island.

Pennant did not land on Staffa during his Hebridean tour in 1772, and although he seems to have been close enough to observe its unusual formation, he does not mention having seen Fingal's Cave. He was prevented from landing by the heavy surge. In his book he says:

Nearest lies Staffa, a new Giant's Causeway, rising amidst the waves, but the columns of double the height of that in Ireland; glossy and resplendent from the beams of the eastern sun. Their greatest height was at the southern point of the isle, of which they seemed the support.

Pennant's visit was on the 11th July 1772. A month later, on the 13th August, Banks made his memorable visit. Mr Leach, the gentleman who informed Banks about Staffa, pursued Pennant in a boat for two miles to acquaint him with what he had seen, but, unfortunately, Pennant out-sailed his liberal intentions.

I have found two surprising claims regarding the discovery of Staffa. The first is obviously absurd, but the second is intriguing. I think they are worth recording. In the *Autobiography and Memoirs of George Douglas, Eighth Duke of Argyll*, who visited Staffa in 1846, occurs the following amazing statement: " It does seem a marvellous fact that no knowledge of the wonders of Staffa had ever reached the world till it had been visited and described by a scientific Englishman, Sir Stamford Raffles." As Raffles was not born until 1781 (nine years after Banks discovered Staffa), this is an astonishing assertion—especially in view of the fact that the Duke was himself a learned man. Probably it was because Raffles and Banks were both distinguished naturalists that he confused their names.

My second discovery was that of a rival claim to Mr Leach having been the person to inform Banks of Staffa's wonderful formation. In *The Tour of the Duke of Somerset and the Rev. J. H. Mitchell through parts of England, Wales and Scotland in the year 1795,* (published in London, 1845) there is an entry:

At Aberdeen, August 23rd. Attended the English Chapel where I was permitted to preach twice, before a numerous congregation. There are two English Clergymen, who are residents, who have the care of the chapel. One of them, Mr Alcock, was the gentleman who first discovered the Isle of Staffa to Sir Joseph Banks.

One would not expect a clergyman to make this claim if it were not true, yet we have to reckon with Mr Leach. The Hon. Mrs Murray of Kensington, who visited Staffa in 1880 and 1802, says that Mr Leach was "a speculative gentleman from Ireland. In Mull he went by the name of Leach, but it was thought it was not his real name. His speculation in the Hebrides was farming." Sir Joseph Banks, however, says in the description of his discovery of Staffa that Mr Leach was " an English gentleman."

Here is Sir Joseph Banks's account of his discovery of Staffa, in his own words:

August 12th, 1772. In the Sound of Mull we came to anchor, on the Morven side, opposite to a gentleman's house called Drumnen, the owner of it, Mr MacLeane, having found out who we were, very cordially asked us ashore; we accepted his invitation, and arrived at his house, where we met an English gentleman, Mr Leach, who no sooner saw us than he told us that about nine leagues from us was an island where he believed no one even in the Highlands had been, on which were pillars like those of the Giant's Causeway; this was a great object to me who had wished to have seen the Causeway itself, would time have allowed. I therefore resolved to proceed directly, especially as it was just in the way to Columb-kill: accordingly, having put up two days' provisions and my little tent, we put off in a boat about one o'clock for our intended voyage, having ordered the ship to wait for us in Tobirmore, a very fine harbour on the Mull side.

At nine o'clock, after a tedious passage, having had not a breath of wind, we arrived under the direction of Mr MacLeane's son and Mr Leach. It was too dark to see anything, so we carried our tent and baggage near the only house upon the island and began to cook supper, in order to be prepared for the earliest dawn to enjoy that which from the conversation of the gentleman we had now raised the highest expectations of.

The impatience which everybody felt to see the wonders we had heard so largely described, prevented our morning rest; everyone was up and in motion before the break of day, and with the first light arrived at the southeast part of the island, the seat of the most remarkable pillars: where we no sooner arrived than we were struck with a scene of magnificence which exceeded our expectations, though formed as we thought upon the most sanguine foundations; the whole of that end of the island is supported by ranges of natural pillars mostly above fifty feet high, standing in natural colonnades according as the bays or points of land formed themselves; upon a firm basis of unformed rock, above these the stratum which reaches to the soil or surface of the island varied in thickness as the island itself formed into hill or valley, each hill which hung over the columns below forming an ample pediment; some of these above sixty feet in thickness from the base to the point, formed by the sloping of the hill on each side almost into the shape of those used in architecture.

Compared to this, what are the cathedrals or the palaces built by man? mere models or playthings, imitations as diminutive as his works will always be when compared with those of nature. Where is now the boast of the architect? regularity, the only part in which he fancied himself to exceed his Mistress. Nature is here found in her possession, and here it has been for ages undiscovered.

Banks adds a footnote here in which he says:

Staffa is taken notice of by Buchanan, but in the slightest manner, and among the thousands who have navigated these seas, none have paid the least attention to its grand and striking characteristics till the present year.

He continues his soliloquy thus:

Is not this the school where the art was originally studied, and what has been added to this by the Grecian school? a capital to ornament the columns of nature, of which they could execute only a model, and for that very capital they were obliged to a bush of Acanthus: how amply does Nature repay those who study her wonderful works!

With our minds full of such reflections, we proceeded along the shore, treading upon another Giant's Causeway, every stone being regularly formed into a certain number of sides and angles, till in a short time we arrived at the mouth of a cave, the most magnificent, I suppose, that has ever been described by travellers.

I have given Banks's account of Fingal's Cave in Chapter VII, which is devoted wholly to a description of this natural wonder.

A Miss Barker of Caldbeck, Cumberland, who spent two days and nights on Staffa along with several friends during the month of August 1928, made a very interesting discovery. She found the initials "J.B., 1772"—presumably those of Sir Joseph Banks—cut into a column at the very inner end of Fingal's Cave, the part which faces outwards towards the entrance. The footing here consists of a single, but not continuous, row of column stumps about one foot in diameter, with a sheer drop beneath of several feet into the sea, and the cavern wall rises perpendicularly from the upper ends of the broken columns. It is possible that these initials were cut by some practical joker, but there is reasonable evidence against this assumption. For instance, no visitor is likely to penetrate so far into the cave unless he, or she, possesses a very enquiring nature. Even should any steamboat tourist desire to reach this point, considerable hustle would be necessary owing to the brief time allowed ashore. Needless to say, there would not be sufficient time to carve initials in the rock face. In the case of visitors having time at their disposal, such as those from neighbouring islands, it is not likely that anyone possessing such a perverted sense of humour as to perpetrate a practical joke of this kind would have sufficient interest in geology to carry a hammer and cold-chisel to perform the carving operation. The employees of the steamboat company, who use tools in the cave, are not the type of men to risk limb and life merely to attempt a joke which might remain undiscovered. The letters are apparently two inches high with their edges weathered to a considerable extent, indicating that they have existed for many years. It is reasonable, therefore, to suppose that they were cut into the rock by Sir Joseph Banks himself in 1772, yet he does not mention them in his description of Staffa. That these initials should have remained undiscovered, or at least unrecorded for so many years, is not surprising when one considers how difficult it is to get near them. I happen to know of a more tangible record, consisting of the usual contents of a memorial stone, in a glass container, which has lain hidden within this cave since 1900. The intrinsic value of this memento does not yet amount to much but some day its discovery, if ever it is discovered, will prove of great interest to the finder.

What is probably the second recorded description of Staffa is given in a letter from Dr John MacGuarie (or MacQuarrie) of Ormaig, Ulva, to Murdoch Maclaine, Merchant, Back of the Fountain Well, Edinburgh, whom he addresses as "Dear Cousine." The letter is dated 24th November 1773, and is now among the Lochbuie Papers (No. 36) in the Scottish Record Office, Edinburgh.

Dr MacGuarie was aware of Banks's description of Staffa, as he mentions having seen it in the newspapers, but the doctor does not seem to have made use of Banks's description to any great extent, and he mentions features of Staffa with which Banks was not acquainted.

If Staffa was not known as an outstanding natural pheno-menon to persons other than the neighbouring islanders before Banks discovered it, his account of the island must have at-tracted visitors very quickly, because Dr MacGuarie, in a pre-vious letter to Murdoch Maclaine, dated 6th September 1773, says: "Staffa continues to be visited; it's generally thought it should be advertised for sale, which I truly think would not be improper." That statement was made exactly one year after Banks landed on Staffa, therefore visitors must have hastened to the island during the first summer after the announcement of Banks's discovery appeared in the *Scots Magazine* and the *Gentleman's Magazine*, as his account in Pennant's *Tour* had not then been published: stormy weather would prevent their arriving sooner.

It is surprising that Dr MacGuarie says, in September 1773, that he thinks Staffa should be advertised for sale when Sir Joseph Banks says, in August 1772, "it is now to be disposed of," and Boswell says, in his *Journal*, that when he and Dr Johnson visited Ulva in October 1773: "I was distressed to hear that it [the Ulva estate] was soon to be sold for payment of his [the proprietor's] debts."

Perhaps what Dr MacGuarie really meant was that he thought Staffa should be sold by itself apart from the remainder of the Ulva estate.

Though it is quite a lengthy document, Dr MacGuarie's description of Staffa is of special value because of its early date, and therefore deserves to be quoted in full:

Ormaig [Ulva]

24th November 1773.

Dear Cousine,

As you was pleased to command me to give you my remarks upon Staffa, sensible of how little entertainment or amusement it could give you at any time, I thought as I had so much time allowed it would be improper to defer it any longer. You'll observe that the description we had of it from Mr Banks in the newspapers,[1] I have set down, placing (*B*) as a mark over his part, after which my own remarks. To proceed then.

The Island of Staffa is one of the Hebrides or Western Isles of Scotland, (*B*) which is reckoned to be one of the greatest natural curiosities in the world. This island is three miles in circumference.

The situation of this island lengthways is N. & by W.—S. & by E. The island is mostly arable; its produce is the same with the rest of the adjacent isles, but more fertile of their kind.—(*B*)   This island is surrounded by a row of massy pillars of different shapes, such as pentagons, &c. They are about 55 feet high, and near five feet in diameter, supporting a solid rock of a mile in length, and about 60 feet high above the pillars. There is a cave in this island, which the natives call the "Cave of Fingall"; its length is 371 feet, about 115 feet in height, and 51 feet wide; the whole sides are solid rock, and the bottom is covered with water 12 feet deep.—Here I beg leave to observe that Mr Banks's interpreter has either misapplied or misunderstood the name of this cave, since in the Gaelic language it is called *Ua Bhin*, which signifies sweet or melodious; which name seems to be more proper, from its excellent echo.—this cave lies to the south part of the island. At low water one may be very well entertained by observing a suction at the upper part of this cave; every third or fourth gentle wave it receives, is again expelled with a good deal of violence, and then begins afresh. In this observation I was first obliged to yourself. I have already observed that the echo here is excellent, which by having a band of musical instruments the delight is so very great that in short it excites more pleasure than I am capable to form an idea of, or even can you conceive the delight it affords. You have experienced what a noble report there is from firing a shot in the body of it.—There are a number of other caves in this island; the greatest number of them have nothing remarkable, E. & N. of Fingall's Cave there is another cave, called *Ua Ad*, or Long Cave, which is variously cut; at the entry to this cave the stones are shaped like the outward part of the concave clam shell; there is nothing else remarkable about it. West of Fingall's Cave is a cave called *Ua Nea'ire*, or Boat Cave, which is vastly pretty at its entry; it resembles a very handsome gate, at the bottom is covered with water, and very deep; the sides are smooth, running narrower inwards; its length is supposed to be that of the island. S.S.W. part of the island there is a cave in the face of a large rock, called the Canon [*sic*], which name

---

[1] Apparently he refers to *The Scots Magazine,* as his quotations are similar to that account.

it derives from its resemblance in every respect to that machine; at the entry to this Canon there is a bason [*sic*] full of water, the depth of which is about 2 foot and a half, and about 15 inches in diameter, in the bottom of which there is a stone lodged; its shape is round, and about 5 pound in weight; when there is anything of a storm, especially at west, this Canon is set agoing, and plays so violently that the island is sensibly shook. E. & by N. of the Canon in the face of a rock of great height there is an herb called the carrot; the root is agreeably sweet; it has a long, fine, large leaf; it throws its seed in August.—About the middle of the island is the safest place for landing, which should be at low water, as at any other time, unless the weather be very favourable, landing cannot be attempted without danger. That is all the remarks I have made as yet, which would be more complete, but ere I had finished half of the other side, I was obliged to hurry on the rest, caused by the death of Balligartan, who died of a short sickness.

The glowing descriptions of Staffa which were circulated by its early visitors caused many strangers to form fantastic ideas of the appearance of the island. One pilgrim arrived at Ulva, a few years after Staffa's discovery, and asked to be ferried to the island. He said he wished the boatmen to sail in and out between the marble pillars. Apparently he imagined the columns to be spaced apart like trees in a forest. When told that the columns were massed together and were not composed of marble but of black rock, he "packed up" and returned home without visiting the goal of his pilgrimage. Another gentleman had his ardour to visit Staffa cooled completely by a storm arising when half way from Ulva in an open boat. This visitor became so violently sea-sick that he ordered the boatmen to turn back and said he would leave in his last will a forfeiture of every penny of his property if his heirs ever dared to visit Staffa.

There was some excuse during the past century for strangers, especially foreigners, forming fantastic ideas of Staffa. Until the present century many of the pictorial representations of the island and Fingal's Cave published, even in standard books, such as encyclopedias and science text-books, cannot be described as anything less than caricatures of the subjects. Most of them show defective perspective at least. There is reason for believing that Banks's drawing of Fingal's Cave has been reversed in the process of printing. If we hold his drawing up to a strong light and view it from the reverse side, it appears more correct than when viewed in its published form.

Although most of the early representations of Staffa are poor likenesses, some of them indicate considerable skill in the process of engraving. In a large folio (twenty-five inches by eighteen inches) published in Paris in 1816, entitled, *Vues pittoresques de L'Ile de Staffa et de la Grotte de Fingal aux Iles Hebrides,* by M. Picquenot and his daughter E. Picquenot, which is now very rare, there are three magnificent, though inaccurate, engravings of Staffa. One of them shows a view of the island from the south, a second shows an exterior view of Fingal's Cave, while the third shows a view of the interior of Fingal's Cave, looking out. Each of those plates is of double-page area, which, allowing for margins, makes them twenty-six inches by nineteen inches. They are very impressive, though to some extent this effect is due to their size and exaggeration of the scenes. There are also two similar plates of the Giant's Causeway, Ireland. There is no indication in the folio that Picquenot ever visited Staffa. Indeed, it seems probable that he never did so. There is a note under each of the first two engravings of Staffa which reads: " Painted from Nature by J. A. Knip. Engraved by E. Picquenot and finished by her father, Member of the Society for Agricultural Sciences, Letters and Arts of Rouen." Under the engraving showing a view looking out of Fingal's Cave, there is a note: " Drawn by M. Faujas. Engraved by E. Picquenot." Picquenot died after having done the work up to the beginning of the third engraving of Staffa. His daughter completed the work with the assistance of H. Guttenberg, a distinguished engraver, and of B. Faujas de St Fond, the famous French geologist (of whom we shall learn more later), who visited Staffa in 1784. The letterpress of the folio amounts to eleven pages, consisting of a preface and a descriptive chapter accompanying each plate. Although written by Picquenot's daughter, the description of Staffa in the letterpress appears to have been derived mainly from Faujas's book, as it repeats even his phrasing in many parts; it also repeats his error for the length of Fingal's Cave—one hundred and forty feet (French feet, or *pieds*).

I have been unable to locate any reference to the visit of J. A. Knip (the artist from whose paintings Picquenot made his engravings) to Staffa. He was a Dutch landscape and animal painter (born 1777 and died 1847), who resided for the greater part of his life in Paris. He became blind in after-life, which may account for his not leaving any written description of his visit to Staffa. The phrase "Painted from Nature" appears to leave no doubt that he visited the island, yet it is remarkable that his paintings of Staffa (according to the engravings which Picquenot made from them) are almost identical with the drawings which appear in Faujas's book, which was published in 1797, only that Knip gives the sea a more dramatic appearance. It would be a remarkable coincidence for two persons to visit Staffa at different times from one another and the second person portray it from exactly the same viewpoint as the first person in so similar a manner as to repeat the many errors of the first. Indeed, it is the repetition of these inaccuracies that makes the similarity of their drawings so obvious. In their view of the south of Staffa, both Faujas and Knip show as their immediate foreground an elongated islet or causeway of column stumps extending so far out into the sea from Staffa as to enable them to obtain a view of the whole of the south of the island from it. From there they appear to have made their sketches. They both show this islet, or causeway, the same shape, though in actual fact there is no such islet or causeway off the south-east of Staffa. In their view of Fingal's Cave they both give an erroneous impression of depth and regularity, and show the west wall of the cave as a comparatively thin structure, though in reality the thickness of this wall extends to almost the full width of Staffa. Like Banks's drawing, they both appear more correct when viewed from their reverse side—a strange coincidence.

I have found that most of the early Continental visitors to Staffa based their drawings and descriptions of the island on those of Faujas, and apparently Knip and Picquenot were no exceptions.

We should not be too severe in criticising the ultra-dramatic and contorted nature of those early drawings of Staffa, however, for in some cases, at least, the exaggeration may have been intentional, in order to impress the beholder with the "awefulness" of the scene; they evoke rather than depict. The true atmosphere of Staffa cannot be conveyed by a straightforward pictorial representation. In the actual scene there are several factors contributing to its solemnity in addition to its form, such as its lonely situation in the ocean, its volcanic origin, the music of surging waves, the sighing of the wind and the plaintive cry of the sea-birds, mingling with their echoes in the chilly gloom of its vast caves; things like these must be left to the imagination. It was probably in an attempt to suggest this collective atmosphere that the early artists exaggerated the form of the island and its caves on their drawings, just as some modern artists try to convey an impression of life and movement in their apparently grotesque compositions. During those early days, before the cold logic of science had given a clear explanation of its formation, Staffa was invested with a much more mystical and dreadful atmosphere than it is now. It was also much more difficult of access at that time. Indeed, actual dangers had to be overcome by its early visitors, far from what was then regarded as civilisation. If those drawings of the island do not present what appeared to the eye they present what was revealed to the mind.

Although allowance may be made for dramatic representations of the scene, there is no excuse for the glaring inaccuracies in some of those early drawings, where the draughtsman appears to have allowed his imagination to run riot. The "plum" is surely an illustration entitled "Fingal's Cave," which appeared in twenty-five editions of *Elementary Geology*, by Dr Hitchcock, published during last century. This example of perverted ingenuity shows no cave at all, but is evidently a distorted picture of part of Clamshell Cave and the little rock nearby called " The Herdsman." To guard against awkward questions, Dr Hitchcock describes Fingal's Cave as " a chasm," as the passage between the Herdsman and Staffa, in his drawing, is shown bounded by sheer close-set cliffs, like a canyon. The columns appear as circular hollow tubes, like large upturned drain pipes.

It is a far cry from those early drawings to the photographs of Staffa taken from an aeroplane, and reproduced in this book.

CHAPTER III

EARLY TRANSPORT TO STAFFA
AND THE ISLAND'S OWNERSHIP

AT the time of Sir Joseph Banks's discovery of Staffa, in
1772, and for many years afterwards, conditions in the
West Highlands and Islands of Scotland were very
primitive, and those conditions lasted longer on the Islands
than on the mainland. Touring in those regions at that time
was a considerable undertaking for strangers; indeed it was an
adventure, the conditions being comparable to travelling in
Tibet at the present day. Risks and discomforts had to be
overcome, while the accommodation, with the exception of the
lairds' houses, was mostly wretched: low, turf-roofed huts
almost indistinguishable from the surrounding ground, with
heather laid on the bare ground for bedding. Inns were few
and far between, and very primitive. When referring to his
famous tour to the Hebrides with Dr Johnson, in 1773, Boswell
says: " When I was at Ferney, in 1764, I mentioned our design
to Voltaire. He looked at me as if I had talked of going to the
North Pole." He refers to the Highland inns as " wretched,"
and describes his bed in one of them as " a stye." Dr Johnson
also refers in forceful language to these inns. Incidentally,
the learned doctor's adaptation to the rigours of travel and
primitive conditions in the Hebrides at that time, after the com-
forts and boon companions of London life to which he was
accustomed, proves that he was a stout fellow in more ways
than one.

Thomas Campbell, the poet, writing in 1795, says: " When
one came to an inn the usual bill of fare announced was,
Skatan agas spuntat agas usquebaugh [*sgadan agus buntata agus
uisge-beatha*] which is to say herrings and potatoes and whisky."
The private still which was common in the Highlands at that
time would account for the generous supply of whisky.

As we have learned from Dr MacGuarie, doughty travellers
had commenced to visit Staffa within one year of Banks's

discovery of the island. They would probably have arrived sooner, but weather conditions would prevent them landing during the late autumn, winter and spring following Banks's visit.

Perhaps it will not be out of place here to describe briefly the conditions of travel for early visitors to Staffa.

Sir John Carr, who visited Staffa in 1807, says in his *Caledonian Sketches:* " It is generally thought that nothing is more easy than to accomplish the survey of these islands [Staffa and Iona] in two or three days [from Oban], whereas it is frequently an undertaking, and a very arduous one, of ten days or a fortnight, if the wind and weather prove unfavourable."

The usual means of reaching Staffa at that time, before the advent of the steamboat, was to set out from Oban for Mull on the first boat available, usually a fishing smack, or to hire an open boat, manned usually by two boatmen, and sail or row, or both, to Aros in the Sound of Mull, a distance of about twenty-five miles. A shorter boat journey but longer land journey was to sail to Loch Don, in Mull. A start was often delayed by unfavourable weather, as even the fishing smacks were small. The fare for a boat when hired with two boatmen for the voyage to Aros was one and a half guineas. When De Saussure came by this route in an open boat with boatmen, it took him ten hours sailing and rowing from Oban to Aros, and he still had to proceed through Mull to Ulva, where he arrived after midnight.

From Aros it was necessary to tramp, or ride on one of the sturdy little ponies or garrons for which Mull was famed at that time, about eight or nine miles over a rough track leading through heather, bracken and rock, as there was no road, to Ulva Ferry on the west coast of Mull. From Loch Don there was an almost equally rough journey overland of about thirty miles. At Ulva the traveller was rowed across a channel about a quarter of a mile broad to the island of Ulva, where there was a public inn and also the home of the laird of the island where his guests were accommodated. Some visitors, who had an invitation from the proprietor of Torloisk, set out from Aros for that place, which is also situated on the west coast of Mull, but about five miles to the north-west of Ulva Ferry. That was the route traversed by Faujas and his companions, who resided as guests at Torloisk House, while Sir Walter Scott, on the occasion of his first visit to Staffa, travelled from Aros to Ulva, where he was the guest of the laird of that island.

Sir John Carr, when describing the ride from Aros to Ulva Ferry on a hardy little Mull pony with a piece of rope for a bridle, says: " The date of my saddle would have puzzled an antiquarian . . . . However, I was fortunate in procuring this much valued rarity, as I found a large fresh *sod* is generally used as an ingenious substitute." Sir John also mentions that although conditions were primitive in this region at that time, there were occasions when rejoicings brightened the lives of the inhabitants. During his stay on Ulva he met some travellers who had been on Iona a short time before when the Duke of Argyll visited that island. They said the presence of His Grace produced almost as great a sensation as if St Columba, attended by St Patrick and St Bridget, had arisen from his tomb to revisit this his favourite island. All the monuments had been washed and scrubbed for the occasion, and to welcome His Grace the local schoolmaster had prepared an address of welcome, but alas! when it came to delivering the speech, his powers of oratory deserted him and he was only able to bow respectfully. To show that there was no lack of enthusiasm, however, the men and women of the island, in fine white mob caps and without shoes or stockings, danced an Iona fandango to welcome the Duke.

After reaching Torloisk or Ulva, the visitor had to await a favourable day for the sail to Staffa, which is not frequent, as local boatmen do not attempt a landing on Staffa during a southerly or south-westerly wind, and these are the prevailing winds in this region. In addition, these winds would be head-winds on the way from Torloisk or Ulva to Staffa.

The sail from Torloisk to Staffa, which would be in a small open sailing boat out into the open sea, and unsheltered from spray and rain, would be about nine miles by rounding the west of Gometra. From Ulva House it would be about the same distance by the south of Ulva. Both places were used as starting points for Staffa before, and for some years after, the steamboat made its first appearance in this region. The cost of hiring a boat with four men (the minimum, as they often had to row much of the way) from Ulva for a return journey to Staffa and Iona was one and a half guineas.

There is an interesting chapter devoted to early visitors to Staffa, before the days of the steamboat, in *Reminiscences of a Highland Parish*, by Dr Norman MacLeod.   He says that some of these pilgrims arrived in Mull on their way to Staffa with beads and trivial trinkets to " trade with the natives."

It was more than fifty years after Banks discovered Staffa that steamboats began to sail to the island.   Lumsden's *Steamboat Companion*, published in 1820, describes the route to Staffa as being by sailing boat to Loch Don or Aros, and thence overland through Mull.   During the eighteen-twenties regular weekly visits to Staffa during the summer months were commenced by steamboat, or steam packet-boat as it was called at that time, from Glasgow.   During the late eighteen-thirties a twice-weekly service to Staffa from Oban was commenced and during the eighteen-fifties and sixties the service from Oban to Staffa had become a thrice-weekly one.   On the other days of the week, the steamboat sailed on the Oban—Fort William— Crinan route.

The earliest visit of a steamboat to Staffa to which I have found reference is that of the paddle steamer *Argyll* during part of the summer of 1823.   Her visits would probably be once-weekly or once-fortnightly, and she was not on this route after 1823, as she was transferred elsewhere.   This reference is merely a two-line mention in *Clyde and Other Coastal Steamers* (p. 131), by Duckworth and Langmuir.

Diligent search has failed to reveal any further mention of steamboat visits to Staffa until two accounts of visits to the island in the steamboat *Highlander*, in 1826, which will be described later.   At that time it was a once-weekly visit.

The next mention which I have found is an announcement, in the *Glasgow Herald* of 18th June 1828, that the paddle steamer *Highlander* would sail during the summer months, "from Glasgow every Monday for Oban, Tobermory and Staffa; and from Tobermory every Friday for Oban and Glasgow."   As the *Highlander* was plying on this route in 1826 she was probably here also in 1827.

Another notice appeared in the press during the month of March 1827, intimating that "The Steam Packet *Maid of Islay No. 1* sails with passengers and goods from Glasgow every Tuesday morning for Islay, Staffa and Iona." That vessel, however, was on this route only during the summer of 1827. During 1828 she was on the Glasgow to Skye, *via* Oban route and her owners did not advertise her as sailing to Staffa after 1827. Mention is made, however, in Fowler's *Commercial Directory of Renfrewshire* for 1833-4, of steamboats plying from the Clyde, of the *Maid of Islay* (presumably No. 2, as No. 1 was sold in 1831) sailing to Islay, Staffa, Iona and Skye.

As those paddle steamboats to Staffa from Oban, and from Inverness *via* Oban, were, naturally, very slow, they usually sailed to Tobermory and lay there overnight. On the following morning they sailed to Staffa and Iona, returning to Tobermory in the evening, where again they lay overnight, before proceeding to Oban. Only on very rare occasions, when the weather was unusally calm, did they return to Oban by the exposed south coast of Mull, and the dangerous Torran Rocks.

Duckworth and Langmuir refer, on p. 5 of their book already mentioned, to a very ambitious cruise arranged and carried out during the summer of 1827. The paddle steamer *St Andrew* sailed from Glasgow to Portballintrae, Co. Antrim, Ireland, allowing passengers ashore to visit the Giant's Causeway, and arrived at Londonderry the following day. From Londonderry she sailed direct to Iona and Staffa, where passengers were allowed ashore for one hour. She proceeded to Tobermory on the same day and early next morning sailed for Fort William. From Fort William she returned to Glasgow, calling at Oban and Campbeltown and rounding the Mull of Kintyre on her route. This cruise was continued for several years as an annual event during Glasgow Fair Holidays.

About the eighteen-forties, steamboats commenced to sail from Oban round the Island of Mull, visiting Staffa and Iona on the route, and back to Oban in one day, but it was a long day's sail. When the King of Saxony and his physician, Dr C. G. Carus, sailed by this route to Staffa, during the month of July 1844, on the steamboat *Brenda*, they left Oban at 4.30 a.m. and arrived back in Oban at 8 p.m.—fifteen and a half hours.

As the visits to Staffa by steamboat in those days were uncertain owing to the weather being often too rough for those small paddle boats, a gun was fired when they came within a few miles of the island to warn the boatmen of Ulva, who sailed across to Staffa to ferry visitors ashore.

The earliest description that I have found of a visit to Staffa by steamboat is that of a Yorkshire gentleman who visited the island on 19th July 1826. He had travelled overland from Inveraray to Oban, where he joined the steamboat *Highlander*, which was on her weekly voyage from Glasgow to Staffa. On the *Highlander* he sailed to Tobermory, where she lay overnight. At 5.30 a.m. on the following morning they sailed to Staffa and Iona, and returned to Tobermory late in the evening, where again they spent the night before proceeding to Oban. This description is given in an unpublished manuscript entitled *Journal of a Yorkshire Gentleman's Tour in Scotland, 1826;* it is now in the Mitchell Library, Glasgow.

The next recorded visit to Staffa by steamboat that I have been able to locate is that of M. Ducos, Governor of the Bank of France. He visited the island on the *Highlander* on 26th July 1826—exactly one week after the Yorkshire gentleman mentioned above. Ducos joined the steamboat *Stirling* at Inverness and sailed south on her to Oban, where he transferred immediately to the *Highlander* and proceeded on board her to Staffa, spending **one** night at Tobermory on the outward journey and another night there on the return journey to Oban. He mentions " the weekly call of the steamboat." Ducos's account of his visit is given in his book *Itinéraire et souvenirs d'Angleterre et d'Ecosse*, VOL. III, published in Paris in 1834.

Beriah Botfield, F.R.S., who sailed from Inverness on the *Ben Lomond* during the month of August, 1829, was carried right on to Staffa, *via* Oban, on the same boat after spending a night in Tobermory. In his *Journal of a Tour through the Highlands of Scotland in 1829*, he refers to " the recent introduction of steamboats to Staffa." The *Ben Lomond* carried Botfield back to Oban by the south of Mull because the weather happened to be " particularly fine." He mentions that only on rare occasions did the steamboat return to Oban by this route.

(*Above*) An acquatint by William Daniell, 1818, of MacKinnon's Cave;
Daniell erroneously refers to it as 'Cormorants Cave'; (*below*) this sketch
by C. L. F. Pancoucke (1830) is the only known representation of the island
which shows the building before it fell into ruin

The view seawards from Fingal's Cave; the low island on the horizon is
Iona

C. L. F. Panckoucke, a Frenchman, who visited Staffa by steamboat in 1829 or 1830, sailed from Glasgow to Skye, *via* Oban and Tobermory, and returned from Skye to Staffa and Iona, then back to Tobermory, where they stayed overnight, before proceeding to Oban the following morning. He completed the whole voyage on the *Maid of Morven*.

In McPhun's little *Pocket Guide to the Western Highlands and Islands* (now very scarce), published in 1835, it is stated that visitors to Staffa usually procured a boat at Oban to convey them to Mull. They then traversed Mull to Ulva, from which island they were rowed or sailed over to Staffa. It adds, however: " Steamboats sail pretty frequently during the summer to Tobermory, in Mull, and sometimes visit Staffa and Iona." After describing these islands it mentions " returning from Iona to Tobermory "; thus they did not usually return by the south of Mull to Oban.

The first mention I have found of a steamboat visiting Staffa and Iona by sailing regularly round Mull is a press advertisement of Messrs David Hutcheson & Co., in 1851 (the year in which they acquired the West Highland steamboat services of Messrs G. & J. Burns), that their steamboat p.s. *Dolphin* sailed round Mull three times weekly, calling at Staffa and Iona, and reached Oban in the evening.

Apparently, the first screw steamer to visit Staffa was the *Fairy*, which came on a cruise with specially invited guests on the occasion of Queen Victoria's visit to the island on 19th August, 1847. William Keddie, in his book *Staffa and Iona*, p. 54, says, when describing Queen Victoria's visit: " The *Dolphin* [the regular paddle steamboat to Staffa at that time] had, for an hour and more, found a rival in the swift steamer *Fairy*, which is propelled by a screw; and wanting paddle-boxes, paddles, and sails, yet working her way through the water at a dashing pace, astonished the Highlanders ashore, who were on the lookout for the *Bhan Righ* [the Queen] and who were at a loss to account for the power by which the *Fairy* moved." The *Fairy* was a trim little vessel with a tonnage of 317 and was built to act as a tender to the first royal yacht called the *Victoria and Albert*—a paddle steamer. She was the first screw steamer to carry royalty, and when her designer suggested screw pro-

pulsion for her, he met with considerable opposition in the
Admiralty, as there were very few screw steamers at that time,
and the Admiralty looked upon them with suspicion.   She had
a speed of over thirteen knots, which was very good considering
that she was built in 1845, only seven years after the first
appearance of a screw steamer.

Although Staffa has had a regular steamboat service during
the summer months for over one hundred and thirty years, and
the route is very exposed, it seems surprising that until the year
1931 (one hundred and eight years) they were all paddle
steamers.

OWNERSHIP OF STAFFA

The ownership of Staffa has changed several times since
Banks "discovered" it, in 1772, and proclaimed its wonders to
the world.   In a footnote to his description of the island, he
says: " This island is the property of Mr Lauchlan MacQuaire
[later spelled MacQuarrie] of Ulva, and is now to be disposed
of." When Staffa was eventually advertised for sale, Dr Lind,
an eminent physician and intimate friend of Banks, told Banks
that if he wanted to buy it, he (the doctor) thought he could get
it for him without Banks's name appearing in the transaction,
for about two hundred pounds.   I happen to know from private
information that this assumption was highly optimistic.

That Lauchlan, or Lachlan, MacQuarrie, of Ulva, mentioned
by Banks, was sixteenth and last chief of the Clan MacQuarrie
in direct succession.   Although he had succeeded to the Ulva
estate, which for generations had included Staffa, as heir to his
father, John MacQuarrie, on 27th October 1739, he was really
not the proprietor of Staffa when Banks "discovered" the
island.   The proprietor at that time, and as far back as 1761,
at least, was Hector MacQuarrie of Ormaig, Ulva.   Lauchlan
MacQuarrie was only the superior, which means that the proprietor, Hector MacQuarrie, paid him a feu duty (a purely
nominal one).

It is an interesting coincidence that Sir Joseph Banks and a
famous son of Ulva, namely, Major-General Lachlan Macquarie
(he spelled his name with a small q and one r), were both
intimately associated with the early development of Australia.

Banks was one of the real founders of Australia as a British settlement and in its turbulent and mismanaged infancy it owed much to his guidance. Indeed, he has been described as the Father of Australia and when a name was discussed for that great southern continent, Linnaeus, who has been described as the "Father of Botany," suggested that it should be named Banksia in recognition of the great work which Banks had done for it. The name Australia was adopted, however, owing to the prominence of this continent in the southern hemisphere. No one did more to further the early development of Australia than Major-General Macquarie, who, in 1809, was appointed Governor of New South Wales, which at that time really comprised the eastern half of Australia; the western half was then practically unknown territory. It was during Governor Macquarie's term of office that the name Australia was finally accepted to designate the whole continent. The names Banks and Macquarie are thus intimately associated with the history of that vast southern continent and are perpetuated in several prominent place-names of Australia. As if to complete the coincidence in the lives of these two men, Governor Macquarie was of the same family as Hector MacQuarrie of Ormaig, who owned Staffa when Banks discovered it to the world.

The Ulva estate, including Staffa, was owned by the Mac-Quarries of Ulva for nine hundred years previous to its ownership by the direct descendant Lauchlan MacQuarrie. He made this statement to Dr Johnson and Boswell when they visited him in Ulva in 1773. I have found definite records that Lauchlan MacQuarrie of Ulva was the seventh heir in direct line to own the Ulva estate, including Staffa, and their ownership probably extended back beyond my research.

Some time previous to 1761 (I have been unable to locate the exact date) Lauchlan MacQuarrie disposed of a small part of the Ulva estate, including Staffa, to a distant relative, Hector MacQuarrie of Ormaig, Ulva, but he retained his right as superior. Thus Hector MacQuarrie was owner of Staffa when it was "discovered" by Banks in 1772 and also when Dr Johnson and Boswell visited Ulva in 1773. The actual superiority of the whole island of Mull and its attendant islands, including Ulva and Staffa, was originally held by MacLean of Duart as far back as 1683 at least, but it seems to have passed to the Duke of Argyll after the Revolution of 1689, when the lands of Mac-Lean of Duart were forfeited and the stars of MacQuarrie and MacLean waned under the rising sun of the Campbells. The Duke of Argyll still seems to be the superior of these islands.

Owing to financial embarrassment, caused principally by profuse hospitality, Lauchlan MacQuarrie had to forfeit the whole of his Ulva estate, which included parts of western Mull, to his creditors in 1777. For some reason, which I have been unable to discover, the small portion of the Ulva estate, including Staffa, owned by Hector MacQuarrie was put up for sale at the same time as the remainder of it owned by Lauchlan MacQuarrie. Perhaps Hector wished to dispose of it or perhaps, like Lauchlan, he found it necessary to do so. A separate notice for the sale of each of the two portions of the Ulva estate, but both inserted by the same firm of solicitors, appeared in the *Edinburgh Evening Courant* from 3rd May to 12th July, inclusive, 1777, and concurrently in the *Caledonian Mercury* and *Edinburgh Advertiser*. The notice of sale of Hector MacQuarrie's portion of the Ulva estate included: " To be sold by public roup . . . The Lands and Estate of Hector MacQuarrie of Ormaig . . . holding blench of Lauchlan MacQuarrie of Ulva, and comprehending . . . the Forty-Shilling-Land of the celebrated Island of Staffa." The notice of sale of Lauchlan MacQuarrie's portion of the Ulva estate included " the Right of Superiority of . . . the Island of Staffa."

The whole Ulva estate, including Staffa, was purchased by Captain Dugald Campbell of Auchnabaw, late of the 87th Regiment of foot. In the *General Register of Sasines*, VOL. 680, it is stated: " Decreet of sale of the estate of Ulva in favour of Dugald Campbell of Auchnabaw, Recorded Register of Acts and Decreets 26th November 1777."

That laird retained possession until 2nd February 1780, when he sold the estate (still including Staffa) to Colonel Charles Campbell of Barbreck, who was retired from the Army after serving for a considerable period as an officer in the Madras Army with the Honourable East India Company.

It was one of the Barbreck Campbells, but of the Lochnell branch (Colonel Charles was of the Argyll family), namely

Colonel John Campbell of Barbreck, who raised the old Argyll Highlanders, the 74th,[1] in 1777, and one of the first to receive a commission in the regiment was Lauchlan MacQuarrie, mentioned above. Although sixty-three years of age and bereft of his ancestral lands, this " Chief of Ulva's Isle " had not lost his warrior spirit. Indeed, he served throughout the American War campaign of the 74th and remained an officer till the regiment was disbanded in 1783. Lauchlan MacQuarrie died in 1818 at the age of one hundred and three years without male issue, and his line thus became extinct.

Colonel Charles Campbell owned the Ulva estate, including Staffa, until 8th June 1785, when he disposed of these lands to Colin MacDonald of Boisdale, in South Uist. It is worthy of note that this new proprietor's father, Alexander MacDonald of Boisdale, was the first person summoned on board the armed brig *Du Teillay* in the hope of obtaining his services by Prince Charles Edward Stuart—Bonnie Prince Charlie—when he arrived on the west coast of Scotland to raise his standard n 1745.

To return to the ownership of Staffa. When Colin MacDonald purchased the Ulva estate, Ranald, his elder son by a second marriage, was infeft in the fee, the father reserving a life-rent in 1790. When Colin MacDonald died on 31st July 1800, his son, Ranald, became sole proprietor.

Although Ranald MacDonald was only twenty-three years of age when he inherited his father's property of Ulva, Staffa and other areas, he proved himself of sterling quality, and his memory was long cherished with affection by the inhabitants of this region. At the age of twenty-one, Ranald had been elected, and for thirty-nine years continued to be, ruling elder for the Presbytery of Mull to the General Assembly. He qualified as an advocate in Edinburgh in 1798 and was, later, Sheriff of Stirlingshire for twenty-six years. He was elected Principal Secretary to the Highland Society in succession to Donald MacLachlan of MacLachlan on 12th January 1813. He was the third holder of the office, which became that of Hon. Secretary by the Charter of 1834, when the name was changed

---

[1] This regiment is not to be confused with the Argyll Highlanders, the 91st, raised by the Duke of Argyll in 1794, which later became united with the Sutherland Highlanders.

to "The Highland and Agricultural Society of Scotland."
Like the majority of Highland lairds, Ranald MacDonald was
known by his territorial title. In this case he choose the title
" Staffa,"[1] the most famous part of his estate, in preference to
" Ulva." That custom was, and still is, necessary in the
Highlands to distinguish the different families of the same name
and clan.

In George Seton's *Law and Practice of Heraldry in Scotland*
(1863), p. 145, appears an illustration of the coat-of-arms
shield registered by Ranald MacDonald of Staffa, about 1810.
The design on it is described as " a galley moored in front of
Fingal's Cave off the cliff of the Isle of Staffa." A salmon is
shown superimposed upon the sea. Although granted by the
Lord Lyon of the time, it seems inferior heraldry.

As Ranald MacDonald changed his name after he was married, his name sometimes causes confusion. On 23rd January
1812 he married Miss Elizabeth Margaret Steuart, only
daughter and heiress of Henry Steuart of Allanton, LL.D., who
was created a Baronet on 22nd May 1815, with a special remainder to his son-in-law.

In 1835, when Ranald's wife succeeded in right of her mother
(Lady Steuart had been heiress of Hugh Seton of Touch) to
the estate of Touch (on the death of her maternal uncle),
Ranald MacDonald assumed the additional name of Seton.
Finally, on the death of his father-in-law, Sir Henry Steuart,
in 1836, he succeeded to the Baronetcy and to Allanton and
became Sir Reginald (or Ranald) MacDonald Steuart Seton
(or Seton-Steuart) of Staffa, Allanton and Touch, Bt. The
names Reginald and Ranald are interchangeable; they are
alternative forms of Raghnald. Burke's and Debrett's *Peerage*
give him the title " Sir Reginald," but the *History of the Clan
Donald* describes him as " Sir Ranald."

---

[1] I have seen the title Marquis of Staffa mentioned in two books on the
Hebrides, but with no other indication who that person was. On searching
registers of old peerages I was unable to locate the title and on communicating with the Keeper of Registers and Records of Scotland was informed
that there never has been such a title. The name is probably a confused
reference to " Staffa " (Ranald MacDonald), or it may refer to the Marquis of
Stafford. A daughter of the Marquis of Stafford married the first Baron
MacDonald and thus the Marquis may have visited some of the Western
Islands of Scotland.

Sir Ranald died at his Edinburgh house, in Rutland Street, on 15th April 1838, and was buried in Greyfriars Churchyard. His wife died in 1866. Although they had three sons and two daughters the title is now extinct. The last holder was Sir Douglas Archibald Seton-Steuart of Allanton, 5th baronet, who died in 1930. Colonel Henry Steuart Lockhart-Ross, who died in 1935, claimed the post of Hereditary Armour-bearer to the King as grandson of Elizabeth Lady Seton-Steuart.

To return to Ranald MacDonald's ownership of Staffa. Financial difficulties were, unfortunately, once again the cause of Staffa and all other parts of the Ulva estate changing possession, and again this embarrassment was caused to a great extent by liberal hospitality and generosity to tenants.

On 24th December 1816, Ranald MacDonald granted a trust disposition in favour of his creditors which conveyed the Ulva estate, including Staffa, into the hands of a trustee, Claude Russell, Accountant in Edinburgh; this transaction is registered in the Particular Register of Sasines for the shires of Dumbarton and Argyll, etc., on 21st March 1817.

On 3rd August 1821, this trustee for Ranald MacDonald and his creditors sold Staffa to Alexander Forman, accountant in Edinburgh, as trustee for Major Robert MacDonald, R.H.A., and others. The purchase money was paid by John Forman, W.S., Edinburgh, brother of Alexander Forman. The other parts of the Ulva estate passed into different hands.

Alexander Forman was nominal proprietor only, as he neither paid nor received any money in connection with the expenses of Staffa. John Forman being the real security for the principal sum paid for the property desired ultimately to have the island conveyed to him in his own name. On 10th April 1837, Alexander Forman made over the island to him as trustee for Major Robert MacDonald and others, which he held as such trustee till his death.

These Forman brothers were sons of a Stirling baker. They established a legal business in Edinburgh and since then the family have been prominent in the legal life of Edinburgh. John Forman, who was born in 1775, died in 1841. His wife, who survived him by eight years, was the daughter of the minister of Pittenweem, the Rev. Dr James Nairne of Claremont.

On 1st April 1851, Colonel (formerly Major) Robert Mac-
Donald and others renounced all claim to Staffa and John
Nairne Forman, w.s., Edinburgh, eldest son of the above John
Forman, having completed the necessary legal formalities,
became the rightful owner of Staffa on 9th December 1857,
free from all trust purposes.   He held the ownership of Staffa
until his death in 1884, when his grandson, Dr Bernard Gilpin
Forman, m.b.e., Medical Officer in the Scalby district of Scar-
borough, succeeded him as owner of Staffa.   The doctor's
mother was a daughter of Bernard Gilpin Cooper of Hazel
Grove, Cheshire.

On the death of Dr Bernard Gilpin Forman, in June 1949,
the ownership of Staffa passed to his elder son Bernard Gilpin
Vincent Forman, of Moorfield, Morton, near Bingley, Yorkshire.

In 1967, Bernard Forman put Staffa on the market.   In
1968, it was bought by Captain Gerald Newell, a former Army
chaplain, of Worthing, Sussex.   Later, Captain Newell sought
planning permission for a £1,000,000 development of the
island, including a hotel, chalets and an improved pier but this
proposal attracted widespread objections and the application
was called in by the Secretary of State for Scotland.

In 1972, Captain Newell decided to offer Staffa for sale, and
in that year it was bought by Mr Alastair de Watteville, of
Chichester, Sussex.   There was general approval when Mr de
Watteville announced that he does not intend to introduce any
changes on Staffa and to keep it open to the public as one of the
natural wonders of the world.

It is worthy of note that Mr de Watteville, the present owner
of Staffa, is a direct descendant of Colin MacDonald of Boisdale,
the highly respected owner of the island from 1785 until his
death in 1800.

I have dealt with the ownership of Staffa at some length
because the subject has been discussed several times in the press
and a good deal of confusion was evident, owing to Ranald
MacDonald having changed his name, and also to the recur-
rence of the same Christian names in the Forman family.

CHAPTER IV

HOW STAFFA WAS FORMED

THE first question one feels inclined to ask when viewing Staffa is: "How was this island formed?" Various theories have been offered in answer to this question, some credible, others quite incredible. As even a summary of the subject will prove rather lengthy, it is perhaps best to devote this chapter to the way in which the island is believed to have come into existence and the next chapter to the theories regarding columnar rock formation.

Celtic mythology saturates the life of western Scotland and has been quick to invest each peculiar hill, rock, valley, headland, and island, with its own especial significance. It is thus only natural that Staffa should have stirred the Celtic imagination to ascribe its peculiar formation to the work of a giant.

A local legend tells us that a great giant named Torquil MacLeod, whose home was in the island of Eigg, while one day doing some work at the Giant's Causeway, in north-east Ireland, decided to take a piece of the Causeway home with him. Choosing the best bit he could find—Staffa—he put it in a sack, slung it over his shoulder and set out for home, wading across the sea. When he was passing the Island of Mull the weight of the rock caused it to cut through the sack and a few small fragments fell out. Those pieces are supposed to be the small rocks which lie to the south-west of Staffa. Observing what happened and realising his predicament, Torquil grunted, " *Hiv! Haw hoagraich!* " and hastened to reach the nearest land, which was the Island of Ulva, but alas! the sack burst, and Staffa splashed into the sea. Being tired and angry, Torquil left it where it lay. So much for legend.

A novel hypothesis to account for the origin of Staffa appears in a recent book entitled *The Riddle of prehistoric Britain*, by Comyns Beaumont. According to this belief, Staffa and other basaltic rock formations in this region are the remnants of a comet which struck or grazed the earth, travelling from north-east to south-west across the north of Europe and Britain, *circa* 1322 B.C. (Beaumont discredits the vast periods of time assumed by anthropologists and geologists for human and geological development, a belief also held by some modern mythologists). The concussion was so violent that it caused the earth's axis to wobble and alter its position, thus causing changes in the climate of many parts of the earth's surface, as revealed by geology. This collision, he states, ended the pre-existing civilisation by the most destructive natural catastrophe ever known in the annals of mankind, because of its magnitude and severity, and included the submergence of the continent of Atlantis, or a great part of it, which, he believes, was the real Flood of Noah. The centre of that pre-existing civilisation, he suggests, lay in the region now occupied by Scandinavia and Britain. Some time after the terrestial cataclysm, and owing to a gradual chilling of the climate, survivors of this old northern civilisation spread gradually southward to a sunnier clime, carrying with them their traditions and legends, and founded the civilisations of the Near and Middle East, that is, Greek, Phoenician, Egyptian and Biblical: a reversal of the generally-accepted belief that civilisation spread northward from the Middle and Near East. He deduces that the Ionians, Corinthians and Dorians drew their inspiration for colonnades from their racial traditions of Staffa, and that Fingal's Cave was the original Judgment Hall of Amenti where Osiris judged the souls of the dead, as related in the Egyptian *Book of the Dead:* " whose roof is fire, whose walls are living serpents, whose floor is a stream of water." He also interprets other classic legends as having their origin in scenery surrounding Staffa and elsewhere in Scotland. He believes that Satan, or the Devil— Donald Dubh, himself—is under Staffa, and not as a mere bogey but in reality. Here is how he reasons it out. Before the great terrestial catastrophe, the early inhabitants of the earth observed the comet that caused it sweeping across the sky with long curving tail and small excrescences like horns from the head. They regarded it as some malevolent, sinuous, fiery dragon, or devil, which they named Satan, or the Evil One, and which, in later mythology, developed into grotesque human form possessing the same features; and he presents evidence for this belief. He considers Staffa to be the only remaining part of the nucleus of that comet which has survived the disaster when it struck the earth, other parts of the comet being scattered in the sea. This evidence, he suggests, explains the Apocalyptic story of Satan being cast down from heaven to earth—"I beheld Satan as lightning fall from heaven"—Luke x. 18—and the almost similar description of the same event given in the Egyptian *Book of the Dead*. Again, Plutarch says that Satan was thrown down from the sky deep into a fiery region of the earth (suggesting volcanic activity) beneath the sea, and covered by an island of fiery rocks and stones which lay " at the ends of the earth in the west," suggesting the original heated nature of the rocks of Staffa. (The word rendered "west" in this quotation has also been translated as "north.") Harold T. Wilkins, in his book *Secret Cities of old South America*, p.411, says, "Hell, or Hades, which the ancient Greeks and Romans swore was in the northern part of the British Isles, land of ancient awe and mystery. Satan—Seth—Thoth was sunk into the watery abyss in the Great Cataclysm." Incidentally, Ifrinn, the hell of the Gaels, and Niflheim, the hell of the Norse, are regarded by them as being wet and cold rather than hot and dry. Lewis Spence says, in *The Magic Arts in Celtic Britain*, p. 123: " The Greeks thought it [Britain] another world to which the souls of the dead were ferried by night, as Procopius assures us." The Egyptians also believed that the "Other World" lay far to the west (or north).

The geological aspect of Beaumont's book seems to be somewhat similar to the theory of the old " Catastrophic," or " Cataclysmic," school of geologists, who believed that the main geological features of the earth were determined by periodical terrestial catastrophes, rather than by the modern scientific belief of slow, continual change, or "Uniformitarian" theory. Although his hypothesis is certainly very unorthodox and may not be regarded seriously by those qualified to judge, his obviously diligent research into unusual and little-known sources, and also his ingenious reasoning and interpretations, deserve respect.

We shall now consider scientific beliefs regarding Staffa.

The island has been accepted as a product of volcanic action since Sir Joseph Banks visited it in 1772. Banks makes no definite pronouncement on this point, but vaguely describes the rock as "Basaltes, very much resembling the Giant's Causeway in Ireland." He also compares some of its appearances with those of lava. His companion, Dr Uno von Troil, is less hesitant, and says in his *Letters on Iceland*, when describing Staffa: "The stratum beneath the pillars here mentioned is evidently *tuffa*, which has been heated by fire, and seems to be interlarded, as it were, with small bits of basalt; and the red [bed?] or stratum above the pillars, in which large pieces of pillars are sometimes found irregularly thrown together . . . is evidently nothing else but lava."

The first geologist to visit Staffa and pronounce it definitely as of volcanic origin was B. Faujas de St Fond, who came in 1784. He was well acquainted with the volcanic rock formations in Central France, and had no hesitation in pronouncing Staffa to be a product of volcanic action. Faujas was followed, in 1788, by a vulcanist named Abraham Mills, who also described Staffa as being formed of lava.

At that time the study of volcanic phenomena was in its infancy. Werner, one of the leading geologists of the period, even taught that volcanoes were really burning mountains, mere accidents due to combustion of subterranean beds of coal set on fire by lightning or by the decomposition of pyrites. He asserted that they had no connection with the geological structure of the earth. That opinion was gradually superseded by the belief that volcanoes were caused by the earth's crust settling and squeezing out, as lava, the material of the earth's interior, which was believed to be molten, through any vent which permitted. Another belief was that a volcanic mountain was due to the uplift of a blister-like mass of the earth's crust, like the viscid bubbles which form upon the surface of hot porridge. Those hypotheses have now been discarded.

A volcano is essentially a vent, or channel, up which hot gases, molten rock and fragmental products rise and are discharged at the earth's surface.[1] The gases are mostly steam,

[1] Sir Edward B. Bailey, who examined this chapter, does not agree with the modern tendency to describe a volcano as a vent, or channel. He defines a volcano as "an accumulation of material brought up to the earth's surface either in a molten condition or by hot explosive gases." He emphasises the accumulation of materials rather than the vent.

and they occur at great depths and pressures dissolved in the molten material, or *magma*, upon which they have the effect of lowering its melting point. The molten material poured out at the earth's surface is called *lava*. The fine fragmental products are called *ash*, though there is only trifling combustion in volcanic activity; the subterranean material is melted, not burned. American scientists have found recently that ascending Hawaiian lava is hotter near the surface than it is as deep down the volcanic pipe as they can plunge their instruments. This increased heat they ascribe to near-surface combustion of volcanic gases, but this belief is not yet confirmed definitely.

When ash becomes cemented into a coherent mass it is called *tuff*.

I have defined these few terms, as they will occur occasionally later.

The shape of the volcanic pile formed by the ejected materials is determined by the nature of these materials and by the extent of the orifice. Ash or viscous lava (technically known as *acid* lava), supplied from a small pipe, will build a steep cone. Fluid or *basic* lava, such as basalt will build gentle slopes, and if it rises from a fissure, the result may be a lava plain, or plateau. The eruptive activity may be continuous or spasmodic, and may be explosive or quiet.

Some geologists believe that all volcanic action is confined to a comparatively thin outermost layer of the earth's crust, or lithosphere, (which is estimated to be about thirty miles thick), and is caused by water percolating into the earth, where it becomes superheated. They assert that this theory accounts for many volcanoes bordering the sea, as the coast-line is usually a locality of great earth-folding and contains fissures which would allow the over-lying water to penetrate into the earth. The majority of geologists, however, consider that the region in the earth's crust where lavas originate is much deeper than the zone to which surface water can descend. They believe that the water which causes volcanoes is that which is an essential constituent of nearly all rocks and is really subterranean, or plutonic, water. This theory would account for volcanoes occurring at sunken areas inland as well as at the sea coast. These geologists admit that volcanic *explosions* occur at comparatively shallow depths and may therefore be caused by rain or sea water penetrating into the earth.

These theories account reasonably well for all ordinary volcanic phenomena, such as can be observed at the present day, but modern geologists consider the very extensive volcanic activity of which Staffa is a product to have occurred at the close, or *revolution*, of one of the earth's geological *cycles*. These cycles are believed to be caused by the substratum of heavy basaltic rock in the earth's crust becoming fluid, or at least fluidable, periodically. This substratum occurs beneath the lighter rocks forming the continents and is exposed in the ocean bed, where it is free from sedimentary rocks. Its periodical melting is believed to be caused by the gradual accumulation of heat generated by the radioactive minerals which it contains. The adjustment of the earth's crust to accommodate this process would cause it to rupture at certain parts, thus permitting the expansion of the temporarily increased volume of basaltic rock welling out at suitable openings.

As already mentioned, Faujas was the first geologist to describe Staffa definitely as a product of volcanic action. But he regarded the island as the denuded stump of a submarine volcano and not as a remnant of lava which had issued from a distant volcano, as is now believed. In his *Voyage en Angleterre, en Ecosse et aux Hebrides* (Paris 1797), an English translation of which was published in Glasgow in 1907, Faujas says: " The extinct volcano of the isle of Staffa has been exposed for so many ages to the action of a sea full of currents, and subject to so many tempests, that one may well say that nothing but the skeleton of a volcanic isle can here be seen which was once much more considerable; the sea attacking the island from every side has carried away or destroyed everything that it could overcome. We should not, therefore, be astonished to find here neither the remains of a crater, nor scoriae, nor light lavas." Again, when describing Fingal's Cave, he refers to it as " this supreme monument of a grand subterranean conflagration, the date of which has been lost in the lapse of ages"; and he describes the volcanic tuff at the base of the "Colonnade" as " the result of a volcanic eruption in which water has entered into co-operation with fire."

Faujas also believed that the terraced escarpments of lava, or *trap terraces*, which are the most prominent features of the landscape in this region, were caused by lava descending in cascade after cascade from the heights to the shore, the molten material moulding itself upon the irregularities of the slope, like icing over a cake. These escarpments are really the truncated outer edges of successive lava flows piled one above the other like the horizontal layers of sponge in a cake.

Abraham Mills does not make any suggestion as to the vent from which Staffa issued.

Panckoucke, to whose work I have referred in the Preface to the second edition of this book, was familiar with the views of the early Continental geologists who had visited Staffa, and believed, like Faujas, that Staffa was the denuded stump of an extinct submarine volcano. When offering his opinion as to how the caves were formed, in his *L'Ile de Staffa et sa grotte basaltique*, he says :

Just where the heated columns stand the tide must have covered them. There, where the waves have most power they have forced the basaltic shafts to curve, but in the interior parts the columns, having had a long space of time to cool, have remained upright. The groups which form the whole island have cooled down more slowly and have thus acquired all their prismatic perfection.

He did not realise that these columns had cooled and solidified ages before the sea had access to them, and it would be interest. ing to know where he saw curved columns in Fingal's Cave.

The first geologist to attempt a systematic description of the rocks of the Hebrides was Dr John MacCulloch, who was selected in 1811 to undertake a series of geological investigations in Scotland. In 1814 some of his remarks regarding those explorations were published in the *Transactions* of the Geological Society. His first comprehensive work on the subject, however, was his *Description of the Western Islands of Scotland, including the Isle of Man*, published in 1819. But though he distinguished the volcanic and plutonic rocks in those islands, he did not offer any suggestions as to how they were produced; he was more concerned with collecting facts than with theorising.

The modern theory of geologists is that Staffa is a small detached remnant of the volcanic, or eruptive, rocks which are so extensive in Mull, of which Staffa was evidently once a part. It will thus be understood why a summary of the geology of Mull is necessary in order to explain satisfactorily how Staffa came into existence.   To deal with the geology of Staffa without mentioning that of Mull would be like describing a twig without mentioning the tree from which it grew.

Although Staffa is the best-known example of columnar rock formation in the Mull area, there are many other beautiful examples of this structure in Mull and several of the surrounding islands.   Indeed, had Staffa not existed, the neighbouring island of Ulva might have become famous for its examples of this form of rock.

The first suggestion that the lavas of Mull were of subaerial origin was made by Ami Boué in his *Essai géologique sur l' Ecosse*, published in Paris about 1820.   He recognised the soils on the basalt tops and deduced subaerial eruption.   This belief was confirmed in 1850 by the discovery at Ardtun, by Charles MacQuarrie, of leaf beds between the bedded lavas.   Mr MacQuarrie brought his discovery to the notice of the Duke of Argyll.   The Duke had samples of the leaf beds examined by an expert, who declared them to be of Tertiary date, and tentatively ascribed them to the Miocene Period, thus dating the Mull volcanic activity.

It was not until 1874, when Professor J. W. Judd read a paper " On the ancient Volcanoes of the Highlands," before the Geological Society, that it was suggested that the lavas of Mull had issued from a great central volcano.

It may be mentioned here that the reason why the names of the men of science who visited Staffa and described it are not so well known to the general public as the names of its literary and other eminent visitors is that science is concerned more with what's what than with who's who.

During the geological era known as the Tertiary, or Kainozoic (before man had made his appearance on the earth), violent volcanic activity developed in many parts of our planet, which caused them to assume, more or less, their present configuration. During that time Europe experienced the most stupendous succession of volcanic phenomena in the whole of its later geological history.   The most outstanding feature was the great floods of basaltic rock, in a molten condition, which welled out through numerous vents in the earth's crust, overflowed and covered the older rocks over large areas.

The most important region of that volcanic activity and out-pour of lavas extended from what is now north-east Ireland to what is now Greenland. The remnants of those lavas now occupy a large part of Antrim, and in disconnected areas extend through the Inner Hebrides and the Faroe Islands into Iceland, Jan Mayen, and east Greenland; in Iceland the volcanic activity has not yet ceased. It has even been suggested that the basalt plateau of Portugal is another fragment of that vast volcanic region. At any rate, the basalts of Antrim, Mull, Skye and Iceland have been found to be similar. The position of these centres indicates that they developed along a line of weakness in the earth's crust.

There is a diversity of opinion as to the type of vent from which those Brito-Icelandic lavas issued, and this also involves their lateral extent, whether they formed one vast lava plateau or smaller plateaus at different centres. Professor Judd ex-explained the British volcanic vents of that time as of a central nature and as represented at the present day by the volcano of Kilauea, in the Hawaiian Islands. The visit of Sir Archibald Geikie to the Snake River basaltic plain in Western America led him, on the other hand, to attribute them to eruptions through extensive systems of parallel longitudinal fissures in the earth's crust, and for long this explanation was generally accepted.

The supporters of Geikie's theory believe that during the first, or regional, phase of volcanic activity, the vents consisted of many fissures in the earth's crust. Those fissures later became partly blocked and ordinary volcanoes developed at the re-maining openings, thus producing a local phase at different centres. That feature was succeeded by a final regional phase which resulted only in the injection of *dykes* into the overlying lavas, but those dykes did not reach the surface, though they are now exposed by denudation. This fissure-eruption theory leads these geologists to believe that the lateral extent of the lavas was enormous, being probably continuous from Antrim to Iceland, and may have been even greater. Dr Tyrrell, in his book *Volcanoes*, says: " If the Wyville-Thomson submarine ridge which connects the Hebrides with Greenland through Iceland is covered with basalt, as there is reason to believe, the total area of the Thulean basalt flood is of the order of a million square miles." Apart from the relics, or remnants, still existing, that huge area of lavas would naturally break up and founder at the same time as the foundering of the land mass or masses over which it spread. That land will be described presently. Much of it probably lies under the comparatively shallow sea covering what is known as the Scoto-Icelandic Divide, which curves in an arc from Britain and Scandinavia to Iceland, Greenland and North-Eastern Canada; the eastern portion is known as the Wyville-Thomson Ridge. This feature is shown on any map or chart indicating the ocean depths.

There is visible evidence in other parts of the earth's surface of gigantic lava areas formed in past ages.

Recent intensive geological work in Scotland has raised grave doubts regarding the longitudinal system of fissure-eruption theory and tends to support Judd's belief in a central type of vent, or at least that there were huge central volcanoes as well as fissure eruptions. For instance, many volcanic dykes in this region cut through the lava flows and must therefore be younger than the flows which they penetrate. Even more significant is the discovery that these dykes are not evenly distributed, but occur in *swarms*, which points to localised centres of activity. There is no evidence on the mainland of Scotland to indicate that the Hebridean lavas reached to any great lateral extent. It would be risky to stake too much upon this absence, however, for though the Chalk of the Cretaceous Period was probably widespread in Scotland in early Tertiary times, comparatively few fragments remain, and these have been preserved principally by protecting basalt lavas. Sir Edward B. Bailey, formerly Director of the Geological Survey of Great Britain, who played a major part in surveying the Mull area, and who compiled the geological *Memoirs* of Mull, Staffa, etc., believes that the Tertiary volcanic activity of the Hebrides commenced with central eruptions and was followed, later, by fissure eruptions. In the geological *Memoir* of Mull (1924), he says: " The present writer thinks that this centre [Mull] has repeatedly served as a focus of fissure-eruptions; but he is doubtful whether the lavas still spared by erosion are not, in the main, the products of a central volcano." He believes that some of the Mull swarm of dykes communicated with the surface.

In the Memoir, *Scotland: The Tertiary Volcanic Districts* (1961), Dr Richey goes further than Sir Edward Bailey, and considers that few, if any, of the Mull swarm of dykes reached the surface and therefore that almost the whole of the lava pile was built up from a central volcano.

Detailed survey has also revived the belief that the Hebridean volcanoes were of the Hawaiian type, as these fulfil many of the conditions demanded by the facts observed in the Hebrides. In this type a broad flat dome is formed, with a shallow cauldron, or caldera, on its blunt summit, and there is an absence of explosive activity, the lavas welling out quietly. Evidence has been found in Mull of the existence of a great volcanic crater six miles in diameter in the centre of the island.

Before proceeding further I would like to explain my reason for making a change in this edition of a geological term which will appear at intervals. In this edition I have used the term "Tertiary" instead of the term " Kainozoic," which was used in previous editions of this book, to denote the geological Era in which the Hebridean volcanic activity developed. My reason for using the term "Kainozoic" in previous editions was that when I wrote the first edition several eminent geologists had adopted the term "Kainozoic" and advocated its use in preference to the older term "Tertiary." I think they were right in doing so because the names still generally used for the two earlier Eras are "Mesozoic" and " Palaeozoic." Within recent years, however, the term "Tertiary" seems to have come back into use, though some geologists prefer to retain the term " Kainozoic." The principal factor which has led me to use in this edition the term "Tertiary" in preference to "Kainozoic" is that the Geological Survey *Memoirs*, to which I refer frequently, use the term "Tertiary" and not " Kainozoic." Perhaps it should be mentioned that the term "Kainozoic" includes the two most recent Periods of geological time, which are not included in the term " Tertiary." These two Periods, however, are infinitesimal fractions of the geological age of the earth.

The great volcanic activity of the Tertiary era of which Staffa is a very small relic is now believed to have accompanied the rupturing and drifting westward of the north America continent from Europe.

When the third edition of this book was written and previous to that time most geologists believed that, as stated in that edition, the north Atlantic Ocean had been formed by the break up and foundering of a vast Thulean, or north Atlantic, continent, or land bridge, which, they believed, had previously connected Europe to north America in pre-Tertiary time. They also believed that at one time there had been a similar land bridge, or continent, in the area now occupied by the south Atlantic Ocean connecting the adjacent continents.

During the time that these beliefs were held by most geologists, a small section of geologists believed in what is known as the Continental Drift Theory, first brought to serious scientific attention about 1912, by Professor Alfred Wegener, the German geologist. This theory explained the formation of the north Atlantic Ocean by the rupturing and drifting westward of north America from Europe. Indeed, Wegener's theory offered the same explanation for the formation of major oceans of the earth, since the Carboniferous period, about 300 million years ago, and he gave reasons for these colossal land movements. Wegener believed that before the Carboniferous period the present continents of the earth formed one vast land mass and that it gradually broke up into several pieces which drifted apart to form the present continents. There is much evidence geological, botanical and zoological to support Wegener's theory of continental drift, but for many years most geologists did not accept it because they thought that more evidence was necessary to confirm it.

Whether the North Atlantic Ocean was formed by the subsidence of a great land bridge or by the rupturing and drifting apart of America from Europe, which are by no means fantastic ideas, this great earth movement would be accompanied by violent volcanic activity, and it is of that action that Staffa is believed to be a relic.

The geological Period, or time, when that volcanic activity, including the lava floods, commenced is estimated from fossil plant-beds found between the lava flows near the base of the volcanic pile at Ardtun, Mull, and elsewhere. It is ascribed by the Geological Survey *Memoir* for Mull to the Eocene Period—that is, the earliest part of the Tertiary Era.

When writing the first edition of this book I mentioned this estimate given by the Geological Survey, but the late Professor J. W. Gregory, who kindly read over and checked my work at that time, told me that he did not agree with this opinion. He said that it was based upon the evidence of Mr Starkie Gardner, which had the high, though tentative, support of Professor Seward, but this view had been rejected for areas where the evidence was much fuller than for Scotland. He advised me to adopt the earlier opinion that the Mull volcanic activity commenced about the beginning of the Miocene Period, that is the Middle Tertiary Era. In support he added, " The Early Tertiary was a tropical flora with palms, etc., while the fossil plants of Ardtun indicate a much colder climate more in keeping with the Middle Tertiary."

In that first edition of this book I inserted a footnote expressing Professor Gregory's disagreement with the Geological Survey on this subject. Since that edition was published, however, I have found that many authoritative writers, when mentioning the Hebridean volcanic activity, adopt the verdict of the Geological Survey—that it commenced during the Eocene Period, or Early Tertiary. I was therefore strongly tempted to accept this decision and omit from the next edition of my book Professor Gregory's dissension. Recent research on the subject, however, seems to cast doubt on the Geological Survey estimate and tends to corroborate Professor Gregory's opinion.

For many years Dr J. B. Simpson, of H.M. Geological Survey, studied the pollen grains associated with the Ardtun leaf beds and various coal seams in Mull. He announced at the British Association meeting in Edinburgh, 1951, that " lavas above the Ardtun leaf beds are no older than Late Miocene "; and these leaf beds are low in the Mull volcanic pile. Reference is made to Dr Simpson's results in the second (1953) edition of Professor

John Walton's *Introduction to the Study of Fossil Plants*.

The Miocene Period is geologically very recent, and therefore Staffa may be said to be of comparatively modern formation. By contrast, it is worthy of note that the neighbouring island of Iona is composed of pre-Cambrian rocks, Lewisian and Torridonian, which are among the oldest known rocks in the earth's crust; no part of the original rock surface of the earth has been found.

During the late 1950s, extensive and continued investigation of palaeomagnetism (the ancient magnetism of rocks) revealed new reasons for continental drift. It was not until the 1960s, however, when the study of palaeomagnetism was applied to the rocks of the ocean floor that further evidence caused a complete swing of scientific opinion towards the acceptance of the theory of continental drift, and the abandonment of the land bridge theory, regarding the formation of the present continents and oceans. The evidence leads to the belief that all the continents formed one vast land mass until about 200 million years ago.

There is now general acceptance that, like other major oceans, the north Atlantic Ocean was formed by continental drift, that is, by the rupturing and drifting westward of the north America continent from Europe, and not by the foundering of a vast land bridge. The fracture is believed to have originated in the south not more than 200 million years ago but the drift apart did not commence until between 150 million and 100 million years ago.

The Continental Drift Theory accounts for the similarity of the contours of opposite coastlines of adjacent continents, which could be fitted into one another like the pieces of a jigsaw puzzle, also for the similarity of plant and animal life in adjacent lands now widely separated by the sea. The great fold mountain ranges of the two American continents stretch north and south along their western seaboard as if these coasts were being crumpled as the continents drift westward.

The rupturing of north America from Europe was at one stage accompanied by extensive volcanic activity, including vast floods of basaltic lava, and it is of that lava that Staffa is a very small fragment. The line of that rupture and the volcanic activity which accompanied it now appears in the extinct volcanic centres of Antrim, Mull, Ardnamurchan, Rum, Skye, Faroe Islands, Iceland and east Greenland. The drifting apart of north America from Europe still continues, and in Iceland where the volcanic activity has not yet ceased the continental rift, or rupture, is visible.

Readers who wish to pursue this very interesting subject should consult, *The Origin of Continents and Oceans*, by Professor Alfred Wegener. English translation, 1924: *Our Wandering Continents*, by Alex L. Du Toit, 1957. A clear modern account of the subject is given in *Continental Drift*, by D. H. and M. P. Tarling, 1971.

As already mentioned, the drift apart of the north America continent from Europe is now believed to have commenced between 150 million and 100 million years ago but the drift of north America away from Europe was not so much a westward movement but rather a twisting north-westward. This means that the drift commenced in the south of what is now the north Atlantic Ocean and very slowly continued northward. Consequently, the north part of the rupture and drift, the part which separated northern Canada and Greenland from Britain and Scandinavia, is believed to have commenced about 80 million to 70 million years ago.

Although the geological Period when the Antrim to Greenland volcanic activity and lava floods commenced was at first estimated from fossil plant-beds found near the base of the volcanic pile at Ardtun, and the Geological Survey *Memoir* for Mull gives the date of these fossil plants as about 70 million years ago, later work, based upon pollen grains associated with the Ardtun leaf-beds and various coal seams in Mull gave the date of the volcanic activity as the Miocene period which is the middle portion of the Tertiary era, and which commenced about 30 million years ago. Still later research, based upon radioactive gabbro and granite intrusions in Mull date the eruptions about 60 million years ago, which is a mere geological yesterday. Staffa is considered to be one of the basal lava flows of Mull. This age of Staffa is of course its age as part of a lava flow, and not as an island. The erosive forces of nature wrought unceasing for millions of years after this date before they had carved out Staffa as an island.

After learning the age of the rock of which Staffa is composed the reader may wish to know what is the scientific estimate age of the earth. According to the most modern scientific estimates, based upon the study of radioactivity (the spontaneous disintegration of certain chemical elements) in the earth's crustal rocks, and the study of meteorites, the earth has a geological (crustal rock) age of at least 3,000 million years. Its age since its origin as a gaseous or cosmic dust planet of our Solar System is reckoned to be about 4,500 million years.

Geological ages are of such vast duration and the methods of calculating them are so difficult that geologists are hesitant about stating them in terms of years. The figures given above, however, are the nearest estimates of modern science, and may help to give readers of this book a more definite idea of the geological age of Staffa than the vague phrases which are sometimes used on this subject, such as " Staffa was formed an infinitely long time ago," " Staffa was formed in the remote past," etc.

The rock of which Staffa is composed is a dark greyish-black, fine-grained basalt, which becomes a rusty brown on weathering, but decomposes no further. The fine grains, or crystals, indicate that the rock cooled and solidified from a molten condition at the earth's surface. If it had cooled and solidified underground (*plutonic*) the crystals would be larger: the deeper underground (and consequently the slower the cooling), the larger would be the crystals. The brownish surface colour indicates oxidisation of the iron which is present in the rock. Indeed, if a piece of rusty iron be broken, an almost exact replica of Staffa rock is revealed—the brown oxide on the outside surface and the greyish-black interior. On grinding down a section of the rock until it is sufficiently thin to be transparent, the microscope shows it to be composed of lozenge-shaped crystals of pale green olivine (fewer in number than in the later lava flows of Mull), laths of clear feldspar, and a granular greenish mineral called augite, together with numerous small pieces of opaque iron oxide. This assemblage constitutes the type of rock called a basalt. The crystals are arranged in rows, or strings, as if they floated along, thus preserving the

effect of the movement of the fluid lava.   On a larger scale, the
direction of flow of the lava is indicated by the steam or gas
cavities in the solidified lava.   These cavities may be empty,
lined with crystals or even completely filled with minerals.
They originated in globular form, but the movement of the
fluid lava lengthened them in the direction of its flow, causing
them to be round at one end and drawn out to a point at the
other end, resembling the shape of an almond.   For this reason
they are called *amygdales*, meaning almond-shaped.   They are
less frequent in compact basalts than in other types of lava.

During the great terrestial disturbances of the Tertiary Era,
when Staffa was formed, what is now the island of Mull was one
of the principal centres of volcanic activity.   According to the
evidence of modern geological survey, Mull includes the most
complicated extinct volcanic centre as yet accorded detailed
examination anywhere in the world.   It presents almost every
conceivable type of eruption in its lavas, agglomerates and
intrusions, and the innate complexity of these formations has
been increased greatly by a shifting, several miles, of the focal
centre of the volcano.   In the *Geological Magazine* review of the
Geological *Memoir* on Mull, the reviewer says: "The reading
of the geological story in the field in Mull was a matter of
extraordinary difficulty."

The calderas that formed at the two centres of the Mull
volcano were repeatedly renewed by subsidence—owing,
probably, to decrease in the pressure of the reservoir of *magma*,
or molten material, beneath.   During the subsidences of these
calderas, the magma welled up the circular fractures round the
subsiding blocks and that process has resulted in the formation of
a remarkable series of *ring dykes*, or curved, concentric outcrops
of igneous rocks (*i.e.*, rocks which have consolidated from a
molten condition).   These ring dykes could have been formed
irrespective of any volcanic cone and they may, or may not,
have reached the surface of the ground.   They are now laid
bare by denudation.   The subject of ring-dykes, however, is
very complex and is not yet understood clearly.   Owing to the
shifting of the volcanic centre of Mull the ring-dykes occur in
two groups—one group round each centre—which overlap and
cut one another at two points on their circumferences.   One of

these ring-dykes, in the locality of Loch Ba, is believed to be the most perfect example of this geological formation known to science. It has a maximum diameter of five miles and averages about one hundred yards in thickness.

The lowest Tertiary rocks in Mull rest upon a thin development of Cretaceous rocks (which in turn overlie the Jurassic) and consist of a few feet of sand, in which what are taken to be wind-rounded grains are prominently represented. This sandstone indicates that desert conditions existed in this region when it was being formed, but gradually the climate changed from arid to warm and moist, which caused swamps and forests to develop, and it was at that stage that volcanic activity broke out. The moist climate continued to prevail during the accumulation of the lavas, but it changed gradually from warm to temperate. Successive lava tops weathered in their turn to soil in which vegetation grew. The evidence thus indicates that the Mull lavas were not of submarine origin, but were poured out on a land surface that stretched, at least, from the mainland westward beyond what are now the Treshnish Isles.

Ben More, in Mull, is often described as an extinct volcano, but neither Ben More nor any other mountain or hill in Mull is an extinct volcano in itself. They are merely the vertical projections of denuded lavas that were ejected from a large volcano which had its first centre between Loch Sguabain and the head of Glen Cannel. Later, the volcanic centre moved north-west to the region around what is now the southeast end of Loch Ba. The remnants of those lavas now form the surface of Mull, with the exception of the Ross, and in outlying fragments appear in Ulva, Gometra, Staffa, the Treshnish and other islands, but not Iona. These areas are the basal wreck of a great volcano worn down to its roots by millions of years of denudation. When at its zenith, this volcano is believed to have been at least ten thousand feet high. It may have been higher but existing evidence does not allow of a more definite estimation of its height. (At the close of the Tertiary volcanic activity the average surface of Scotland must have been above the level of the highest present-day mountains).

The average thickness of a bed of lava in the Mull area is about fifty feet, but the total thickness of all the lava flows in

Mull still reaches to a height of over three thousand feet.

Although Mull was once deluged with lavas, it was never a burning, fiery furnace, as some persons believe. There is no burning, fire, smoke or ash connected with volcanic action. The term "ash" is still used by geologists, but it is a relic of the time when volcanoes were believed to be burning mountains. To modern geologists the term "ash" does not convey any idea of combustion, but denotes fine-grained volcanic debris which is usually blown into the air by the explosive action of liberated subterranean gases, through volcanic vents, and which settles ultimately on the surrounding land surface. The supposed smoke in a volcano is steam and gases carrying fine volcanic dust in suspension. The supposed flames are the reflection of the glowing mass of lava on the clouds of this dust overhead, though there are pockets of inflammable gases.

The volcanic rocks of Mull, like those of all other volcanic regions, were ejected in a molten condition, caused by the alloying of mineral substances in superheated water underground, and heat within the earth's crust. They merely changed their condition and not their composition, as would have occurred if the process had been combustion.

Every evidence found in the Mull area indicates that the lavas were poured out, at intervals, with a minimum of explosive activity. The occurrence of a widespread layer of mudstone, several feet thick, which is believed to be weathered volcanic ash, at the base of the lava series, however, betokens considerable explosive activity at the very beginning of the volcanic history of the district. There is also evidence that violent explosions occurred later at widely different intervals. But considering the volcanic period as a whole, there was relatively little explosive activity. A long interval of volcanic repose followed the initial explosion.

The duration of the volcanic action appears to have been of unusual longevity, one indication being the occurrence of sedimentary material, including coal and leaf beds, with well-preserved terrestrial vegetation between some of the basalt sheets. This evidence means that considerable intervals occurred sometimes between successive outflows of lava—sufficient time for the surface of a flow to disintegrate into soil and allow trees, shrubs and other plants to grow to full maturity, die and become buried.

The fossil leaf-beds of Ardtun, Mull, have become world-famous in geology, as they date the Hebridean volcanic activity; they occur between lava flows which are low in the Mull volcanic pile.   These leaves appear to have been shed autumn after autumn by deciduous trees and have been preserved by falling into a still, shallow lake, or backwaters of a river-system, round the marshy borders of which the trees grew, and layers of clay were deposited on top of them.   They accumulated on the bottom of the lake, one above the other, fully expanded and at perfect rest, as they are found in a wonderful state of undamaged preservation.   Some of them retain even their original withered colours.   In the Glasgow Museum and Art Gallery there is a fine collection of leaf-impressions and leaves in the clay taken from Ardtun.   During a visit to the leaf beds at Ardtun, I found several leaf impressions and one actual coloured leaf set in its double impression in greyish clay which to my unqualified inspection looked like a hazel leaf in autumn colouring.

Sir Albert Seward, in his Presidential Address to the British Association, in 1939, said that if we could survey the vegetation of the present geographical position of the Hebrides as it appeared during the volcanic period of the Tertiary Era, when Staffa was formed, " we should be impressed by its luxuriance: at first sight the general aspect would seem familiar, but on a closer examination of the trees and shrubs we should find only a few recalling modern European species; many would remind us of exotic plants of eastern origin"; that is, plants of the modern Far East.   In the second (1953) edition of Professor John Walton's *Introduction to the Study of Fossil Plants*, however, Dr J. B. Simpson is quoted as saying: " It is suggested that the nearest natural habitat of that flora [Mull Tertiary] now would be Portugal, Spain, and Northern Africa, that is to say, at least 20° of latitude nearer the Equator."

A much larger fossil than those in the leaf beds of Ardtun was discovered by Dr John MacCulloch, the geologist, in the base of the lofty sea cliffs of Burg, in the promotory of Ardmeanach, Mull, directly opposite Staffa.   This very interesting feature is, or rather was, a fossilised tree trunk, now called " MacCul-loch's Tree " or " The Fossil Tree of Burg," standing in a vertical position embedded in columnar rock of a lava flow. The fossil tree originally stood about forty feet high and varied from three to four feet in diameter, but its comparatively soft texture has caused it to weather away until all that remains is a stump about four feet high at ground level. The cast, or impression, of the tree in the rock is, however, still quite clear to its full height. Although sheltered in a recess in the cliff, this fossil tree is really difficult of access and is very seldom visited, because it is far from habitation and the cliff in which it is situated forms the outermost part of a high headland which is open to the Atlantic and is fringed with a rocky, boulder-strewn shore.

There is a much smaller fossil tree in the rocks over the entrance to a cave about two hundred yards to the north of " MacCulloch's Tree." There is also another fossil tree near Tavool House on the north shore of Loch Scridain.

When considering Staffa, it should be remembered that it was not always an island, but was originally a small portion, situated near the base, of the Mull series of lavas. It is an island now because great portions of the surrounding and overlying land have disappeared through various causes. There would be disruptions and subsidences from subterranean disturbances, and as soon as the volcanic activity subsided finally, intense natural erosion would commence and continue ceaselessly, such as the devouring sea and the weathering action of rain, frost, and air, which causes decomposition and dis-integration of the rocks, also rivers washing away the debris and automatically scouring their channels deeper. These erosive forces of nature are usually described as the agents of denudation.

When describing this region, Sir Archibald Geikie says: "There is the most stupendous evidence of change in the topo-graphy." The main form of this district, however, was shaped by erosion, or land-sculpture, before the onset of the Pleistocene Ice Age. That Ice Age really had several recurring inter-glacial stages when the climate became milder and the ice retreated temporarily. The retreat of the ice front was not continuous but oscillatory. The general flow of the ice sheet in western Mull was in a westerly direction.   As it crept over the landscape, boulders became embedded in it which were carried along and, combined with the ice, scoured smooth pre-existing contours.   When the ice began to melt these boulders were deposited far from their original site and are now known as *erratics*.   There is a number of red granite boulders of this type forming conspicuous objects on the Island of Iona where there is no native red granite.   They were probably carried over from Mull.

Comparatively recent elevation of Mull and its attendant islands is indicated clearly by the pre-Glacial and post-Glacial *Raised Beaches* which appear in many parts of their coast-line.

Whether the volcanic area of Mull formed part of a great Brito-Icelandic plateau of lavas, or was a distinctly separate centre, the amount of land removed by erosion from this district since the cessation of its volcanic activity has been colossal. There is visible evidence that the lavas have been furrowed from the height of Ben More to sea level at least, that is, to a depth of over three thousand feet.   Indeed, erosion has cut up the sur-face of Mull to such an extent that a relatively slight depression would turn it into a group of islands.   Also, the coast-line of the greater part of Mull consists of sheer cliffs—clearly the work of the sea, as lava flows much too slowly to end so abruptly. Moreover, this area has been dislocated by many faults by which different portions have been shifted greatly in level.

That movements subsequent to the solidification of the Mull lavas have taken place is shown by the inclination of some of the basaltic sheets, of which Staffa is a good example.   This in-clination of Staffa causes the actual top of the Fingal's Cave lava to be at sea level near the north end of the island, the over-lying rock being the base of a later lava flow.   The tilt of the island appears quite clearly on the aerial view of Staffa.   It slopes down from the cliff-tops at the south and west to the low ground at the north and north-east.   The settling of the Staffa lavas appears to have been even more than a single tilt because the southern part of the island, from the extreme southern cliffs at the Colonnade north to the little valley, has a greater tilt towards the east than the part of the island north of the little valley.   This little valley may have originated as a fracture, or *fault*, in the solidified lavas when the southern portion of the island tilted downward toward the east more than the northern portion.

The nearby island, called the Dutchman's Cap, which, like Staffa, is a remnant of the basaltic floods of Mull, also indicates movement subsequent to the solidification of this part of the Mull lavas as it dips gently towards the south-west—that is, in the opposite direction to the dip of Staffa.

Staffa is believed to be a detached remnant of one of the basal lava flows of Mull. This belief is based upon the columnar structure and petrographical similarity between Staffa and the lower flows of Mull, where these are exposed. But as Staffa has been altered in level by earth movements which occurred after the lavas had solidified, it is not possible to say to what depth the lavas extend beneath it. It is not known whether or not lavas floor the sea bottom continuously from Mull to the Treshnish Isles. To whatever depth the lavas continue beneath Staffa, it is probable that they rest upon a tin development of Upper Cretaceous rocks overlying some low member of the Jurassic (such as the Lias of Gribun), and that below the Jurassic should occur Triassic resting in violent unconformity on Moine Gneiss (again as at Gribun), and not on Lewisian Gneiss such as occurs in Iona. Briefly stated, the foundation of Staffa is probably very like what is seen at Gribun.

While exploring Staffa, the visitor can see for himself the relationship which it bears to Mull if he will look across to that island, especially to the headland of Burg, or Ardmeanach, which is directly opposite Staffa. There he will observe, if the weather be clear enough, that the outline of the upper portion of the landscape rises in a series of steps or trap terraces (a geological term derived from the Norse word *trapp* meaning steps, or a stair). Each of these terraces consists of a solidified individual lava flow truncated by erosion similar to the one seen so clearly at the south end of Staffa. The greater part of this magnificent headland, like the major portion of Mull, is composed of superimposed horizontal beds of lava. In the face of an escarpment here Sir Archibald Geikie counted twenty separate lava beds piled one above the other.

In order to make clear the relationship which Staffa bears to

Mull, we may describe Burg as being composed of many large Staffas rising in a regular level sequence. Conversely, if a series of Staffas surmounted the existing one, we should have a representation of the Mull coast as it appears at Burg and many other parts. From this statement it will be realised that the upper portion, at least, of the submarine hill of which Staffa forms the exposed summit, is, probably, of similar formation to that seen above water, though sloping more gradually towards the bed of the sea than the sheer cliffs of the island.

The Fingal's Cave lava—that is, the principal flow forming Staffa—is generally divisible into a lower zone of massive regular columns, a middle zone of narrow, close-spaced, wavy columns, and a top zone largely of slag. The two columnar zones are exposed, typically, at Fingal's Cave, and the line of demarcation between the two tiers of columns is even and definite. It is not a line of separation, however, for they both consist of one rock and are merely differentiated by their jointing. The massive and straight columns, forming the lower zone, have developed through comparatively slow regular cooling of the lower surface of the lava. The close-spaced wavy columns, forming the middle zone (really the top portion of the island at the Colonnade and Fingal's Cave) have resulted from rapid irregular cooling of the upper surface after the lava had solidified. The slaggy lava forming the upper zone occupies the east coast of the island for about three hundred yards south from Goat Cave.

The basement of reddish conglomeratic tuff which appears at sea level, beneath the range of regular columns at the Colonnade and elsewhere, was formed by the eruption of rock debris during intervals between the successive outflows of basalt.

We may summarise the story of Staffa's formation thus: At the beginning and until long after the middle of the Tertiary Era, the districts of Scotland which we now call Lorne, Morvern, and Mull, were united in one continuous land mass. There was no Firth of Lorne, no Sound of Mull, and no sea between what is now western Mull and the Treshnish Isles (these channels were formed after the cessation of the volcanic activity). In other words, there was no island of Mull. It was really part of the mainland, which, at that time, stretched

The landing place (centre right) with Clamshell Cave behind; the Causeway path can be seen leading towards Fingal's Cave which is immediately behind the headland on the extreme left

(*Above*) The Herdsman, *Am Buachaille*, seen from the plateau; (*below*) the packed columnar rock formation in *Am Buachaille*

westward continuously beyond the present position of the Treshnish Isles. That land was much flatter than it is now and the
climate was warm and moist.

Towards the middle of the Tertiary Era earth tremors and
rumblings commenced in this region. Those disturbances
were followed by the outbreak of a volcano, or lava caldera, in
a wide area around where now lies Loch Sguabain, in Glen
More, Mull. At first, violent volcanic explosions blew rock
debris high into the air. That action was followed by a long
period of quiescence, but again the volcano broke forth. This
time the activity was much less violent, the principal feature
being a great outpour of basaltic lava which spread over the
surrounding landscape for many miles in all directions. That
lava flow was probably about fifty feet thick and in a westerly
direction it reached at least as far as the present position of the
Treshnish Isles. Slowly the volcanic activity subsided and,
during the ensuing phase of quiescence, the solidified lava was
weathered into soil in which vegetation grew. Again the
volcano broke forth and issued another great flood of lava which
spread over the landscape of the first lava flow and, in its turn,
solidified slowly. This new surface was also weathered into
soil in which plants grew, but again only to be deluged by a
subsequent flood of lava. The process was repeated again and
again with a minimum of explosive activity, the interval between
some of the outpours being of sufficient duration to permit of
trees growing to full maturity. During these outbreaks, the
volcanic centre shifted north-west to the region around what is
now the south-east end of Loch Ba. Ultimately, the pile of
solidified lavas reached to a height of at least ten thousand feet
at their centre and, as they sloped gradually as they spread
outward, were probably over two thousand feet high above
what is now Staffa. At that stage the volcanic activity subsided
finally, and the erosive forces of nature attacked the landscape,
carving, gouging, and weathering, thus gradually stripping off
the solidified lava flows one after the other, assisted, no doubt,
in their work of destruction by fissures and subsidences. There
may have been faults in the earth's crust in the region of what is
now the sea bed between western Mull and the Treshnish Isles,
or perhaps there was shattering of belts of rock by tension clefts.

As gaps appeared in this western area, the relentless battering of the sea, and other forces of erosion, would slowly but surely break up and engulf huge portions of that land, until now all that remains above water are a few detached fragments of one of the basal lava flows of Mull. One of these fragments is Staffa, and others are the Treshnish Isles.

In a south-westerly direction, the last remnants of the Mull plateau lavas may be the small islets, or rocks, of Reidh Eilean and Stac MhicMhurchaidh, which lie west of Iona. They show columnar formation, but the rock is of coarser grain than most of the Mull lavas, and there is no proof that they are not part of a sill.

As we ponder on the tremendous changes that have taken place in the Mull area since the outbreak of its volcanic activity, we should bear in mind that in the building-up and in the wearing-down of its colossal volcanic pile the mighty forces of nature have wrought unceasing for millions of years. So also, when we consider the enormous amount of erosion that has occurred here since the cessation of its terrestial disturbances, we realise that much as we are impressed by what remains of this volcanic region, we should be impressed far more by what has disappeared.

NOTE

Should any reader wish to pursue the subject of this chapter further, the following books can be recommended:— *Tertiary and Post-Tertiary Geology of Mull, Loch Aline and Oban*, 1924; *The Geology of Staffa, Iona and Western Mull*, 1925; *The Geology of Ardnamurchan, North-west Mull and Coll*, 1930; and *Scotland: The Tertiary Volcanic Districts*, 1961. These books have a direct approach to the geology of Staffa and Mull without any of the concomitant subjects which I have included in this chapter. They are *Memoirs* published by H.M. Geological Survey and are therefore of the highest reliability, but as they are written for geologists, they may be rather technical for the average reader. As far as I am aware, there is no non-technical description of the geology of this region published. There is a very interesting and readable account of the subject in Sir Archibald Geikie's *Ancient Volcanoes of Great Britain*, 2 vols., 1897, though naturally, it does not include the results of modern research.

CHAPTER V

COLUMNAR ROCK FORMATION

FOR many years considerable discussion took place among geologists regarding the way in which the columnar, or prismatic, formation of the rock composing the greater part of Staffa, and elsewhere, was produced. Theories and experiments were tested over a long period before the problem was finally solved.

Towards the end of last century Robert Mallet, the geologist, said that all the salient phenomena of the prismatic and jointed structure of basalt can be accounted for upon the admitted laws of cooling, and contraction thereby, of previously molten rock possessing the known properties of basalt. The essential conditions are a very general homogeneity in the mass, and slow cooling, principally from one or more of its surfaces. That view still holds good.

From practical experiments and other observations it is agreed that columnar rock formation, which is typical of the more compact, heavy basalts, is due to the shrinkage of the molten material on solidification and cooling; but it cannot be described as crystallisation, as the process of its development is quite different from that which forms a crystal. At one time, some geologists believed that basaltic columns were gigantic crystals and that crystals could grow only from aqueous solutions. These erroneous ideas led them to believe that the columns must have formed underwater. The discovery that basaltic columns form on a dry land surface disproved these beliefs.

The development of the basaltic columns began on the upper surface exposed to the atmosphere, and the lower surface exposed to the cold ground, and extended upward and downward into the mass as solidification and cooling proceeded.

When a mass is subjected to a uniform strain, according to the law of least resistance, it tends to assume this prismatic structure. At any point on a surface, three breaks radiating from a centre form the least number of breaks that will relieve a strain that pulls in all directions, as does the strain in cooling lavas. A combination of these breaks results in the formation of hexagons which run through the entire mass of lava. Many igneous rocks, that is, rocks which have solidified from a molten condition, present this mode of jointing. It occurs sometimes in other rocks, such as sandstone and shale, that have been subject to considerable heat; but the structure reaches its most perfect development in basalt. In this rock the columns, which are often very long and regular, are bounded by three, four, five, or six planes, producing triangular, quadrangular, pentagonal, and hexagonal prisms.

In rocks having a very homogeneous texture, such as Staffa, the six-sided prisms are the most prevalent, for in this case the centres of contraction, or tension, through loss of heat and water, are equidistant, and the angles of the prisms fit together without any intervening empty space. Theoretically, all the columns should be hexagonal, but usually neither the constituents of the rock nor the physical conditions are sufficiently uniform to ensure perfect symmetry, and thus they vary. Columns having more or less than six sides are the result of irregular spacing of the contraction centres, caused by these parts of the rock not having a perfectly uniform composition. A common example of contraction into prismatic formation, owing to loss of moisture, can be seen in drying mud or drying starch.

The long axis of the columns has been found to be perpendicular to the surface at which the greatest cooling took place. In accordance with this law, the columns are usually vertical in horizontally-bedded lavas, as at Staffa. Occasionally, the columns are segmented into a series of superimposed short lengths, or drums, by a subsidiary cross-fracturing which developed to relieve the vertical contraction of the lava. These cross features are of ball and socket formation, convex or concave upward, and formed later than the vertical fissuring of the columns.

As mentioned in the previous chapter, there are really two zones of columnar rock in the Fingal's Cave lava: a lower zone of massive, regular, upright columns and an upper zone of smal-

ler irregular columns. The reason for these different formations is that the lower zone cooled by slow conduction, while
the upper zone cooled by comparatively rapid radiation into
the air or crust of slaggy lava. These two zones meet in a
plane which is remarkably even and clear in the Fingal's Cave
lava. The slow cooling of the lower zone led to uniformly-
spaced centres of contraction, or tension. The more rapid
cooling and solidification of the upper zone caused the centres
of contraction to be less regularly disposed, which resulted in
smaller, wavy and much less symmetrical columns.

Professor Watts suggests the following simple experiment to
explain the principle of how this type of rock formation occurs:

If a number of cigarettes be squeezed together in the hand, each one will
become flattened where it touches another and thus the inner ones will
become six-sided. It is a similar cause which makes bee-cells hexagonal;
the bees all start together as near as convenient, and each one tries to build a
round cell; but each cell comes into contact with six others and acquires six
sides by pressure. [Many parts of Staffa resemble a honeycomb in appearance by the six-sided pattern of the columns]. If instead of pressure
throughout the mass, as in the case of the cigarettes, we imagine an evenly
distributed stretching or tension, each particle drawing its immediate
neighbour towards itself, it is easy to imagine that something quite similar
will follow, and evenly distributed hexagons will form on the cooling surface,
packed together so as to occupy the whole space.

Although columnar rock structure occurs frequently in *sheets*,
or *sills*, *bosses*, and *dykes* (veins of lava of different forms injected
into the pre-existing rocks and later laid bare by denudation),
it is usually less regular than in lava flows. The two best
known examples of this rock formation, Staffa and the Giant's
Causeway, Ireland, are relics of lavas that were extruded at the
earth's surface and spread over the surrounding landscape. A
more modern discovery of a large exposure of striking columnar
lava is the Devil's Post-Pile in the Sierra Nevada Mountains,
California, which is also a remnant of a lava flow.

There are larger columns, both in diameter and height, in
the Giant's Causeway than in Staffa, so also there are larger
columns in the neighbouring islands of Ulva and Mull, as well
as in Skye, while the Shiant Isles,[1] north of Skye, present

[1] These islands are remnants of thick *sills* of Tertiary dolerite intruded into
Jurassic sediments and therefore did not originate, like Staffa, as part of a lava
flow extruded at the earth's surface.

columnar cliffs which rise to a height of five hundred feet. But mere size does not stir the aesthetic sense, though in some persons it may cause an open-mouth wonderment, and a group of columns, however striking, appears as a meaningless structure when unrelated to its immediate surroundings. The columns require to form part of a composition whose members are in harmony with one another before they can be said to possess aesthetic qualities. Only in Staffa do we find magnificent natural columns of basaltic rock fulfilling this requirement. Here they rise from an adequate stylobate and are surmounted by a suitable entablature, with no unsightly object nearby to distract one's attention. The natural simplicity and clearness of arrangement of these component parts produce a composition of very imposing effect. It is this artistic appearance of Staffa, combined with its isolation, which makes it unique among all regions of columnar rock; it also has the additional attraction of its remarkable caves.

In popular science and non-scientific literature the statement is frequently made that there is a submarine connection of columnar rock between Staffa and the Giant's Causeway at the present day, but this assertion is wholly unwarranted. When the Antrim and Hebridean volcanoes were in action, and for some time afterwards, there may have been some connection between the lava flows of Mull, including Staffa, and those of Ireland, but there is no existing evidence of that connection. The erosive forces of nature have wrought severely for so long a period that any evidence which might lead to a belief in a connection between the two areas has been obliterated. A line joining Staffa to the Giant's Causeway passes through the western extremity of the Ross of Mull and Rhynns of Islay, yet we do not find any Tertiary volcanic rocks in these districts, with the exception of numerous dykes in Islay. These Islay dykes are intrusives from below, and probably never reached the surface to give rise to volcanoes and lava flows. Again, the sea bed sinks to a depth of about forty fathoms (two hundred and forty feet) between Mull and Islay, and to an average depth of about seventy fathoms (four hundred and twenty feet) between Islay and the Giant's Causeway. The lavas would therefore require to reach to this depth at least in order to connect Staffa to Antrim, yet the geologists who surveyed Mull and Staffa believe that the latter island is a remnant of one of the basal lava flows of Mull considered as a whole. Nevertheless, there seems to be significance in the following statement in the Geological Survey Memoir, *Scotland: The Tertiary volcanic Districts* (1948), p. 42: " It is noteworthy that the columnar lavas of Staffa and the west of Mull are identical in structure and composition with the basalt lavas of Antrim, as developed at the Giant's Causeway."

It should be remembered that the columnar rock structure appears to advantage at Staffa and the Giant's Causeway because the former is an island and the latter a sea-coast promontory. Consequently, the ceaseless pounding by the waves has removed material which might have hidden their most perfect parts had they been situated inland, and has given them a clean-cut appearance. These two areas are regarded as classic examples of columnar rock formation, although it appears in many of the earth's volcanic regions.

CHAPTER VI

DESCRIPTION OF CAVES, ETC.

THE coast of Staffa presents many striking features, with its

> Cliffs of darkness, caves of wonder,
> Echoing the Atlantic thunder.

Even if the island had not possessed its wonderful columnar rock formation, it would have won renown for its great caverns swept to their inner recesses by the sonorous surge of the sea. Like the island itself, these caves have been aptly named:

> Clamshell (or Scallop) Cave
> Fingal's, or the Great Cave
> Boat Cave
> MacKinnon's Cave
> Cormorants' (or Scarts') Cave

On the Ordnance Survey map of Staffa there is one cave in the north-east cliffs of the island named " Goat Cave," but on making enquiries I learned that no modern inhabitant of the neighbouring islands was aware of this name on Staffa. The name appears to have been known, however, to the natives of Mull during last century, because the Ordnance Survey Office informed me that the name Goat Cave, on Staffa, was given to the original Surveyors in 1875-7 by the Rev. J. G. Campbell, Tiree, by Mr D. McLean, Fanmore, Torloisk, Mull, and by Mr H. McCall, Torloisk, and that the name was verified at the revision Survey of 1897 by Mr Hector Black, Ulva.

All the caves have a small beach of coarse black shingle at the inner end, at low tide.

As Clamshell Cave is the best-known landing place in the island, I shall make it a starting point for a description of the coast, travelling in a clockwise direction. The landing place of early visitors to Staffa—Banks, Faujas, Dr MacCulloch, etc.—appears to have been near the east end of the little valley which crosses the island obliquely, for they describe it as being not far to the north of Clamshell Cave. Even William Keddie, who visited Staffa in 1847, mentions that after the passengers were landed from the steamboat by Ulva boatmen they proceeded a short distance south to Clamshell Cave. Those early visitors kept to the shore rocks southward from their landing place to Clamshell Cave and thence onwards to Fingal's Cave, but according to one of Sir Joseph Banks's drawings he and his companions descended from the top of the island, where they had spent the night, down the rock face on the south of Clamshell Cave, that is, where the wooden stair used to be. This rock face is fairly steep.

Surely nothing more remarkable in rock formation than Clamshell Cave can be seen anywhere. One side of the entrance is formed by columns of rock bent into a formation resembling a clamshell or the ribs of a wooden ship. The opposite (north) side is formed by the projecting ends of columns and appears like a giant honeycomb. This cave has a very striking appearance, but has too much of the bizarre to be described as picturesque, though its curved columnar formation is probably of more interest to the geologist than the regular structure of the more renowned Fingal's Cave.

One theory offered to account for the peculiar curved-column formation seen at Clamshell Cave is that when an upper system of close-spaced wavy columns, caused by the rapid irregular cooling of the upper surface of lava, meets with the straighter and more massive system of columns caused by the slow regular cooling of the lower surface, then, instead of coalescing, they sometimes bend abruptly into rough parallelism.

Owing to its shape, it is rather difficult to decide where the cave actually begins, but the following measurements will give an approximate idea of its size:

Length inward	130 ft.
Height	30 ft.
Breadth	16-18 ft.

This cave is well sheltered from the sea, and is therefore one of the best landing places, having a small beach of coarse black shingle with the broken columns on either side forming natural landing stages.

Proceeding southward along the water's edge, a small island, or rather rock, composed of columns without any stratum over them, appears on the left. It is called the Herdsman, or *am Buachaille*, to give it its Gaelic name. Its highest point is about thirty feet above sea level, and it is separated from Staffa by a channel about fifteen feet wide. The name "Herdsman" is often applied in the Scottish Highlands to solitary rocks, hills, and islands, which seem to keep guard over the surrounding ground, or islands, like a herdsman over his cattle. The Lord of the Isles was often referred to as *am Buachaille nan Eilean*, meaning " The Herdsman of the Isles."

Another reasonable derivation is that this rock has received its name by reason that it herds back the heavy seas which roll in from the south, thus adding to the safety of landing at Clamshell Cave; southerly and south-westerly winds are the most prevalent here.

Although wonderful enough when viewed from sea level, the Herdsman has to be seen from the top of the adjacent cliffs of Staffa for one to realise fully its complex formation. Its columns are seen dispersed in orderly confusion, and at one part appear like logs of driftwood piled one above the other. At high water the sea divides this little rock into two parts, the northern portion having a conical form with its columns converging towards an imaginary apex, while the southern part has the majority of its columns laid horizontal. The side facing Staffa is as sheer as if cut with a knife, which shows to perfection the beautiful packed formation of these truncated columns.

The channel between the Herdsman and Staffa is about ten feet deep at mean tide, and the rock on either side is encrusted with greyish-brown barnacles and limpets, white dog-whelks, and crimson sea-anemones, which sparkle like gems through the limpid green water in the sunshine. As there is no sand or silt in the vicinity of Staffa, the waters which break on its rocky shore contain no sediment, and they are as clear as crystal tinged with emerald. Although the sea around Staffa may appear of a dark hue, this effect is really due to the reflection of its black rocky bed.

When heavy seas sweep in from the south they get choked at the entrance to the narrow channel between Staffa and the

Herdsman and, mounting up into tidal waves, or bores, rush through the passage in fierce, hissing torrents to spend themselves in foaming confusion near Clamshell Cave.

John Stoddart, LL.B., who visited Staffa in 1799, says: "As every strange phenomenon in these regions is connected with the Fions [=the Feinne—the army of Fingal], the Buachaille is said to consist of 8000 distinct stones on each of which stood one of these warriors." One imaginative visitor suggested that perhaps the Herdsman was the heap of columns that had been excavated from Fingal's Cave, or perhaps the surplus columns left over after Staffa had been built.

In the cliffs of Staffa, opposite the south end of the Herdsman, there is a peculiar formation resembling a large chair set into a niche in the rock face. This feature is known as Fingal's Wishing Chair and tradition says that if one sits here and wishes, that desire will certainly be granted, but it must be kept strictly private until it is fulfilled. Apparently this feature has not always been named Fingal's Wishing Chair, as Dr Spiker, a German visitor to Staffa in 1816, calls it the Priest (he does not mention the name "Wishing Chair") and says "it is believed that at one time there was an altar here."

On one occasion when visitors were being conducted to Fingal's Cave, the guide pointed out the Wishing Chair and mentioned that any wish made while sitting on it would certainly be granted. Naturally, most of them desired to put it to the test, and one lady, after wishing while seated on the chair, remarked to the nearby visitors, "I wonder if the tradition regarding wishes made here is true?" A gentleman replied, "Oh yes, I have proved it on several visits to Staffa." The lady said, "That is very interesting. May I ask what you wished?" "Well," he said, "on each occasion I wished I would get safely back to Oban."

At the Wishing Chair and onward we are traversing the "Causeway," an irregular shore formed by the upper ends of broken columns giving an appearance of tessellated pavement. Some of these exposed ends are concave while others are convex: these surfaces form the horizonal ball and socket joints of the standing columns. This is the best place to observe the various sectional shapes and sizes of the columns. They range from one foot six inches to three feet six inches in diameter and the majority are five or six-sided, though there are many exceptions. Some have as many as nine sides, while one, at least, near Fingal's Cave, is almost square.

A conspicuous projection of the cliff rising from the Causeway presents what are known as the " Bending Columns," in the lower zone of the lava flow, as they are bent, or curved, inward at the top. This curvature is probably due to the same cause as that which bent the columns at Clamshell Cave, and not, as might be supposed from a superficial inspection, to the weight of the overlying mass of rock—which is really another zone of the same lava flow—causing them to yield. All the columns for a short distance south of the Bending Columns and north-ward to Clamshell Cave are more or less curved at the top, but since the cliff projects at this point the curvature is more apparent here. This bent or curved formation developed when the lava was cooling after it had solidified, and not when the lava was flowing.

Not many yards south of the Bending Columns is Fingal's Cave, but as the next chapter is devoted to a full description of this great cavern I shall pass it by in the meantime.

In order to explore the remainder of the coastline a boat is necessary, as, with the exception of a few small creeks, and a few hundred yards at the north end of the island, the cliffs rise sheer from a rocky platform at sea level.

After leaving Fingal's Cave, in a boat, the " Colonnade," or " Great Face," appears on the right. This part of the island consists of sheer cliffs formed by an extensive range of long regular basaltic columns, having an average height of fifty-five feet. The columns rise from a base of volcanic tuff at sea level and are surmounted by an entablature of amorphous basalt, the whole composition being suggestive of the facade of a Greek temple.

These cliffs appear from close inspection to rise vertically from the sea, but as far as can be calculated from photographs which have the horizon line level, they fall back at an angle of about seven degrees from the vertical. The inclination is caused by these columns being perpendicular to the plane of the rock bed. As this plane dips from south-west to north-east, it follows that they have the same inclination from the vertical as the plane of the bed has to the horizon. This inclination does not detract from the appearance of the cliffs, but rather conveys an impression of majestic challenge in the same manner as the rake of the funnels of an ocean liner. Many people may visit Staffa without noticing that the island is inclined, as it is only from the south and south-east that the inclination is conspicuous.

There is a small cave at sea level scooped out in the form of a long tunnel in the lower stratum of the Colonnade cliff, known as Boat Cave, as it can be entered only by means of a boat. Its dimensions are:

Length inward	..	..	..	150 ft.
Height above high water	..		..	14 ft.
Breadth at entrance		..	..	12 ft.

There is nothing remarkable about this cave, but when viewed from a distance it seems somehow to add a finishing touch to the cliffs, as if it were an entrance to this great columnar facade.

The highest point of the Colonnade cliffs is one hundred and twelve feet above high water mark, this point being situated between Fingal's Cave and Boat Cave.

On rounding the Colonnade, MacKinnon's Cave opens out in the cliffs, where numerous sea-birds haunt every ledge and cranny whitewashed with guano. It has been hollowed out in the tuff up to the base of the columnar zone of rock, which, owing to the tilt of the island, is about fifty feet above sea level at this point, though on the opposite (east) side of the island the top of the tuff is beneath sea level. Thus the overhanging range of upright columns forms the flat arch over the cave entrance. This magnificent cave is almost as large as Fingal's Cave and, though the columnar formation is less striking, would have won renown had the latter cave not existed.

After the remarkable hooded formation of columnar rock over the entrance, the most striking feature of this cave is the flatness of the roof, which, although inclined slightly from the horizontal, presents a surface almost as flat as a plastered ceiling. This roof, or ceiling, is formed by the flat surfaces of the lower ends of the vertical columns from which the tuff beneath has been eroded. Thus the plane of the whole surface is very regular, and it is emphasised even more by being covered with smooth calcareous accretions, resembling a layer of plaster, over the whole area. The tilt of the roof is caused by the inclination of the columnar lava flow which forms it. As this cave faces south-west, it is exposed to the full force of the Atlantic. Owing to projecting ledges of rock at sea level, and the heavy backwash from the cave, the scene here during rough weather is a wild turmoil of rushing, tossing waves and spouting spray, as we learned one stormy evening during our stay on Staffa when we viewed it, at some risk, from a hollow in the cliff-top.

MacKinnon's Cave derives its name from the principal character of the poem *The Abbot MacKinnon*, written by James Hogg, the Ettrick Shepherd, in 1813. The poem is a weird tale founded on an ancient Hebridean legend, and forms one of the series of poetic ballads known as *The Queen's Wake*. This collection consists of Scottish folklore tales said to have been recited before Mary, Queen of Scots, at Holyrood, at a competition for Scottish Bards.

Here is a brief outline, with quotations, of the story as told by Hogg in his poem:

Abbot MacKinnon, Abbot of Iona, having intrigued with " Matilda of Skye," thus breaking his monastic vows and violating the sacred traditions of Iona, was visited, in a dream, by St Columba, who told him:

> The cycle was closed, and the period run.
> He had vowed to the sea, he had vowed to the sun,
> If in that time rose trouble or pain,
> Their homage must pay to the god of the main.

The Abbot was so impressed by the dream that he felt compelled to fulfil St Columba's vow, so gathering the monks mentioned by the saint as also having broken their vows, he sailed for Staffa, according to instructions, where they could seek forgiveness in solitude:

> Up rose the Abbot, up rose the morn,
> Up rose the sun from the bens of Lorne;
> And the bark her course to the northward framed,
> With all on board whom the Saint had named.

On arriving at Staffa they landed at Clamshell Cave:

> Then awed to silence, they trod the strand,
> Where furnaced pillars in order stand,
> All formed of the liquid burning levin,
> All bent like the bow that spans the heaven.

They proceeded over the Causeway to Fingal's Cave and there burned incense and offered up fervent prayers for forgiveness, but a loud voice from the cave was heard, saying: "Greater yet must the offering be." Alarmed at this mystic warning, they retraced their footsteps to Clamshell Cave, climbed to the top of the island and crossed over to the western cliffs near MacKinnon's Cave. As they proceeded northwards along the summit of the cliffs, a small bay[1] at the base came into view:

> A little bay lies hid from sight,
> O'erhung by cliffs of dreadful height.

While looking down from the cliffs they saw a mermaid sitting on a boulder in the bay, and as they listened they heard her sing a song that foretold the righteous retribution which they must suffer. In despair, they rushed back to their boat, but on reaching it they found an old man, with a long grey beard, sitting in the bow chanting:

> Oh, woe is me,
> But great as the sin must the sacrifice be.

He seemed to be a supernatural being, and on being asked what he wanted, made no reply, but his countenance reminded the Abbot of St Columba.

As they pushed off from the island, with the spectre still sitting in the bow, the storm, which had been gathering, broke suddenly, and before the gale had driven them far from Staffa, the old man rose up and, stretching out his arms to heaven, cried, "Now is the time." At that moment a squall struck the boat, swamping it and drowning Abbot MacKinnon and his companions. Perhaps it would be hypercritical to ask who could have related the event if all in the boat were drowned.

According to the traditions of the neighbouring islanders, MacKinnon's Cave is named after Abbot MacKinnon, the last Abbot of Iona, who died in 1500. Tradition says that he

[1] Port an Fhasgaidh.

sheltered his boat in this cave for a short time after having been forced to leave Iona during a religious feud.   Finding that the cave, probably the whole island, did not offer much shelter, he sailed across to Mull, and landed at a place called Gribun, where he spent some time in a cave there, which also was named after him.[1]   A footnote in one edition of Boswell's *Journal of a Tour to the Hebrides, with Samuel Johnson, LL.D.*, states that " this cave at Gribun derives its name from a gentleman the name of MacKinnon, who entered the cave for exploration purposes but never returned."   The first theory seems the more feasible.

In connection with the name of these caves, it is to be remembered that Mull was the original habitat of the clan MacKinnon, who were closely associated with Iona during the fifteenth century.   According to W. F. Skene's *Highlanders of Scotland*, VOL. II, p. 263, the MacQuarries, whose ancestral home is Ulva, and the MacKinnons are descended from two brothers.

Thus it should not surprise us to find the name MacKinnon attached to place-names in this region.

The principal dimensions of MacKinnon's Cave, in Staffa, are:

Length inward	..	..	..	224 ft.
Height	..	..	..	50 ft.
Breadth	..	..	..	48 ft.

It is worthy of note that neither Banks nor Faujas mentions the name MacKinnon in connection with any cave in Staffa, though, of course, they were so enraptured by Fingal's that they paid little attention to any other cave.   They call " the large cave in the south-west of the island " Cormorants' Cave, though cormorants nest in all the caves, with the exception of Boat Cave.   Dr MacCulloch appears to be the first visitor to record this cave by its present name (MacKinnon's)—in a footnote he says, " also called Scart, or Cormorant, Cave "— but he does not give any clue as to the person from whom the cave derives its name.   He merely remarks: " The traditions respecting this hero are nearly as obscure as those which relate to Fingal, although to judge by the places to which he has given his name, his celebrity was not inconsiderable."   Writers since

---

[1] This cave at Gribun is believed to have been used as a hermitage by disciples of the Columban Church, a large flat stone within having served as a table.

Clamshell Cave; the wooden stair has been removed since this photograph
was taken

(*Left*) Looking out from MacKinnon's Cave; the floor is under water except when the tide is right out; (*below*) the back of Fingal's Cave showing the small shingle beach which is only exposed at low water on spring tides

Dr MacCulloch's time have repeated his double name for this cave, without troubling to verify his statement. No doubt their reason for doing so is that he is the most useful authority to quote, as he gives dimensions for all the principal caves in Staffa. While exploring this cave, however, Dr MacCulloch, and others, apparently overlooked an opening in the north wall which would have led them into another cave. This second cave is the one which is recognised as Cormorants' Cave by the present inhabitants of the neighbouring islands, who derived this information from their ancestors.

Cormorants' Cave is situated in the cliffs a short distance north of MacKinnon's Cave and can be entered at or near low tide without the use of a boat by clambering over a region of very slippery boulders and coarse shingle from the little bay in the south-west of the island. Like MacKinnon's Cave, it is hollowed out in the tuff. As it is set back in a recess in the cliffs, and the entrance can be seen only from a few points on the island, and still fewer when in a boat, there is some excuse for Dr MacCulloch not mentioning it. He may have been told that the names MacKinnon and Cormorant were given to caves in the south-west of the island, but failing to find the latter (he mentions that his boatmen were timid about approaching certain rock-strewn parts of Staffa) decided that the two names were alternatives for the one cave.

The inhabitants of Gometra, the nearest inhabited island to Staffa, told me that they and their ancestors have always known these caves by the names which I have given them, and pointed out each one to me.

Cormorants', or Scarts' (from the Gaelic word *sgarbh*, meaning "cormorant") Cave, does not rival Fingal's or MacKinnon's in size, but is more deserving of the name of cave than is Boat Cave.

The principal dimensions of Cormorants' Cave are:

Length inward	6o ft.
Height	40 ft.
Breadth	20 ft.

A few yards into this cave, and on the right-hand side, the narrow tunnel which communicates with MacKinnon's Cave branches off. This winding, dark and slippery subway is about twenty feet long and about three feet wide by about ten feet high. Although it forms a connection between the two caves, it cannot be described as making them into one. It is a flaw in the rock, enlarged by the action of the sea, penetrating from near the inner end of MacKinnon's Cave to meet the south wall of Cormorants' Cave at right angles, and is accessible only at, or near, low tide. This passage from Cormorants' Cave is perhaps the best way to make one's first acquaintance with MacKinnon's Cave, as, after emerging from the darkness of the tunnel, the immensity of the cave, its great entrance and glistening walls lit by the flood of daylight, and the resonant churning of the waves in the cold, dank atmosphere make a lasting impression on the mind.

A short distance north of Cormorants' Cave the coast-line turns abruptly towards the west, and in the apex of the angle there is a small bay with a rough beach of smooth rounded black stones, too large to be called shingle, and boulders, called Port an Fhasgaidh (Gaelic for " Shelter Haven ") on the Ordnance Survey Map. As it faces towards the south-west, that is towards the prevailing winds, it is very exposed and would be more aptly described as the *un*sheltered bay. The local name for this little creek is Port nam Faochag (" Haven of the Whelks "), which is very appropriate, as these molluscs swarm on the rocks and sea-weed here more thickly than I have ever seen them elsewhere. The higher part of the east end of this beach forms the entrance to a little valley, or hollow, which crosses the island at an oblique angle and almost cuts it in two.

At the base of the continuous vertical columns of rude formation, a few yards to the west of the outermost projection of the headland which forms the west side of Port an Fhasgaidh, there is a remarkable aperture in the cliff as regular as the bore of a cannon. This cavity is about four feet in diameter and runs inwards and upwards into the cliff at an angle of about forty-five degrees for about fifteen feet. It has received several names: " Thunder Cave," " Gun Cave," " The Cannon," and " Gunna Mor," or " Big Gun," but the dimensions indicate that the term "cave" is inappropriate here. The most suitable name is Gunna Mor, or Big Gun, as the interior is polished smooth like the bore of a cannon, and the opening remains parallel almost throughout.

The earliest mention of the Gunna Mor which I have been able to locate is given in the letter, dated 24th November 1773, from Dr John MacGuarie to his cousin, Murdoch Maclaine, which is quoted in full in Chapter II. This phenomenon is also mentioned by the Hon. Mrs Murray of Kensington (1805), by Sir Walter Scott (1814), and by W. Keddie (1850); but none of them states definitely where it is situated. Mrs Murray describes it as bring " not far from Boat Cave "; but it is no-where near Boat Cave. Keddie says it is " on the west side of the island," which is rather vague. Scott mentions it as being near the little bay in the south-west of the island. Scott's indication is reasonably good, but does not indicate whether it is to the east or west of the bay, and the lofty cliffs at this part have many nooks and crannies. I have not found mention of the Gunna Mor by any modern writer on the Hebrides, and was unable to obtain any satisfactory information as to its whereabouts from the neighbouring islanders, the majority of whom were unaware of its existence. Ultimately, I had the good fortune to learn from the late Mr John MacDonald, Gometra, who gave me much local information about Staffa, that he had visited the Gunna Mor several times, and he kindly instructed me how to find it. Mr MacDonald was senior Staffa boatman for many years and fished the lobsters on the coast of Staffa for the greater part of his lifetime.

During the month of July 1931, I set out alone to search for this little-known feature of Staffa after being landed at Clam-shell Cave by Iona boatmen. According to the instructions of Mr MacDonald, I crossed over the island to Port an Fhasgaidh and scaled the narrow ledges of rock at the base of the cliffs on the west side of the bay, which can be done only at, or near, low tide. On reaching the outermost part of the headland I scanned the cliffs carefully without seeing any aperture and began to doubt my directions. Suddenly, on proceeding a few steps further, I found the Gunna Mor in a recess in the cliff several feet above the level of where I was standing. There could be no mistaking this aperture. I tried to clamber up into the bore in order to ascertain its length, but the angle is so steep and the interior so slippery, there was considerable risk of slipping and being shot out over a rock face into deep water about fifteen feet below.   Therefore I did not undertake the venture, especially as I had left the boatmen on the opposite side of the island and they did not know exactly where I was exploring.

By inserting a three-foot measuring rod into the bore and judging the length in terms of this measurement, I estimated the Gunna Mor to reach inwards and upwards for about fifteen feet.   It may be longer, for at that point the darkness obscured my vision and a lighted bunch of matches failed to penetrate the gloom at the inner end, though I thought I could discern the extremity glistening with moisture at about fifteen feet.   At the entrance there is a pot-hole fourteen inches in diameter and two feet deep, of very regular formation, filled with water.   Unfortunately, the ledge at the entrance is much too narrow to permit of a photograph being taken of this interesting feature of Staffa, and from the sea the opening appears quite insignificant: I viewed it from the sea later.

An early account of the Gunna Mor is given by the Hon. Mrs Murray of Kensington in her *Guide to the Beauties of the Western Highlands and Hebrides*, VOL. II., published in 1805.   She visited Staffa in 1800 and again in 1802, and says: " In the year 1800 I was the ninth female stranger who had ventured to Staffa, but none of them had gone valiantly alone as I did."   Although she does not mention having seen the Gunna Mor, or Thunder Cave as she calls it (her description of its position would seem to indicate that she did not see it), she says:

The reason of its being called Thunder Cave is as follows. By some means or other a very large round stone incorporated in the mass of rock, supporting the pillars not far from Boat Cave, became loose in its socket, and afterwards, by continual friction, made itself a large aperture in which it was in storms violently agitated.   When driven with great force by the billows to the back of its socket, it rebounded with a noise like loud thunder which was heard at a great distance.   I had not a chance of hearing one clap, for not many years ago (I was told) some Irishmen came to Staffa to view its wonders.   They, on coming to the Thunder Cave and hearing of the miracle performed by the round stone, said amongst themselves, "By —, boys, let us carry it over to Ould Oireland," and they did so.   A terrible noise, however, is still to be heard when the sea roars into the cavity the stone once filled.

Dr MacQuarie says the stone weighed about five pounds.

The fine pot-hole at the entrance to the Gunna Mor was formed, no doubt, by debris from the bore being churned by the sea, in the same manner as pot-holes are formed in the rocky bed of a river. It is difficult, however, to account for the formation of the bore itself, as there are no sloping columns at this part which might have become dislodged to form it. The action of the sea alone would not account for it, as sea caves are usually wider at the entrance than further in, whereas the Gunna Mor is practically the same diameter throughout. In any case the waves can reach it only during a very high tide or during a storm. It could hardly have been formed by the method described by Mrs Murray as the friction would have worn away the boulder before it had formed a cavity even much smaller than the aperture here. The rebounding of a five-pound stone would not cause much noise.

If ever there has been a loose boulder in the Gunna Mor, as described by Mrs Murray, it is difficult to understand why it did not rebound into the sea. Were the angle of inclination of the bore less steep and the pot-hole at the entrance shallower, it might have been trapped in the pot-hole. But the angle of inclination being about forty-five degrees, the boulder would not come to rest so suddenly after shooting down such a steep slope. If the boulder were small enough to enter the pot-hole completely it could not be lifted out by the sea, owing to the cavity of the pot-hole being so deep compared with its diameter.

The coast of Staffa, from Port an Fhasgaidh to the western extremity of the island, consists of high precipitous cliffs exposing rude columnar structure, not of striking appearance, with a flat rocky marine-erosion platform projecting to a considerable distance from their base near sea level. About half a mile to the south-west a few small, but dangerous, fangs of rock jut out of the sea which are almost always collared with a swirl of surf.

On rounding the westernmost headland, and proceeding northward, the cliffs continue to be of rude columnar formation and decrease gradually in height until east of the north end of the island they fade out and the coast becomes low and flat. There is only one cave in this western coast of Staffa and it hardly deserves this term. Until after the publication of the

1957 edition of this book (not the abridged edition) I did not
have a close-up view of this part of the island from the sea and,
unfortunately, had accepted the statement of others that there
were several caves here.   Since that time, I have twice sailed
along the west of Staffa, close to its rocky cliff-bound coast,
which can be done only during very settled weather and even
then the Atlantic swell breaks heavy here.

During my first sail I saw rock crannies and undercuttings
but did not see any caves.   On the second occasion, however,
which was a more leisurely sail and allowed more minute
examination, I saw one large cavity in the cliffs, at sea level,
which might be described as a cave, though it is not comparable,
either in size or appearance, with the other caves in the island.
It is excavated in the tuff at the base of the cliff, in the apex of a
recess in the coast, on the south side of a prominent headland
about mid-way between north and south of this westermost
coast of Staffa.

The heavy swell which was breaking during that second visit
made close approach too dangerous an undertaking and the
boatman had to consider the safety of his boat, far from any
form of assistance.   I was therefore unable to learn how far this
cave, or cavity, penetrates into the cliff.

The probable reason why I did not see this cave on my first
sail along the west coast of Staffa is that when sailing from
north to south, as I did on both occasions, one has to look backward to see it, as on the approach from the north it is screened
by a headland and is in the apex of a deep recess in the cliffs.

The base of the greater part of these cliffs cannot be seen from
their summit owing to the irregularity of their form, and as it is
inaccessible except by means of a boat no one could tell from
their summit whether or not there were caves here.   Few
boatmen care to sail close to this grim and lonely coast of cliffs
and skerries continually beaten by the heavy Atlantic surge and
miles from the nearest inhabited island.   The booming of the
waves as they beat in the undercutting of these wester cliffs may
have led persons on the summit plateau of Staffa to assume that
there were caves in this part of the island.

At the extreme north end of Staffa, towards the west, there is
a small island, or large rock, called Eilean Dubh, and in the

coast of Staffa near this little island there is a deep cleft, or geo, in the low cliffs where the column formation is very conspicuous, especially when the sun gleams and glints on the spray-drenched rocks. A short distance east of it, where the coast is flat and low, there is a small natural harbour which forms one of the two best landing places on Staffa; the other landing place being at Clamshell Cave.

During the latter part of last century, when weather conditions were favourable and on the days on which the steamboat approached from the north, visitors were landed at this little creek in the north end and allowed to walk over the island and down the wooden stairway which used to be at Clamshell Cave, and thence to Fingal's Cave. During their traverse of the island, the steamboat sailed round and anchored off Clamshell Cave or Fingal's Cave, where they rejoined her. Passengers disinclined or unable to walk the length of the island were landed at Clamshell Cave or Fingal's Cave and allowed to remain ashore while those who had traversed the island and had visited Fingal's Cave were being embarked.

On rounding this northernmost point of Staffa and turning southward, the coast rises gradually to a small eminence called Meall nam Faoileann (" the rounded hill of the seagulls "), though the birds most numerous here are puffins. At sea level, in this part of the island, there are two large hollows in the east face of the cliffs, but of insufficient depth to be described as caves. In the southern part of the cliffs here there is, however, a definite cave, named Goat Cave by the Ordnance Survey, but it is just a large normal sea cave with no special features.

Proceeding southward, the coast becomes comparatively flat again, but with a rough rocky shore of rude columns splotched with lichen, and continues so, presenting no conspicuous feature except irregular columnar formation, till near the east end of the little valley which crosses the island. Here the rock stratum seems to have an inclination to the bent form of columns which appear presently.

After passing the end of the little valley, the coast rises to form a steep and irregular, but not inaccessible, front of curved columns. Playfair, in his *Description of Scotland* (1819), describes this part of Staffa as " a vast basaltic mass, where the columns appear to have been removed from their perpendicular site and laid horizontally; but before they were completely consolidated their support in the middle yielding, gave them the bended concave form they now bear." Although that theory is incorrect, the description of the appearance is very apt. As it is here that Clamshell Cave cuts into the island, we have arrived back at our starting point in our description of the coast of Staffa.

Dr Carus, who visited Staffa along with the King of Saxony during the month of July 1844, mentions that a wooden stairway was affixed to the cliffs at Clamshell Cave to give access to the surface of the island. This mention of the wooden stair is the first that I have found. William Keddie, who visited Staffa in 1847, also mentions this wooden stairway.

In an article entitled "The Island of Staffa" published in *Hogg's Instructor*, VOL. VI (1851), the writer, who does not give his name or the year of his visit to Staffa, says that when visitors returned over the Causeway from Fingal's Cave: "They are now made to ascend the sloping precipiece [at Clamshell Cave]; and they accomplish this feat by the aid of a rude handrail and stepping stones of column-tops." Although this article was published in 1851, the writer may have visited Staffa before Dr Carus and Keddie.

Apparently there was no wooden stairway here when Botfield visited Staffa by steamboat, in 1829, because he mentions that visitors were landed at Fingal's Cave, and, after exploring it, they walked northward over the Causeway to Clamshell Cave. He adds: " By the continued basaltic causeway on the northern side [of Clamshell Cave] access is obtained to the table-summit of the island."

A new wooden stair to the summit of the island, at Clamshell Cave, was erected about 1885 to replace the previous one which had become badly decayed. Professor J. P. MacLean in his *Report on Fingal's Cave*, submitted to the Smithsonian Institution in 1887 (therefore he must have visited Staffa in 1886 or 1887) says: " The summit is gained by a stairway recently constructed."

Shortly before the outbreak of the Second World War, the Steamboat Company removed, and did not replace, the wooden stairway leading to the summit of the island at Clamshell Cave, as, for many years, tourists have not been allowed sufficient time ashore to visit the plateau of Staffa's surface, and thus the stairway was not being kept in repair and might have become dangerous. About the same time they levelled the upper surfaces of the concave and convex column ends of the Causeway to aid tourists when traversing it. Although certainly helpful to persons paying a hurried visit to Staffa, the concrete infillings have been made unduly conspicuous by the use of untinted concrete which now appears like a white line drawn along the dark rock of the Causeway. The concrete used, if actually necessary, should have been tinted with oxide of iron to make it blend with the surrounding rock.

Since the termination of the war, further aids (one cannot describe them as improvements) have been built on Staffa, such as a small concrete landing stage and a large flight of concrete steps at the landing place at Clamshell Cave. These modern structures save visitors the rough scramble that was necessary previous to their erection when visiting Fingal's Cave but they have lessened the adventurous atmosphere which used to add to the thrill of a visit to Staffa. Unfortunately, they are built in the most renowned and most conspicuous part of the island and, while they are minor in regard to the island as a whole, they provoke an expression of reproach, as they lack the aesthetic consideration due to such an outstanding work of nature as Staffa.

With the exception of a few small creeks no loose stones are found round the coast-line, the heavy Atlantic swell washing every part of the rock smooth and bare of any loose material. Below low water mark, however, large fronds of bronze tangle sway in the ebb and flow of the waves, anchored to the rocks by a tough leathery stem about two inches thick.

Though the lava of which Staffa is composed is thought to have been extruded and spread over the land surface about sixty million years ago, which gives the island this geological age, it was not then an island but was part of Mull, which at that time stretched in one continuous land mass westward beyond the position of the Treshnish Isles at least. Since that time great changes have taken place in this region. Enormous masses of land have been worn away and the sea has encroached greatly upon the land.

The excavation of Staffa's caves is, with minor reservations, the result of sea action; their formation is therefore of a very much later date than the solidification of the lava. Indeed, they are believed to have been formed in very recent geological time, which can be expressed in mere thousands of years. Their excavation could not commence until the surrounding land had been eroded sufficiently to allow the sea to surround and attack Staffa.

Although the sea could not have advanced to its present position around Mull, thus making it an island, until long after the cessation of the volcanic activity, according to the Geological Survey *Memoir* for Mull it had done so long before the onset of the Pleistocene Ice Age (the last great Ice Age). At a late stage in pre-Glacial time, when the surface of Scotland had been eroded mainly to its present-day surface, the whole of Scotland and its attendant islands, including Staffa, subsided to a level of about one hundred feet lower than they are at the present time. Consequently their coast-lines were submerged to that depth. The one-hundred-foot raised beach indicating that submergence appears clearly in Mull and the Treshnish Isles, and there is also a sea cave at this beach level in the Island of Ulva. From this evidence we learn that much of the present-day coastal form of Mull and its attendant islands was shaped by pre-Glacial erosion and also before the pre-Glacial submergence of the land. Some of the Staffa caves *may* have originated in an insignificant way before the pre-Glacial submergence of Scotland, but much the greater part, if not the whole, of their excavation is believed to have been done since the ice retreated from this region.

The caves of Staffa could not have been formed during the time of the pre-Glacial submergence of the land, because a one-hundred-foot submergence would mean that Staffa would be almost completely submerged and wave action would therefor not have any appreciable effect at the level of the caves. According to the *Memoir* for Mull, the caves were not formed by the pre-submergence erosion but by post-Glacial erosion. Of Fingal's Cave it is stated: "It would be pure speculation to assign any of its excavation to other than modern conditions."

When the Pleistocene Ice Age was at its maximum, Scotland was covered with a vast ice sheet which over the Hebrides (including Staffa) was about 1,600 feet thick. This tremendous load of ice depressed the land, with reference to sea level. As the ice melted and retreated, and for some time after its retreat, the land gradually emerged from the sea to its present level. The emergence halted temporarily for a considerable time at different stages as is now indicated by Raised Beaches at different levels.

The maximum extent of the European ice front during that last great Ice Age reached as far south in Britain as the Thames and the ice covered the whole of Ireland, its western margin stretching west of Ireland and the Hebrides.

Ultimately, the ice front began to retreat and in due course Staffa was uncovered and laid open to the sea. The ice retreated from the region of Staffa about 10,000 years ago. This opinion is based on what is known as radiocarbon dating, a very modern and accurate method of estimating in actual years the age of relics up to about 50,000 years old. This mode of reckoning is based upon the rate at which radioactive carbon (Carbon-14, or C-14) disintegrates. The method is somewhat similar to that by which geologists date the age of the rocks, but they work with different elements.

As the Geological Survey *Memoirs* state that the caves of Staffa are almost certainly of post-glacial formation, we find that their excavation commenced not more than 10,000 years ago. Indeed, much the greater part, if not the whole, of their excavation must have been done much more recently than this date, because time would have to elapse after the recession of the ice front from this region to allow Staffa to emerge sufficiently from the sea for the battering action of the waves to attack the level of its caves.

It is engaging to contemplate what effect the ceaseless work of the sea will have had upon the shape and appearance of Staffa and its caves after a further 10,000 years—whether the island will be almost indistinguishable from what it is today; whether it will be badly eroded, but recognisable; or whether it will have gone for ever.

During most of the period subsequent to the retreat of the ice, Staffa has been an island standing at various levels above the sea. Its emergence has not been uniform continuous elevation but has been erratic. There have been stationary periods punctuated by ups and downs, the downs being caused by return of water to the sea owing to the melting of the ice. Judging from Scottish evidence elsewhere, Staffa's maximum elevation was probably higher than it is at the present day.

Fingal's Cave is believed to have been formed by the pounding waves attacking the bed of tuff under the columnar lava and thus undermining the vertical columns which would then fall down leaving the roof of thin irregular columns. Consequently, there may have been minor erosion of this cave when Staffa was at its highest level—thus causing the bed of tuff to be also at a higher level. During most of post-Glacial time, however, conditions were unfavourable for the excavation of Staffa's caves, because the vulnerable tuff was below the level of the breakers. At the present time erosion conditions for the excavation of Fingal's Cave are at their best, so we may regard this cave as geologically of very modern formation.

It is surprising that the above theory for the formation of Fingal's Cave does not apply to MacKinnon's Cave and Boat Cave. Both of these caves are hollowed out in the bed of tuff, with the bases of vertical columns forming their roofs, and these columns have not fallen.

MacKinnon's Cave is probably the oldest cave in Staffa, followed by Cormorants' Cave, Boat Cave, Fingal's Cave and Clamshell Cave, because the top of the tuff at MacKinnon's Cave is about fifty feet above sea level, from which point it slopes down, owing to the tilt of the island, to about sea level at Fingal's Cave; the higher the tuff the sooner wave action would reach its level as Staffa emerged from the sea.

As Fingal's Cave has its bottom submerged by about twelve feet of water even at low tide, geologists consider this cave to have been excavated since the twenty-five-foot post-Glacial raised beach of this region emerged from the sea.

Toward the end of last century part of the earliest remains of human habitation in the Highlands, believed to be of the Bronze

Age, were found in caves at Oban on a raised beach about thirty feet above sea level. This beach must therefore have been above sea level when the Bronze Age people lived on it. On the Geological Survey sheet for the Oban district this beach is named " the fifty-foot post-Glacial raised beach." The corresponding post-Glacial raised beach on western Mull has an average height of about twenty feet above sea level and on the Geological Survey sheet for western Mull this beach is named " the twenty-five-foot post-Glacial raised beach." This Mull beach, however, is really of the same horizon as the fifty-foot beach at Oban, because this particular beach has been elevated to heights which differ slightly in various parts of Scotland. These distinctive names for the same raised beach in separate areas are liable to cause confusion.

From the evidence of human relics of Bronze Age in the Oban Caves on a beach which corresponds to the twenty-five-foot post-Glacial raised beach on Western Mull, we may say that the excavation of much the greater part, if not the whole, of Fingal's Cave commenced about the time man first appeared in the West Highlands, and that was from about 5,000 to about 6,000 years ago.

The caves of Staffa are generally believed to owe their origin to the action of the sea, but the inclination of the rock has probably had something to do with the origin of Fingal's Cave and Clamshell Cave. The latter cave is extremely well protected from the action of the sea by natural breakwaters, and also is on the sheltered side of the island, namely the east.

In *The Scottish Geographical Magazine* for October 1887, there appeared a thesis entitled " The Caves of Staffa " by Mr Cope Whitehouse, M.A., F.AM.G.S., in which he claimed that the caves of Staffa were not formed by the forces of nature, but by the hand of man.

At least two writers have ascribed to Mr Whitehouse the belief that the whole of Staffa had been built by man, but that was probably because they received an inaccurate report of his paper from some second-hand source. Mr Whitehouse made no such assertion. What he did say was that the caves had been formed by human agency, quite a sufficiently startling hypothesis in itself.

He viewed Staffa and Iona not only as connected by an accident of geography, resembling an *optical-double* star, which is really composed of two distinct suns wholly disconnected in space, but as a true *binary* (one star divided into two by fission), and said that once in history they had formed a political and social unit and offered mutually an explanation of each other's importance.

Here is a brief summary of Mr Whitehouse's paper:

Refugees from Syria took ship to remote colonies, some of them probably having reached the west coast of Scotland[1]

Staffa was precisely the spot which a Tyrian or a Carthaginian would select for a fortress, owing to its situation in the centre of the great bay formed by Mull and the Treshnish Isles.

This fortress to protect Iona, which was the seat of learning and culture.

The excavation of the largest caves was commenced at the surface of the island, and after piercing the overlying amorphous rock the columns were loosened and extracted. (The rock-hewn temples of Petra and Abu-Simbel were commenced at the top).

The caves were formed to act as shelters and hiding places for the long Phoenician galleys, breakwaters being built to protect the entrance of each cave. (Tyre, Sidon and Ravenna are no longer harbours).

A few of his arguments against the caves having been formed by the action of the sea:

The Treshnish Isles and Iona break the Atlantic swell before it reaches Staffa, hence there is no exceptional force in the seas which strike the island. [This point is not really true, as Staffa is unsheltered from south to west, the direction of the prevailing winds].

Fingal's Cave is wider above sea level, that is, in the hard columnar basalt, than it is at sea level and underwater in the softer tuff.

Columnar basalt under the action of the sea forms a causeway, not a cave.

If formed by the sea, loose drums of basalt would have gathered and formed a breakwater before the caves were properly commenced.

A force sufficient to pulverise the basalt would have destroyed the island, certainly the eastern wall of Fingal's Cave.

There is no yielding of roof in the columnar basalt above Boat Cave [or in MacKinnon's Cave].

The dimensions of MacKinnon's Cave are almost the same as those of Fingal's Cave, that is, two tunnels of almost the same dimensions have been driven under different conditions.

[1] A number of prehistoric canoes were found during excavations in Glasgow and one of them had a plug of cork. This evidence indicates some intercourse with Mediterranean countries where cork trees grow. It was found about twenty feet above the present high water level and must therefore have come before the last land movement had concluded. That was a very long time ago, and before the last Scottish glacier had vanished.

Several points put forward by Mr Whitehouse in the latter part of his hypothesis are undoubtedly correct, but much more convincing evidence will require to be given before anyone will believe that the caves of Staffa are the work of man.   Whatever we may think of his speculation, however, it has, at least, the merit that it raises points which have been overlooked, or at least unrecorded, by any other visitor to Staffa.   It means that the usual explanation of the origin of the caves—that they have been formed by the action of the sea only—requires qualifying. To add even one point in support of those given by Mr White-house—Boat Cave faces Mull and is therefore sheltered; it runs into the cliffs at right angles to the heaviest seas which strike Staffa.   Indeed, even were the sea driven towards this cave it could not strike it direct, owing to a projecting headland intervening.

To scoff at a hypothesis of this kind without appreciating the reasoning which led to it, as is often done, is unfair.   When Mr Whitehouse first offered his theory for harnessing the waters of the Nile to prevent famines in Egypt, it was looked upon as fantastic.   We now know that the harnessing of the Nile has been an accomplished feat of engineering for many years.

CHAPTER VII

FINGAL'S CAVE

THE most imposing and most renowned feature of Staffa is undoubtedly Fingal's Cave, a masterpiece of Nature's architecture which compels admiration. At first sight it appears to be the work of skilled craftsmen, while its pointed-arch entrance, its clustered columns, its size and symmetry, are suggestive of a Gothic cathedral. Another resemblance which it bears to classic buildings is that when viewed close up it shows many detailed mouldings, yet when seen from a distance, though of massive appearance, it impresses by the serene simplicity of its outlines, its stable strength, and the unity of its component parts.

Although within the cave daylight is considerably subdued and the enclosing rock is of a drab colour, under suitable atmospheric conditions the vast interior presents an intriguing play of light and shade. The flickering glints reflected from the choppy surface of its undulating ocean floor dapple the colonnades and fretted roof with varying effects like a wavering mosaic. On a day of clear sky, the quivering shafts of sunlight penetrate its crystal green waters in their ceaseless movement to scintillate in rainbow hues from the multi-coloured lichen-encrusted rocks submerged, flashing like facets on a gem. This play of iridescence appears all the more brilliant against the sombre surroundings in the cavern twilight.

To stand on the narrow ledge of chequered pavement in the solemn atmosphere of this majestic hall of simple, yet superb, natural columns and witness the imposing spectacle of its interior grandeur; to view the beautiful vista which appears through its arched entrance, as if seen through a giant telescope, when bright sunlight illuminates the outer scene of deep blue sea and azure sky with the green isle of Iona resting on the horizon; all in harmony with seabirds' cry and the deep-toned rhythmic music of the waves, inspires a feeling of reverence and invites meditation.

The mouth of Fingal's Cave

(*Left*) The Causeway of broken columns which forms the route from the landing place to Fingal's Cave; (*below*) a heavy sea breaking over the Causeway at the Bending Columns; this photograph by the author could only have been taken by someone living on the island, since landing would be impossible in such weather

It requires a sensitive mind as well as an observant eye to obtain a correct impression of this great cavern. It must be observed with thought as it is more eloquent of the past than of the present. We have to contribute our own share to the scene by bearing in mind the titan forces of nature that have built and carved it, the historic events and legends which its name recalls, and the romantic associations of the surrounding scenery. As Wordsworth says:

> Minds that have nothing to confer,
> Find little to perceive.

Louis Albert Necker de Saussure,[1] the Swiss geologist, who visited Staffa during the month of August 1807, felt the true atmosphere of Fingal's Cave. In his *Voyage en Ecosse et aux Iles Hebrides*, he says:

Added to the pleasure which the beauty of the cave itself gave me were some impressions which lent still more to its charm, namely, the feelings inspired by its situation in the middle of the stormiest of oceans, in the less frequented parts, immune from the destructive hand of man, in an island for a long time undiscovered and for ever beaten by the angry waves and tempests; the idea of the possibility that volcanic action had at one time contributed to its formation; the distant view of Iona; but especially the memories recalled by the name of Fingal given to this cave. Fingal, Ossian and his bards have perhaps in bygone days gathered under its vaulted roof, the beautiful music of their harps would accompany the sound of their voices, and, mingled with that of the waves and winds, has perhaps more than once made every crevice of this cave resound. There they would sing of their wars and victories, would commemorate the death of those heroes whose shades they seemed to see wandering by the light of the moon at the entrance of this dark cave.

In an article on Fingal's Cave which was published in *The Architectural Review*, August 1948, the writer considers that the discovery of Fingal's Cave may have had some influence on the

---

[1] This Necker de Saussure was a grandson of the famous (Horace Benedict) de Saussure, who was distinguished for his early studies of the rocks and physical features of Switzerland, and who has the credit of being the first to christen the science of the earth's structure with the name by which we now know it— Geology. Necker de Saussure first visited the Hebrides while studying in Edinburgh, in 1806, 1807 and 1808, and they appealed so much to him that he returned later in life, made them his adpoted home and died and was buried at Portree, in the Island of Skye, in 1861.

famous architects of that time. The editor, in a commentary on that article, says: " Few natural wonders of this sort can have played so large a part in the visual re-education of a whole generation, and memories of the columns of this stupendous cavern haunted the imagination of architects and artists for half a century."

Fingal's Cave is more impressive when viewed from the rocky shore of Staffa, as far back as the tide will allow, than when seen from a distance on the sea. As the southern cliffs of the island increase in height from east to west and as the cave is situated in the eastern extremity of these cliffs, it appears somewhat dwarfed by the higher cliffs extending westward, when viewed as part of the whole southern face of Staffa from the sea. When near to the cave, one's gaze is concentrated on its massive proportions and is not distracted by the higher cliffs to the west.

The prinicpal dimensions of Fingal's Cave are:

Height from sea level, mean tide, to apex of arch	65 ft.
Height from apex of arch to top of cliff above	30 ft.
Breadth at entrance, at top of broken columns	50 ft.
Distance from entrance to innermost part	230 ft.

These dimensions and many other dimensions of the interior of the cave were carefully measured in June 1900 by a qualified architect whom my father assisted in this work. My father acted as representative of Messrs David MacBrayne Ltd., the shipping company, who commissioned the measurements to be taken for the purpose of making a model of Fingal's Cave. Several days were spent on Staffa measuring and sketching the interior and exterior of the cave, ashore and in the boat used by the Gometra boatmen who at that time landed tourists on Staffa. Unfortunately, the model was never completed. The depth of water at the entrance to Fingal's Cave at mean tide is about twenty-five feet and about fifteen feet at the inner end. Spring tides rise about twelve feet, neap tides about eight feet and range about four feet. There is a narrow causeway along both sides of the cave formed by the upper ends of broken columns, which enables visitors to explore the cave almost to its inner end.

The dimensions given in this book for Clamshell Cave, Boat Cave, and MacKinnon's Cave are those given by Dr MacCulloch, as his measurements are regarded as the most reliable. In the case of Cormorants' Cave I have given the dimensions measured by myself, as Dr MacCulloch does not mention this cave. So also, I have given my own measurements for Fingal's Cave and have mentioned the source from which I obtained them. They will be found to differ very little from those of Dr MacCulloch.

The principal dimensions of Fingal's Cave given by others are as follows:

DIMENSION	BANKS	FAUJAS[1]	DE SAUSSURE[1]	DR MACCULLOCH
Height (a)[2]	117' 6"	59' 7"	124' 7"	66' 0"
(b)[3]	—	21' 2"	53' 3"	30' 0"
Breadth[4]	53' 7"	37' 3"[5]	—	42' 0"
Length[6]	250' 0"	149' 0"	266' 3"	227' 0"

NOTES

[1] *Faujas and De Saussure give their dimensions in French feet, here converted into English (1 French 'pied' = 1.065 English ft).* [2] *Sea level to apex of arch.* [3] *Apex to top of cliff.* [4] *At entrance.* [5] *At sea level.* [6] *From entrance to innermost part.*

It is surprising that Sir Archibald Geikie, who is responsible for the translation of Faujas's book into English, does not comment upon the error which this French geologist makes in his length from the entrance to the innermost part of the cave. Indeed, Geikie gives all the measurements of Faujas in French feet, or *pieds*, as they appear in the French edition of his book, describing them as feet, without translating them into English feet or explaining that they are French feet, or *pieds*. Faujas says that his tape measured one hundred French feet, or *pieds*. Evidently, he forgot to note the dimension obtained by the first full stretch of his tape when measuring the length of Fingal's Cave, for one hundred plus one hundred plus forty French feet amount to about two hundred and fifty-five English feet—a more reasonable length for the cave than the one hundred and forty French feet (equal to one hundred and forty-nine English feet) which he gives. The repetition of this error by Panckoucke gives a clue as to the source from which he derived his dimensions of Fingal's Cave.

Banks's figure for the " Height of the Arch at the mouth "
(of the Cave), is equal almost to the height from the sea bed of
the cave to the top of the cliff over the cave entrance. This
dimension may really be the sum of three figures—the depth of
water at the cave entrance plus the height from sea level to the
top of the arch, plus the height from the top of the arch to the
top of the cliff over the cave entrance.

De Saussure, in the original (French) edition of his book,
seems to have quoted Banks's measurements for Fingal's Cave
without translating them into French feet or mentioning that
the figures he (De Saussure) gives are really English feet.
Thus, if we translate the figures De Saussure gives in his book
back into English feet we find them exceeding the original
figures given by Banks.

The columns which form the entrance to Fingal's Cave
appear, at first sight, to be vertical, but from the photograph
looking out of the cave it will be seen that they are inclined
from the vertical, the west side more than the east; the photograph has the horizon line level.

Here is Sir Joseph Banks's description of the cave:

The mind can hardly form an idea more magnificent than such a place,
supported on each side by ranges of columns and roofed by the bottom of
those which have been broken off to form it; between the angles of which a
yellow stalagmitic matter has exuded, which serves to define the angles
precisely; and at the same time vest the colours with a great deal of elegance
and to render it still more agreeable, the whole is lighted from without, so
that the furthest extremity is very plainly seen from without, and the air
within being agitated by the flux and reflux of the tides is perfectly dry and
wholesome, free entirely from the damp vapours with which natural caverns
in general abound.

We asked the name of it.   Said our guide, ' the cave of Fhinn.'   ' What
is Fhinn?' said we.   ' Fhinn MacCool, whom the translator of Ossian's
works has called Fingal.'

The Rev. Leigh Richmond, the famous divine, who visited
Staffa during the month of August 1820, says in a letter describing his visit: " When I first beheld the cave of Fingal, in
Staffa, I knew not whether to close my lips in mute astonish-
ment, or to fall down and pray to the true God of such a temple.
I wanted new faculties for such a new demonstration of Al-
mighty power."   He would, no doubt, receive this impression

on a comparatively calm day, otherwise he would be unable to land on the island.   Yet, when the elements rage this scene can arouse dread rather than sentiment.

During our stay on Staffa we visited Fingal's Cave one stormy evening at high water during spring tides with dark cloud-wrack racing across a lowering sky to learn what the scene here is like when Nature is roused.   There was a very heavy sea running as it was the third evening of a four-day south-westerly gale and the ponderous surges were sweeping high on the Causeway and on the Herdsman.   It was a rather dangerous undertaking to reach the cave in these conditions, but we regarded it as a unique opportunity worthy of reasonable risk, though we set out with some trepidation.   There was no concrete track over the Causeway at that time, and even if there had been one it would have been of little use to us on that occasion.   By keeping a wary eye upon the onsets of the monstrous seas and scampering backward or forward to safety when one threatened we scrambled as quickly as possible over the length of the rough Causeway to its highest part at the cave entrance.   Here it projects in the form of a long spit which cleaves the waves as they strike it.   On that evening its inner end was several feet above the highest reach of the sea, though exposed to the biting wind and showers of stinging salt spray, but fortunately the heavy rain had taken off.   The steel-wire guide-rope, which we had fitted here two days previously, provided a good handhold.

We were amply rewarded for our exertion by the spectacle of the tremendous forces battling in this war of the elements.   It was an astounding scene of savage grandeur, while the noise was dreadful.   In a striding cavalcade, the huge seas with hissing crest stormed into the cave.   Piling up in the restricted channel, each mighty mass of water rushed through with the devastating force of an avalanche to burst against the inmost barrier with a thunderous crash.   Every titan shock and its reverbrating roar seemed to send a shudder through the rocks.   With a resounding rumble, the backwash gushed and churned in a wild welter of tumbling torrents and seething foam, only to be overwhelmed by the next onrushing sea.   Viewed from our stance on the gale-swept causeway at the entrance, the waters trapped within the cave presented a fearsome turbulence of sea fury as they snarled and lashed in all directions among the crevices and truncated columns in the drenched atmosphere.   Outside the cave, the plunging waves in their impetuous charge smashed themselves against the cliffs and rocks in a riot of surf and flying spray.   Through the uproar of the sea the blustering wind bellowed and whined dismally.

In the dull light of that stormy evening, when grey sea and sky seemed to mingle, we received an ineffable impression of the supreme grandeur and stupendous might of nature as we stood in respectful awe by this

> chancel of ocean,
> And saw her waves rush to their raving devotion.

It seemed as if an irresistible force was meeting with an immovable object.   At first sight the "immovable object" appeared to win, but the rugged coast of the island bears eloquent testimony that it is the "irresistible force" which wins ultimately.   Unfortunately, bad lighting conditions, restricted viewpoint and the atmosphere being saturated with mist and spray, prevented a photographic record being made of this wonderful scene.

It is difficult to control the use of superlatives when trying to convey an impression of a close-up of the scene at Fingal's Cave during storm, but lest any reader may think that I have exaggerated, let him look at the photograph facing page 135 (which has not been retouched in any way), showing a heavy sea breaking at the Bending Columns, and try to imagine the violent commotion and noise when waves of this size crash into Fingal's Cave.   On the occasion I have described above we saw larger waves than the one shown but I was unable to photograph them owing to the showers of heavy spray which they scattered over the rocks on which we stood.   Indeed, at intervals the waves seemed to increase in size and force.

These waves, or rather seas, which beat against the Colonnade and Fingal's Cave from the south and south-west during stormy weather are not rollers of surf but huge masses of solid water which strike with tremendous force as they have the full fetch of the Atlantic behind them. There is no fringing reef or shelving shore at this part of the island to lessen their impetus. John McCormick, who was a native of the Ross of Mull, says in his book, *The Island of Mull*, that during stormy weather people on the north side of the Ross of Mull can sometimes hear "the thunder-like roars emitted from Fingal's Cave." I mentioned this statement to several Ross of Mull and Iona friends and asked them if they had ever heard the roar of Fingal's Cave at this distance. They seemed surprised and said that they had never heard it or had known of it being heard in these localities, even during winter storms. In order to reach the Ross of Mull or Iona, the sound would require to travel about six miles against the wind, because it is southerly or south-westerly winds which drive the heavy seas into Fingal's Cave, and the Ross and Iona lie south of Staffa. Friends on the Island of Gometra, however, told me that they had heard the noise of the waves beating in Fingal's Cave during winter storms. They said the sound, which they called *mactalla* ("the echo"), was not a roar but a deep boom. Their statement is more feasible than that of Mr McCormick, because Gometra lies about four miles to the north-east of Staffa and thus a south-westerly gale would carry the sound in this direction. From this evidence the reader can form some idea of the dreadful noise which we experienced when at the entrance to Fingal's Cave on the stormy evening I have mentioned.

In his book, *The Green Ray*, Jules Verne, the French writer of scientific romances, who visited Staffa in 1859, gives his imagination rein in a dramatic description of the scene inside Fingal's Cave during a wild night of autumn storm when the hero and heroine were trapped there for hours by the sea, but ultimately escaped. Only in fiction, however, could they have survived that ordeal.

As for the scene at Fingal's Cave during the furious storms of winter, it must resemble a tempestuous nightmare, or some dread spectacle from Ragnarok, the terrible Twilight of the Gods. Even the most vivid imagination would falter in trying to form a realistic conception of the terrific tumult of plunging, crashing waves, thundering echoes and shrieking winds, which must then rage in the mist and spray-drenched precincts of this huge sea-swept cavern.

Professor J. W. Judd, in his *Volcanoes* (1881), describes the formation of Fingal's Cave thus:

> The remarkable grotto known as Fingal's Cave has been formed in the midst of a lava stream. The thick vertical columns which rise from beneath the level of the sea are divided into joints and have been broken away by the action of the sea; in this way a great cavern has been produced, the sides of which are formed by interlacing columns, while the roof is made up of smaller interlacing ones. The whole structure bears some resemblance to a Gothic Cathedral, the sea finding access to its floor of broken columns.

This statement is not quite accurate. The thick vertical columns do not rise from beneath the sea in the cave; they rise from a basement of tuff at sea level. This tuff also forms the floor of the cave, and there is evidence for believing that this cave was not produced by such a direct process as that suggested by Professor Judd.

Professor J. MacLean, who examined the cave on behalf of the Smithsonian Institution, U.S.A., and submitted a report to that establishment in 1887, states that the conclusions he arrived at regarding the forming of Fingal's Cave are:

> (*a*) The dip of the rock of the island of Staffa indicates that there must have been a disturbance after the basalt had been deposited, which must have produced more or less crevices in the rocks.
>
> (*b*) The action of the water has made a large excavation under and in the basaltic tufa (which forms the base), which action was facilitated by a fault or fissure in the rock.
>
> (*c*) The action of the water under, and against, the basaltic tufa caused an erosion sufficient to unsettle the basaltic columns above.
>
> (*d*) This removal or wasting of the pillars was hastened by a flaw or fissure between them.

This supposed flaw, or fissure, between the columns is an important point, for without it the action of the water under them—assuming that a cavity had been formed in the tuff beneath—would not appear to be sufficient to loosen and cause subsidence, as there is no evidence of unsettling of the columns which form the roof of Boat Cave and MacKinnon's Cave. There is at least one point in support of the belief that there was

once a fissure in the face of the cliff here before the formation of
Fingal's Cave. If on a drawing, or photograph, we project
lines parallel to the columns on both sides of the cave towards
one another until they meet at the apex of the arch, we find that
though they meet at this point they are still about two feet apart
at sea level. This evidence seems to indicate that there was a
fissure or flaw in the rock here at one time.

It is worthy of note that the island of Iona is visible from the
innermost part of Fingal's Cave, Dun-I, the highest hill in Iona,
lying practically on a line with the centre of the cave. The
arc of a circumference with a radius of six miles, determined by
the angle subtended by an opening of fifty feet at the end of a
tunnel two hundred and thirty feet long, is almost infinitesimal.
This point was put forward, at one time, in support of the belief
that Staffa, in the past, had been used as a fortress to protect
Iona, and that fire signals could be made to Iona from inside
Fingal's Cave without any outsider being aware.

The exploration of Fingal's Cave was really a strenuous
undertaking for its early visitors, before the advent of the steamboat. They had to clamber along the irregular ledge of broken-
column stumps without the assistance of guide-ropes, supports
or concrete steps. In those days the boatmen held a long oar
or boathook across the deepest hollows in the causeway within
the cave so that visitors could catch hold of it as a support.

The first mention I have found of permanent supports having
been fitted in Fingal's Cave is by M. Ducos, who visited Staffa
during the month of July 1826. He says: " Sir Ronald
MacDonald to whom the island belongs, has fitted two iron
supports and an iron gangway [in Fingal's Cave] which rust
is eating away and which bends when one puts one's weight on
it and will one day cause a grave accident—but who would not
risk it?"

Not until the eighteen-seventies were there reasonably good
supports and guide-ropes in the cave. The sketch of the interior
of Fingal's Cave in Keddie's book, which was drawn about
1848, shows no stanchions or guide-ropes in the cave. Previous
to that time passengers from the steamboat were sailed into the
cave in a rowing-boat if weather permitted, otherwise they were
landed elsewhere and left to scramble about the cave as best

they could.   Iron gratings were originally fitted by the steam-boat Company to span the more dangerous spaces between the broken columns but towards the end of last century those gratings were removed and several spaces filled in with concrete: the cement was taken from Oban and the sand, etc., was ferried in an open boat from the island of Gometra four miles distant.   During 1900, a few concrete steps were built to overcome the remaining difficult rises in the rock within the cave.

A few weeks before the end of the Second World War (May 1945), a floating mine struck and exploded against the Colonnade just outside the entrance to Fingal's Cave, on the west side. The explosion caused the collapse of a considerable number of long vertical columns, and the zone of rock above these columns sheared and collapsed so that now the cliff rises in one plane from base to summit.   Previous to that incident the zone of rock over these columns projected and overhung them.   This large fall of rock left a white calcined mark on the columnar zone but as the zone above it consists of a more amorphous rock, the mark left by its shearing was not noticeable unless examined closely.   That white calcined mark on the columnar zone was very conspicuous for a year or so after the incident, but is now almost weathered away.

During the month of August 1953, fragments of rock weighing several hundredweights (not tons, as reported in sections of the press) broke loose and fell from the upper, amorphous, part of the cliff above the Causeway, outside the entrance to Fingal's Cave toward the east and caused the suspension of landing visitors on the island for some time as they fell on the track which visitors traverse on their way to the cave.   This seems to be the first recorded fall of rock in this part of the island since Staffa was "discovered" in 1772.

Both by its resemblance to a great pillared hall and by the melody of surging waves within, Fingal's Cave is so suggestive of music that occasionally a group of visitors unites in song.   One instance of this kind seems specially worthy of mention.   It occurred on 10th June 1897.   On the previous day a special service had been held in the ruins of the Abbey Church of Iona (it was not restored at that time) to commemorate the 1300th anniversary of the death of St Columba; the first public worship to be held there for over three hundred years. Many of the best-known leaders of the Church of Scotland were present, including Dr Norman MacLeod, Dr Blair, Principal Story, Dr James MacGregor of St Cuthbert's, Edinburgh, Dr MacAdam Muir of Glasgow Cathedral, Dr Mitchel of Aberdeen, and others. On their return journey to Oban on the following day the *Grenadier* anchored off Staffa to allow her passengers—about three hundred—to visit Fingal's Cave. The worthy divines kept together and their boat was the first to reach the landing place on the island, from whence they proceeded on foot to the inner end of the cave. Remaining in the cave until most of the visitors had entered it or were near it, these reverend gentlemen gave expression to their feelings by singing the 103rd Psalm to that grand old traditional tune Coleshill, in which they were joined by everyone present. One of the party said later that " It touched a sympathetic chord in every heart." This paean of thanksgiving sung by so many voices and led by those eminent churchmen must have been very impressive as it mingled with the deep bass of the waves and reverberated in this natural cathedral.

In the soft light of late evening during settled weather, when one can penetrate on the narrow causeway almost to the inner end, a visit to Fingal's Cave is a memorable experience. Naturally, the effect differs greatly from that of the same scene in times of storm, yet it is none the less inspiring. Both aspects arouse a thrill, but while in storm it is a thrill of amazement, a kind of primeval thrill, on an evening of settled weather it is a thrill of reverence; I have never experienced a sinister or depressing atmosphere in the cave.

As daylight wanes there is a unique solemnity in the cool twilight of this great cavern with its colonnades and vaulted roof, swept by the restless sea. Through the vast portals comes the heaving surge of the Atlantic, its sonorous music causing the echoes to break forth in unison. This diapason of the deep swells rapidly in a grand crescendo to a mighty climax as the sea booms against the inner end of the cave with a loud vibrant echo. Then, as the sea recedes, it decreases gradually until all that is heard is the tinkling sound of the little cascades falling from the numerous stumps of broken columns, and a vast sigh from the undertow.   The pause is brief; again, and yet again, the action is repeated as the ocean swell heaves into the cave in its rhythmic motion, recalling the lines from Gray's *Elegy*:

> Where through the long-drawn aisle and fretted vault
> The pealing anthem swells the note of praise.

Indeed, only a poet can hope to give an adequate description of the harmony of sound and structure in this minster of the sea.

CHAPTER VIII

HOW FINGAL'S CAVE RECEIVED ITS NAME

ONE explanation of how Staffa's greatest cavern received the name Fingal's Cave may be deduced from the following description of the Giant's Causeway, Ireland, in *Letters Concerning the Natural History of the Basalts of the Northern Coast of the County of Antrim* (1784),[1] by the Rev. William Hamilton:

> The Causeway was observed by the fishermen, whose daily necessities led them thither for subsistence, to be a mole, projecting into the sea, which answered for several purposes; on closer inspection it was discovered to be built with the appearance of art and regularity somewhat resembling the works of man, but at the same time exceeding anything of the kind which had been seen: and it was found that human ingenuity and perseverance, if supported by sufficient power, might be abundantly adequate to its production. The chief defect in this analogy seems to have been the want of strength equal to the effect! but this was soon supplied in the tradition of a fanciful people, and Fin ma Cool (MacPherson's more modern Fingal), the celebrated hero of ancient Ireland, became the giant under whose forming hand the curious structure was erected.
>
> It was afterwards discovered that a pile of similar pillars was placed somewhere on the opposite coast of Scotland, and as the business of latitude and longitude was not at that time very accurately ascertained, a general confused notion prevailed that this mole was once continued across the sea and connected the Irish and Scottish coasts together.

It seems reasonable to suppose that the principal cavern in the Scottish pile of pillars would be named after this Finn Mac Cool, or Fingal, the giant who was believed to have built the whole formation of Staffa and the Giant's Causeway. William Keddie, who visited Staffa in 1847, says: "The popular notion is not that Fingal inhabited this cave [Fingal's Cave] but that he built it."

In Scotland the name Finn MacCumhaill (*Fin MacCoul*) is usually shortened to merely Finn, or Fionn (*Fewn*)—"the Fair One."

---

[1] These letters appear in *Pinkerton's Voyages*, VOL. III.

Fionn is the central figure of the later heroic cycle of Ireland, commonly called Ossianic or Fenian, and is reputed to have been leader of a band of chivalrous warriors or super-men called the Feinne,[1] or Fianna. The names Fionn and Feinne have been anglicised as Fingal and Fingalians, but though these latter names are now most frequently used in English literature to denote the Gaelic hero and his warriors, according to the late Professor W. J. Watson, D.LITT. CELT., there is no authority for their introduction; the name Fenians is also used as an anglicised form of Feinne. To save confusion, however, perhaps it is best here to use the most familiar names—Fingal and Fingalians.

The Fingalians are said to have been a kind of standing army which was scattered throughout Ireland to ward off enemies, particularly the corsairs from Lochlann (the Norsemen). In times of peace they, and their hounds, proved themselves unequalled in the chase. Irish historians of the tenth century lead us to believe that Fingal usually resided in Almu (Allen), in Co. Kildare, where he was surrounded by some of the contingents of the Fingalians, and give the date of his death as A.D. 283.

Unfortunately, the origin of the stories and poems connected with Fingal and his warriors is obscure, and scholars are by no means agreed on the subject. The *Annals of Ulster* state that Fingal was the father of Ossian, or Oisin, the great traditional bard of the Gaels, and was lineally descended from Niah Neacht, King of Leinster—that he was married first to Grainne, or Grania, daughter of Cormac MacAirt, who was proclaimed monarch of Ireland in A.D. 254. Grainne, having intrigued with Diarmid an Tuirc, was repudiated by Fingal, who married her sister Aibe, the mother of Ossian. Another version of the latter part of this account is that Fingal and his band of warriors came to Tara to seek the hand of Grainne in marriage to Fingal, but while there she eloped with Fingal's lieutenant Diarmid.

Regarding the existence in the flesh of Fingal and Ossian, the last detailed examination of the evidence for and against seems to be that given by William Sharp (" Fiona MacLeod") in his Introduction to the Centenary edition of *The Poems of Ossian*

---

[1] Feinne (*Fayn*), or Fianna, is a collective noun, and is used to designate the whole company of warriors commanded by Fionn.

(1926). Sharp's opinion is summed up in his quotation from Dr Alexander McBain's Address, "Who Were the Feinne?": "Did Fingal live or Ossian sing?—we have to give the answer, that Fingal lived and Ossian sang only in the heart and imagination of the Gaelic race, to embody their ideal of all that is noble and heroic." But this verdict is not necessarily final on the subject, and is not acceptable to all students of Ossianic literature. In the *Encyclopaedia Britannica*, Professor R. A. S. MacAlister, of University College, Dublin, says:

> Finn MacCumhaill [Fingal] was probably the general to whom Cormac MacAirt, King of Tara (*c.* A.D. 250), entrusted the task of organising a standing army whereby he sought to establish a suzerainty over the whole of Ireland. But he has attracted to himself a vast body of popular legend, and has thus become a mythological figure which dominates the folklore of the Gaelic peoples in Ireland, Scotland and the Isle of Man.

Fingal and his band of warriors—the Feinne—are a Celtic parallel to King Arthur and his knights of the Round Table.

For three centuries, from the fifth onwards, the language and literature of Gaelic Ireland and Gaelic Scotland were virtually the same, hence the stories of Fingal and his warriors would, naturally, pass from Ireland to Scotland. Later on many new stories were no doubt composed in Scotland regarding this hero, and Scottish place-names would naturally be introduced, but there is no authentic evidence for the belief, commonly held, that the title applied to Fingal by MacPherson in his *Poems of Ossian*, namely " King of Morven," means the district of Morven, or Morvern, in Argyllshire. According to Professor W. J. Watson, the correct spelling of this place-name is Morvern, or *A' Mhorbhairn*, meaning " Sea-gap." Of course MacPherson may have meant King of Mor-bheinn, meaning King of the great bens or mountains. In Scotland, Fingal's name is pre-preserved in many place-names.

The Gaels had come from Ireland into Scotland but after the Norsemen began their raids intercourse between the two countries was interrupted, and this, in time, under Pictish and Norse influences led to a divergence in the speech of the Gaels in Ireland and those in Scotland; a process which the Reformation accentuated, so that Irish and Scottish Gaelic are now separate dialects.

What is known as the Ossianic Controversy arose through the publication in 1760 of a collection of poems entitled *Fragments of Ancient Poetry collected in the Highlands of Scotland and translated from the Gaelic Language by James MacPherson;* a second volume appeared in 1762, and a third in 1763. MacPherson, who was a young Highland schoolmaster, claimed his work to be translations of fragments of poetry by a third-century bard named Ossian, son of Finn, or Fingal.

These poems breathe the spirit of valour in a mystic vein, with a kaleidoscopic background of wonderful atmospheric effect—turmoil of the tempest and sunshine and mist on land and sea. On publication they took the literary world of Europe and America by storm; their reception has been described as " a universal deluge of approbation." They were read and recited in castle and cottage, and were translated into every language in Europe. Among those who fell under their charm was Napoleon, who carried a copy on all his marches.

In *Fingal, an Epic,* the praises of this hero are sung:

Behold the King of Morven! He moves below like a pillar of fire. His strength is like the stream of Lubar, or the wind of the echoing Cromla; when the branchy forests of night are torn from all their rocks! Happy are thy people, O Fingal! thine arm shall finish their wars. Thou art the first in their dangers, the wisest in the days of their peace. Thou speakest, and thy thousands obey: armies tremble at the sound of thy steel. Happy are thy people, O Fingal! King of resounding Selma.

Again, in these poems, we read of the exploits of Fingal and his warriors; of their skill in the chase, of their prowess and bravery in their fierce battles with the invading forces of Lochlann (Scandinavia); of their victory rejoicings, when at

the feast of shells . . . The voice of sprightly mirth arose. The trembling harps of joy were strung. Bards sung the battle of heroes; they sung the heaving breast of love. Ullin, Fingal's bard, was there: the sweet voice of resounding Cona.

Highlanders generally accepted these poems as Ossian's, but as time went on some English critics began to doubt their authenticity. Those critics held that if such a person as Ossian ever lived, he was only an ignorant Highlander who could not write a line of poetry, and that the poems published were a product of MacPherson's own musings on Celtic imagery. Others believed that MacPherson had found a few fragments of

Fingal's Wishing Chair, a natural seat formed in the rock wall beside the Causeway; a wish made while seated there is said to come true

The Great Face seen on a still day from the south-south-west, with Boat Cave on the right and MacKinnon's Cave in shadow

old Celtic poetry and had mixed them up to form a basis for poems of his own which he presented to the public. A characteristic beginning to these poems is: " A tale of the times of old; the deeds of days of other years," which one writer describes as "Macphersonic trappings."

One of MacPherson's most bitter critics was Dr Johnson, the great literary dictator. Indeed, one of Johnson's reasons for undertaking his famous tour of the Hebrides with Boswell was to search for evidence to prove the non-existence of any poetry by a person named Ossian. Dr Johnson and his supporters in this controversy regarded MacPherson as author rather than as editor of these poems.

MacPherson was asked, and even offered financial assistance, to publish the original Gaelic pieces which he had collected, but, taking offence at personal slanders, he refused to do so and unfortunately the controversy about the genuineness or otherwise of his translations has never been settled satisfactorily. A very interesting analysis of the subject is given in a recent book: *The Gaelic Sources of MacPherson's "Ossian,"* by D. S. Thomson, 1952.

One regrettable feature of the controversy was the personal bitterness that crept into it and diverted the attention of the public away from the literary merit of the poems. Whether of Ossian's or MacPherson's creation, their beauty in presenting the ethnic Gael is undoubted. Matthew Arnold said of these poems: " Windy Morven and echoing Sora and Selma with its silent halls!—we owe to them a debt of gratitude and when we are unjust enough to forget it, may the Muse forget us."

When Queen Victoria popularised the Highlands, the works of Ossian were resuscitated and used by writers as a wreath of twilight-mysticism to intertwine their pseudo-Celtic effusions. Ossian's "Address to the Sun" was quoted almost as often as twenty-fifth of January enthusiasts quote Burns' "Address to a Haggis." Here it is revived again :

O thou that rollest above, round as the shield of my fathers! Whence are thy beams, O sun! thy everlasting light? Thou comest forth, in thy awful beauty; the stars hide themselves in the sky; the moon, cold and pale, sinks in the western wave. But thou thyself movest alone: who can be a companion of thy course? The oaks of the mountains fall: the mountains themselves decay with years; the ocean shrinks and grows again: the moon herself is lost in heaven; but thou art forever the same; rejoicing in the brightness of thy course.   When the world is dark with tempests; when thunder rolls, and lightning flies; thou lookest in thy beauty from the clouds, and laughest at the storm.

I have dealt with Fingal and Ossian at some length because one of the most frequent questions asked by visitors to Staffa is, " Who was Fingal?"

To return to the point at issue, namely, the origin of the name of Staffa's greatest cavern—Fingal's Cave.   The belief that this cave owes its name to Ossian's hero has been opposed by several writers, who maintain that the name Fingal, as applied to this cave, is a corruption of the Gaelic words meaning "musical cave," or " cave of music."   One writer made the dogmatic statement that this cave " is no more associated with the Fingal of Ossian than it is with the Hector of Homer."[1]

The Gaelic words for "musical cave" are *uamh bhinn; mh* in the substantive and *bh* in the adjective have a *v* sound, and therefore *uamh bhinn* is pronounced *oo-a-veen*.

The Gaelic for Fingal is *Fionn* in the nominative, but the Gaelic nouns are declinable, and the genitive of *Fionn* is *Fhinn*. The letter *f* is silent before the aspirate; *Fhinn* therefore becomes *'inn* (pronounced *een*), which makes the pronunciation of the Gaelic for Fingal's Cave *oo-a-een*.   It would be quite an excusable mistake for anyone to pronounce the *f* in *Fhinn*, which would make the pronunciation of the Gaelic for Fingal's Cave *oo-a-feen*.   There would therefore be very little difference in pronouncing the Gaelic for " musical cave " and the Gaelic for "Fingal's Cave."   Sir Joseph Banks's guides might have translated the name as the Cave of Fingal, while the true and literal translation was " musical cave."   The name of Fingal is so well known to every Gael that almost any word approaching any of its inflections in sound is readily associated with him.

---

[1] Ossian and Homer have much in common; that they ever existed in the flesh is problematical; the ancient accounts of their lives are legendary; by some they are regarded as a type of wandering bard, while others consider them to be purely mythical figures typifying an ideal; some scholars ascribe different parts of their epics to different periods of time, so that they could not be written by one author; the Fingal of Ossian and the Hector of Homer are characters possessing many similar traits.

The peculiar musical sounds emitted from Fingal's Cave, apart from the regular boom of the waves striking it, are caused, probably, by the air being trapped in a hole underwater, from which it can be seen bubbling up on a calm day. This aperture is a little below the base of the columnar structure at the inner end of the cave, and may be the mouth of a cavity or even a small cave. It gave rise, at one time, to the fanciful theory that there was a tunnel from Staffa to the Giant's Causeway in Ireland. These musical sounds are heard more distinctly when at a short distance from the mouth of the cave. When inside the cave, the unceasing boom of the waves and the numerous echoes formed seem to drown the higher notes.

Professor Sir A. Geikie, the well-known geologist, says:

There can be little doubt that this etymological explanation [of the name of Fingal's Cave] is correct. The volume of air driven into the internal cavity by the impact of the water is under the pressure sometimes of several tons to the square inch of surface. When the pressure is suddenly relaxed by the sinking of the wave, the imprisoned air at once rushes out and in favourable chinks and passages gives rise to musical sounds as when a trumpet is blown.

The term " musical cave " might also have been applied to the cave from its resemblance to a pipe organ, if the Gaels had seen one. Apparently the Gaels of northern Ireland, who resided in the neighbourhood of the Giant's Causeway, were acquainted with pipe organs long before the "discovery" of Staffa. There is evidence as early as 1694 that they had applied the name "Giant's Organ" to a group of long vertical columns which stand in the side of a hill some distance from the Causeway.[1]

I beg to offer a third explanation as to how Fingal's Cave received its name. I have not seen it mentioned in any other work, but it seems quite reasonable. The name may be a perpetuation of the memory of the Vikings, who at one time possessed the Hebrides, including Staffa. The Gaels made a distinction between the Norwegian Vikings and the Danish Vikings by calling the former *Fionn-ghoill*, white, or fair, foreigners, and the latter *Dubh-ghoill*, black, or dark, foreigners. The usual explanation given is that these distinctions were

[1] *Fingal's Cave* is the name of a reel composed by John Gow, son of the famous Neil Gow, vide *Musical Scotland*, by David Baptie, 1894.

made owing to the fair hair and complexion of the Norwegians, while the Danes had dark hair and complexion. This ethnic discrimination in colour, however, is hardly tenable. The more probable reason for the colour distinction is that the Norwegians wore white garments and carried "pure white" banners, while the Danes wore black garments and carried "jet-black" banners. The Norwegians and the Danes were different peoples and often attacked one another savagely. There is historical evidence for the latter explanation of the colour distinction, as mentioned by W. C. MacKenzie in *The Highlands and Isles of Scotland*.

As it was the Norwegians who conquered the Hebrides and evidently gave Staffa its name, they may have been the original discoverers of the island's greatest cavern. That the Gaels should therefore bestow upon this cave the name "Uamh nam Fionnghall," meaning the "Cave of the White, or Fair, Foreigners, or Norwegians," is, in my opinion, quite feasible. In the English translation the latter part of the name might easily have been confused with the name Fingal. Indeed, some old Gaelic chronicles spell the Gaelic name of the Norwegians "Fingalls," which makes this hypothesis for the origin of the name of Fingal's Cave even more acceptable.

Many of the old inhabitants of Mull call the cave neither *Uamh bhinn* nor *Uamh Fhinn*, but *An Uamh Mhor Staffa*, meaning "the great cave of Staffa." It is better, however, to have some specific name to distinguish it from the other caves and its dimensions indicate that, except for its arched roof, it is almost the same size as MacKinnon's Cave.

We have, therefore, the three foregoing derivations of the name of Fingal's Cave, each with its own merit, from which to choose. To me the first one seems the most appropriate. It is the simplest and most direct; the name "Fingal's Cave" means what it says, a point to be commended always. This name stands for all that is noblest and best in Celtic tradition, and there is also a mystical atmosphere about both the hero and the cave. The name "musical cave," or "cave of music," is applicable to almost any cave into which the sea washes; it all depends upon what is one's idea of music. There are many occasions during stormy weather when the booms and roars emitted by Staffa's greatest cavern can hardly be described as musical, they terrify rather than soothe. To describe that noise as musical is like applying the term musical to the bellowing of a mad bull; *Uamh Fuaim* (" cave of clamour ") would be a more appropriate name on those occasions than *Uamh bhinn* (" cave of music "). Finally, the memory of the Norse possession of the island is perpetuated in the name Staffa.

Let us then regard this great cavern, this regal Hall of Shells (the banqueting hall of the Fingalians), as a worthy shrine for the spirit of mighty Fingal, the greatest hero of Celtic tradition; the hero whose exploits, immortalised by Ossian, greatest of the bards traditional or factual, have stirred the emotions and fired the imagination of the Gael for generations. In fancy's flight we can join with the poet and picture:

> Fingal in his spacious hall,
> That echoes with the ocean's thund'ring fall;
> Whose waves on Staffa's massy pillars roar
> And shake with deaf'ning noise the cavern'd shore.
> There Windy Morven's chief I seem to hear,
> His valiant arm reclin'd upon his spear;
> While thousand demigods, that stand around,
> Catch the great leader's animated sound;
> In song they pass the night, and chant the praise
> Of high-born warriors fam'd in other days;
> Or tune their harps to love and soft desire,
> And strike for Bragela the golden lyre.[1]

---

[1] P. B. Homer, in *Observations on a Short Tour in Scotland: Made in the Summer of* 1803.

CHAPTER IX

FLORA AND FAUNA

ON the undulating plateau of Staffa the pasture varies according to its situation. In the hollows it is rich and verdant, while on the higher parts it becomes somewhat scant, short, and hard, and frequently the rocky skeleton projects through the thin skin of turf. Tufts of scurvy grass are rooted in most of the upper rock clefts. The crumbling volcanic rock forms very fertile soil but it is porous, and on Staffa it is shallow, drying up quickly except in the depressions, where moisture accumulates. The moist climate of this region, however, keeps the vegetation fresh and green.

The flora of the island calls for no special mention, only common flowers being found here, such as sea thrift, or sea pink, sea campion, primrose, daisy, buttercup and a few insignificant varieties which are not likely to interest anyone except the botanist. One of these minor varieties adopts an unusual method, among plants, of supplementing its food supply. This plant is the pretty little butterwort, or bog violet, whose pendulous flower hangs gracefully over its boat-shaped leaves, which radiate over the ground like the rays of a star. In these leaves are many minute glands secreting a viscid fluid by which any small insect alighting on them is held fast. Gradually the leaf curls inwards, making the prisoner still more secure, and slowly the butterwort digests the substance of the insect, ultimately ejecting the shrivelled husk. Thus, like the Venus fly-trap, the butterwort would seem to be carnivorous.

Although humble in stature and bloom, some of these little flowers clothe parts of the surface of Staffa so thickly during early summer that the expanses of colour are very pleasing to the eye, while on the cliff tops and ledges cushions of sea-pink tremble in the salt winds.

There are no trees on the island, the largest plants being a few bramble bushes and at least one small bush of prostrate dwarf juniper on the sheltered, eastern side.

Dr MacGuarie, of Ulva, in his description of Staffa written during November 1773 (included in Chapter II), says: " The island is mostly arable; its produce is the same with the rest of the adjacent isles, but more fertile of their kind." Abraham Mills, a vulcanist, who visited Staffa during the month of July 1788, says that he saw " barley, oats, flax and potatoes growing near the centre of the island," and Thomas Campbell, the poet, who visited Staffa during the summer of 1795, says, in a letter to a friend: " On the top of these [cliffs] are rich plains of grass and corn." Dr John Leyden, the Scottish poet and friend of Sir Walter Scott, says in *A Tour of the Highlands in 1800:* " Although now only used for grazing cattle, it [Staffa] formerly produced a considerable quantity of corn." Being so exposed to the strong Atlantic winds, it is difficult to understand how a satisfactory crop of corn could be grown on Staffa, though it is well known that from time immemorial the West Highlands and Islands of Scotland produced large crops of cereals. They ceased doing so only at the beginning of the nineteenth century, when, owing to improved methods of communication, it was found possible to bring cereals from other parts of the country at a cheaper rate than they could be grown at home. It is hardly possible in the severe Highland climate to grow cereals which can compete, either in price or quality, with those grown in the more favoured South.

Leyden also mentions having seen three deer, which had been placed on the island, and which seemed perfectly tame. The Hon. Mrs Murray, of Kensington, who paid her first visit to Staffa in the same year as Leyden, also mentions those deer. In her *Guide to the Beauties of the Western Highlands and Hebrides of Scotland*, VOL. II, she says:

The first time I was on Staffa I saw only a few sheep and three red deer; the latter on the summit followed our boat as we rowed at the base, and when we came to Fingal's Cave they stood to view us from the tremendous high dome over it. In 1801 one of the deer grew so wild that he was very near killing a man; he on that account was shot; the other two were in the habit of following all boats leaving the island, but having, it is supposed, extended their convoy to too great a distance, they perished on their return . . . . Goats have since been sent to Staffa in lieu of the deer, an animal much better suited to the character and extent of the island.

These deer are also mentioned by George L. A. Douglas,

Advocate, in his *Tour in the Hebrides A.D. 1800* (first published 1927).

For many years fourteen or fifteen head of cattle were landed on Staffa every autumn and left to graze till the ensuing spring. They were withdrawn finally about sixty years ago and substituted by a flock of sheep which were the only large animals on the island until the Second World War, when the high prices paid for beef caused cattle to be landed once again on Staffa for grazing.   At the present time both cattle and sheep are ferried over from Iona to graze on the island.

During summer Staffa, like most of the uninhabited islands of western Scotland, has a large and varied colony of seabirds, including razorbill, guillemot, cormorant or scart, puffin, oyster-catcher, wild duck, storm petrel and various types of gull. Each type of bird seems to have its own particular part of the island for nesting purposes.   The guillemots and razorbills nest on the rock ledges at MacKinnon's Cave, the cormorants in the inner recesses of all the caves except Boat Cave, the puffins at the north-east and the gulls on the west of the island. Other birds have their own secluded retreats.

The gulls are the most noisy residents on Staffa.   Around their nesting sites they are seldom silent, but when a human being intrudes on this territory the noise becomes pandemonium with their " yammeris and yowlis, and shrykking skreeking skrymming scowlis and meickle noyis and shoutis."

It must have been a scene like Staffa with its colony of sea-birds which Thomson had in mind when, in *The Seasons*, he wrote:

> Where the Northern Ocean in vast whirls
> Boils round the naked melancholy isles
> Of farthest Thule, and the Atlantic surge
> Pours in among the stormy Hebrides—
> Who can recount what transmigrations there
> Are annual made?   What nations come and go?
> And how the living clouds on clouds arise?
> Infinite wings!   Till the plume-dark air
> And rude resounding shores are one wild cry.

Included among the gull colony of Staffa are these two rapacious feathered pirates—the great black-backed gull and the skua.   Both are large and powerful birds;   the former, with snow-white neck and underparts and black back and wings, is really a handsome bird, but the skua has unattractive mottled sooty-brown plumage, and is bold and pugnacious even to human beings, as I learned from personal experience. I hope the reader will not think that I am exaggerating when I mention one occasion on which a skua vented its wrath on me by several very determined sallies of dive-bombing tactics. It swooped down swiftly with my head as target until I beat a retreat, when I was alone one evening on the beach at Port an Fhasgaidh. That it would have struck me had I not moved seems certain, as I felt the wind when it shot over me where my head would have been had I not ducked quick and low. Unfortunately, the stones on the beach were too large to use as missiles. It was an incident in my life which I am not likely to forget, and I had two witnesses who saw the attack from a distance of about one hundred yards. Their attention was attracted by hearing me shouting to try and frighten the bird. I experienced a similar, but less vicious, attack on a later occasion when on the Dutchman's Cap, one of the Treshnish Isles, near Staffa. It was noticeable that these birds would not attack when more than one person was present. It is common for skuas to attack anyone who goes near their nest, but as far as I am aware skuas do not nest on Staffa or any of the neighbouring islands.

The most interesting type of bird on Staffa is surely the puffin, or sea-parrot, which must be one of the most quaint of British birds. It has an upright mode of walking, or rather waddling, owing to its legs being near its tail. This peculiar gait, combined with its plumage of black back and neckband and white front, added to its large parrot-like bill, which is brilliantly coloured red, yellow and blue, suggests a miniature red-nosed clown in evening dress. Its behaviour is as comical as its appearance.

This amusing bird, of which there is a large number on Staffa during the summer months, is about the size of a pigeon, but more plump, or chubby, and its short legs and webbed feet are coloured a bright orange or red, which probably accounts for its local name in this district, namely *Seumas Ruadh*, Gaelic for "Red Jimmie." The surface of its brilliant bill peels off in horny plates after the breeding season.

Many an hour have I spent among these feathered comedians on Staffa observing their habits and exploring their nests, which are situated in burrows cut into the terraced soil at the top of the cliffs.   Here they lay their solitary white egg, which seems to get soiled with the surrounding earth.   The burrows reach to a depth of several feet, and appear like rabbit-holes.   Indeed, in some places puffins chase the rabbits out of their homes and confiscate them.   This is not the case on Staffa, however, for, according to the neighbouring islanders, there never have been rabbits on the island, therefore the puffins must have excavated those tunnels themselves.

The puffin has a comical habit of popping its head out of its burrow entrance suddenly and jerking it nervously from side to side to see if the coast is clear.   If all is well, it advances a few paces from the burrow and stands quite pompous, with its chest puffed out, surveying the surroundings like a portly gentleman at the door of his mansion, though, if danger threatens, its scurry back is not at all dignified.

If unmolested, puffins will approach within a few feet of a human being as they seem to be very inquisitive.   Their wide-eyed, solemn expression and quaint method of shuffling forward cautiously, then halting and turning the head sideways to survey one with a cold, stony stare, can hardly fail to raise a smile or even a hearty laugh.   The difficulty in walking properly is caused by the legs being near the tail, which occurs in all under-water swimming birds and assures a more forcible propeller when under water.   In walking birds such as the swan, goose, and surface-swimming duck, the legs come well under the middle of the body.   The cormorant is built on the same lines as the puffin, for the same reason.

The comical behaviour of the puffin appears to be somewhat similar to that of the penguin of the Antarctic, as described by explorers, only that the puffin utters no sound except an infrequent burr.   They fly, or whirr, in a very swift and undeviating line of flight, their wings vibrating with insect-like rapidity, their red legs and feet sticking out behind, wide spread, in a most ungraceful fashion.   Swooping past close along the face of the cliff, then out seaward, they make a circuit, and so pass and repass, again and again, making an aerial puffin procession.

They always seem to keep flying over the sea and seldom come over the land.

Puffins are believed to guide their chicks on their first voyage to sea during the darkness of an August night. According to Seton Gordon, a leading authority on the wild bird life of Scotland,

the young have never been seen to leave their islands; they are very rarely indeed seen at sea. It appears as though the parents take them far out into the Atlantic beyond sight of land—else they would be seen like the young of the guillemot and razorbill, during the months of August and September.

This belief is amended in a recent book, *Island Going*, by Robert Atkinson, where the writer states that he and a friend came across one or two young puffins making their way with difficulty to the sea by night. He mentions that the full-grown young puffins are too fat to fly so their parents desert them and leave them to fast until of their own accord they waddle and tumble to the sea. The night-time journey appears to be nature's way of preserving them in their feebleness on land from birds of prey to whom they would prove very tasty morsels.

At first I thought of killing one of the puffins and having it stuffed, to keep as a souvenir. On further consideration, however, I realised that in all wild bird life it is the glorious freedom and natural actions which appeal to the observer quite as much as any special appearance the bird may possess. Since then, I have seen stuffed puffins and I do not regret my decision to leave them alone, as a dead, stone-like puffin in a glass case does not convey the slightest idea of the pleasure it is to observe these same birds when alive in their natural surroundings. I do not believe in "shooting" wild birds or animals with any weapon more destructive than a camera, and those who have attempted this sport will know that it is much more difficult to stalk, and get within reasonable photographing distance of a wild bird or beast than it is to get within gunshot range of the same creature.

The quaint little puffin has the distinction of having had its name used to designate a denomination of coinage and postage stamp which were issued for local use by the owner of Lundy Island, in the Bristol Channel, until suppressed by the Law Courts in January 1931. Those coins and stamps were so named owing to the numerous puffins which frequent this island.

Other birds on Staffa well worth observing are the guillemots and razorbills which nest on the cliffs at MacKinnon's Cave. Like the puffins, they shuffle their chubby bodies around in an upright position with an expression of dignified curiosity. As their eggs are laid on narrow ledges of rock in the cliffs, in an inaccessible position, the most satisfactory way to observe their habits is to lie on the turf at the top of the cliff on one side of the cave entrance and, through binoculars, watch them on the opposite cliff. These birds build no nest, but lay their large (in comparison with the size of the bird) egg on the bare surface of a rocky ledge. One reason offered to account for the eggs not rolling off the rock surface when disturbed is that owing to their shape, which is blunt at one end and sharp at the other, they merely rotate on their axis when moved, but observation and experiment indicate that this belief is very doubtful as they often roll off or are knocked off the rock ledges. The eggs are of a very light shade of green, sometimes white, blotched and streaked with dark lines in a very peculiar manner.

The commonest type of sea-bird in the rocky regions of our British coasts, excepting perhaps the seagull, is the cormorant, and Staffa has its full complement. Indeed, the rocky platform at the base of the cliffs in the south-west of the island would not appear complete without its cormorant colony. This large, ungainly, black, sleek bird, with snake-like neck and hooked bill is a familiar object perched on his " rock of the sea," like some prehistoric pterodactyl. Flocks of them are often seen sitting like groups of black bottles, or Indian clubs, on boulders at the water's edge. In the south of England they are known as "Isle of Wight Parsons," owing to their sombre appearance. The cormorant is a heavy flier, rising clumsily from the sea, but is a powerful swimmer and an expert fisherman, as is necessary to appease a ravenous appetite. In Oriental countries it is trained to catch fish for its owners, being usually provided with a tight collar to prevent it from swallowing its captures. When disturbed on its nest the cormorant refuses to budge, but utters harsh cries and pecks viciously with its strong bill. Those birds on Staffa are apparently not true cormorants, but green cor-

morants, or shags. Seton Gordon, when describing the bird
life of this vicinity, says: " The big cormorant is almost entirely
absent from these little Hebridean islands, his place being filled
by the green cormorant, or shag." The colour of the big
cormorant is chiefly black, glossed with bluish-green, and a fine
specimen stands about three feet high. The shag is about one-
fourth smaller than the cormorant, is dark glossy green in
plumage (more glossy than its larger relation) and has a small
plume on the crown of its head. When diving, while swimming, the shag, and the cormorant also, throws itself out of the
water with neck outstretched; this is what causes the splash.

At the highest part of the broken columns which form a narrow causeway along the west side of Fingal's Cave, the opposite
side from that which visitors traverse, a cormorant has made her
nest regularly for many years. Conscious of the security of her
position, no amount of shouting or noise will induce her to leave
it; she merely cranes her neck and casts disdainful glances at
her human visitors.

A few storm petrels, known to mariners as Mother Carey's
chickens, nest among the heaps of stones caused by the crumbling ruins of habitation on Staffa. Mother Carey is a corruption of Mater Cara; the Blessed Virgin Mary. At night-
time they can be heard making a peculiar sound, sometimes a
purring and sometimes a soft clucking. It has been remarked
of these birds that they hatch their young by sitting on the
ground about six inches from their solitary egg and, turning
their heads towards it, make these peculiar sounds day and night
until it is hatched, which may account for the Gaelic name for
storm petrel, which is *Gur-le-gug* meaning, " hatch with, or by
means of, a cluck."

Although we heard those storm petrels on Staffa several
times, only on one occasion did we see them, and that was one
night, or rather morning, about one a.m., when we heard their
purring sound and searched for them. On gently removing a
stone from each of two places where we heard them and flashing
a torch we saw a petrel in each cavity cowering on a crude nest,
a mere depression in the ground, but there was no egg in either
nest. The birds were quite tame and did not move on our
approach, but crouched closer to the ground and ejected

a small quantity of dark yellow oil from their bill when handled.

The storm petrel is the smallest web-footed bird, being about the size of a swallow and of a black colour. It derives its name from its fluttering, rather than flying, over the sea surface with dangling legs, which often seem to tread or run up a wave, thus representing Saint Peter walking on the sea, hence its name, petrel, meaning " little Peter." A schoolboy, when describing the storm petrel in his essay, spelled the name "storm petrol," to which the schoolmaster added a marginal note: " Hail to thee, blithe spirit! bird thou never wert."

One beautiful type of nest found on Staffa is that of the eider duck, which is lined with down plucked by the bird from her own breast. This layer of down is about two inches thick, and when the bird leaves her nest she pulls part of the down over her eggs, thus helping to keep them warm and also hiding them from any birds or persons likely to steal them.

The beautiful oystercatcher, in its black and white plumage and brilliant orange-coloured bill and legs, is also a resident of Staffa. Its shrill piping cry is regarded by those who have the Gaelic as " *bi glic, bi glic, bi glic*," pronounced " bee gleechk " and meaning " be wise," " be prudent," " take care." It is a familiar sound around Staffa in calm and storm. This bird is a favourite with the Gaels and, from an old Celtic legend, they have given it the name *gille-bridean*, meaning "the servant of St Bride, or St Bridget."

An occasional gannet, or solan, may be seen winging its way on straight and steady course over the surrounding waters in search of prey. It is a strong handsome bird about three feet in length with a wing-spread of about six feet. Its plumage is snow-white with black wing tips, and its long sharp bill gives it an arrow-like appearance when in flight. Its powerful wings rise and fall with measured beat as it glides through the air, the very poetry of motion. The solan does not circle and watch over one spot when hunting, like the gull, but flies straight on over the sea until some fish attracts its attention. It then springs up into the air to a considerable height, and, after a few moments' pause, shoots down perpendicularly with a velocity which has to be seen to be appreciated, throwing up a white spout of water as it plunges beneath the surface. It usually remains under water for from ten to fifteen seconds. To witness a solan on its lonely patrol and fishing in the rich glow of evening sunlight against an azure sky or indigo sea is a thrilling sight of dynamic beauty revealed with a vividness which is lost in the glare of noonday.

James Wilson, brother of "Christopher North," who visited Staffa during the month of July 1841, while travelling as the guest of the Secretary of the Board of Fisheries, says, in *A Voyage round the Coasts of Scotland:* " We perceived two black ravens [on Staffa], and we were afterwards informed that this felonious pair had not left alive a single lamb." Personally, I have never seen a raven on Staffa, but my father became aware of one in a rather startling manner. On one occasion, many years ago, when unforeseen circumstances caused him to be the sole inhabitant of the island, he was awakened in the early hours of the morning by a tap-tap-tapping on the window of his bothy. At first he paid no attention, but as the tapping continued he got up to investigate, and saw a black figure moving in front of the window, but the dim light of breaking day made the form indistinct. On closer inspection the figure proved to be a large raven which had ventured near the hut, and on approaching the window was attracted by a plate of meat within. The tapping was caused by the raven striking the window with its beak in an endeavour to reach the food.

The large grey, or Atlantic, seal is a frequent visitor to the waters surrounding Staffa and in good weather can sometimes be seen basking on the rocks and skerries. The smaller common, or round-headed, seal is seldom seen in this vicinity though it haunts the river mouths over in Mull. The average length of the grey seal is between seven and nine feet and a bull may weigh over fifty stones, whereas the common seal has an average length of between four and five feet. Their sense of smell is acute, also their sense of hearing, though their organs of hearing are hidden beneath the skin. In the common or round-headed seal the ear orifice consists of a small vertical slit in the skin close behind the eye, while in the grey seal the ear opening is a small circular hole. The grey seal is sometimes called the dog seal, owing to the shape of its head, which has a long muzzle and a space of bare skin round the nose. Although timid, seals seem prompted by curosity, and though very agile when swimming, they enjoy basking lazily on the rocks.

It is a common belief among West Highland fishermen that musical sounds attract and fascinate the seal. Sir Walter Scott mentions this notion in his *Lord of the Isles:*

> Rude Heisker's seal through surges dark
> Will long pursue the minstrel's bark.

Naturalists tell us that, owing to the difference in the structure of the hearing organs of common seal and grey seal, it is only the former which is influenced by music; it has no effect on the grey seal, though I have heard fishermen say that the grey, or Atlantic, seal is also attracted by music.

Many years ago, some Mull fishermen caught a young grey seal near the Treshnish Isles, which lie about five miles to the north-west of Staffa, and took it home with them, where it became very tame and, when hungry and unable to obtain fish, waylaid hens and ducks. Ultimately, the fishermen decided to take it back to its natural haunts and dumped it near its old home at the Treshnish Isles. Imagine their surprise when, several weeks later, they found their pet seal lying sleeping among the bracken near their own cottage. No one discovered how it managed to return to its dry land home in Mull.

When fish are plentiful, a school of porpoise may be seen gambolling in the sea off Staffa. Their round glistening black backs as they slip in and out of the water in graceful curves, are suggestive of the undulations of a half-submerged sea-serpent.

As far as I am aware, no one has seen a sea-serpent near Staffa (there is no "license" on the island), though any of the caves would supply the fiction writer with an ideal lair for one of these problematical monsters of the deep.

The grampus, which is a close relative of the porpoise, is an occasional visitor to these waters and, like its relative, travels usually in groups, or schools, but, unlike the porpoise, is a ferocious creature. A school of grampus, and sometimes an individual, will follow and capture a seal and rend it in pieces to appease their ravenous appetite. Another habit of the grampus is to shoot up from below and snap any unwary seabird which happens to be swimming on the surface of the sea.

Flocks of duck have been seen to disappear quickly in this manner. The grampus has also been known to attack lobster creels containing a capture, while the fishermen were hoisting them from the bed of the sea, crushing the creel like paper and swallowing the lobster. Sometimes they strip an entire long-line of fish as these are being brought to the surface. The grampus is much larger than the porpoise, though this may not be very enlightening to anyone who does not know the size of a porpoise—if such there be: the porpoise is about six feet long, the grampus about twelve. The most obvious point of distinction between the two, in addition to size, is that the porpoise appears as a round, shiny, jet-black object as it tumbles over, head foremost, in the sea, appearing and disappearing very quickly. The grampus, on the other hand, appears above water as a slaty-grey object and emerges and submerges more leisurely than the porpoise in a forward roll, somewhat like the motion of the swell on the sea. This type of grampus is a dolphin, and not the killer whale, which is also known as a grampus.

We never saw any whales near Staffa, though they are probably casual visitors to this region when following a shoal of fish. Neither did we see any sharks, though the huge basking variety is quite common on the west coast during summer. It should be remembered that the whale family, which includes the porpoise and grampus, but not the shark, are sea mammals and not fish, that is, they bring forth their young alive and suckle them. Fish, on the other hand, produce their young in the form of eggs, or roe, which are hatched outwith the parent. Another feature which distinguishes sea mammals from fish is that the former have their tail in a horizontal plane, while the latter have their tail in a vertical plane.

If one is very careful, an occasional otter may be seen on the rocky platform which stretches from the base of the cliffs in the south-west of Staffa, but they appear to be very sensitive to sound and make themselves scarce on the slightest alarm.

In the quieter waters of the creeks in the eastern side of the island the globular sea urchin with its sharp needles clings to the underwater rocks, while the lobster is sufficiently numerous around Staffa to repay " setting the creels " by the men of

Gometra. And to the edible qualities of the lobsters, crabs, dulse, whelks and other marine produce of this locality, I can personally testify.

On several occasions, when we were boiling a lobster or crabs which were given to us by the Gometra boatmen, in an improvised pot (an old bucket) over our evening fire in the open, we were kept busy driving off scores of swooping and screaming seagulls, which were bent on stealing the contents; as their numbers increased they became very aggressive. The sight of our pot of crabs was sufficient to attract the gulls in large number, and their eagerness for those tasty morsels made them almost frantic with excitement.

CHAPTER X

INHABITANTS

ALTHOUGH Staffa is now uninhabited, and has been since
the beginning of the nineteenth century, it was not always
so. When Sir Joseph Banks and his companions landed on
the island in 1772 they found it occupied by a solitary herdsman.
Uno von Troil, one of Banks's companions, says in his *Letters on
Iceland* (*vide* footnote in Faujas's *Travels in England and Scotland*
(1784), VOL. II, p. 39, though the incident is not related in the
English translation of Troil's book): " There is only one hut
which is occupied by a peasant, who attends some cattle that
pasture there. To testify his joy for our arrival, he sang all
night over in the Erse language, which we did not understand.
He regaled us with fish and milk." Faujas says, in his own
words in VOL. II, p. 24, of his book, when referring to Banks's
visit to Staffa:

On their arrival at Staffa they erected a tent, to pass the night under it;
but the only inhabitant then on the island pressed Sir Joseph so strongly to
come and sleep in his hut, that he out of complaisance consented, and left his
companions under the tent. On leaving the hut next morning he discovered that he had acquired a colony of vermin. He mentioned the
circumstance to his host in terms of mild reproach. But the latter, who was
touched to the quick, perked himself up, and assuming a tone of consequence,
retorted haughtily and harshly that it was Sir Joseph himself who had im-
ported the lice into his island, and adding, that he had better have left them
behind in England.

As this incident is not recounted in Banks's own description
of Staffa, Faujas probably had it related to him when he visited
Banks in London at the outset of his journey to Staffa.

Thomson's reference to a lone herdsman, in *The Seasons*,
seems applicable to Staffa when Sir Joseph Banks visited it:

Here the plain, harmless native his small flock
And herd diminutive of many hues
Tends on the little island's verdant swell,
The shepherd's seagirt reign; or, to the rocks
Dire-clinging, gathers his ovarious food,
Or sweeps the fishy shore.

When the Bishop of Derry (Lord Bristol[1]) and his Italian artist friend, Bitio, visited Staffa, during the month of July 1776, they found the solitary tenant still occupying the island. The Bishop, being unable to speak Gaelic, told one of his guides to ask the herdsman what he wanted most. The answer was simple and moderate, " a razor and some soap." The worthy prelate gave him a purse containing ten guineas, and later sent three razors and several pounds of soap, which made the poor fellow pity and despise the rest of the world till his presents were worn out and expended. When this reverend visitor first beheld Fingal's Cave, he was so impressed by its sublimity that he fell on his knees and prayed.

It is difficult to imagine how the lone herdsman occupied his time all the year round. Dr MacCulloch, that cynical savant, who hammered Highland sentiment as well as Highland rocks, says:

> I know not what this tenant could have found to do; unless like St Magnus, he had employed himself in "ploughing his heart with the plough-share of repentance," in contemplating his nose, like the Brahmins, till he saw a blue flame at the end of it, or in catching fleas.

Sometimes, in the isolation of his island home the solitary inhabitant may have seen those visions of the supernatural which the old legends of western Scotland tell us appeared to lonely shepherds, and which Thomson mentions in *The Castle of Indolence:*

> As when a shepherd of the Hebrid Isles
>   Placed far amid the melancholy main,
> (Whether it be lone fancy him beguiles,
>   Or that aerial beings sometimes deign
> To stand, embodied, to our senses plain),
>   Sees on the naked hill, or valley low,
> The whilst in ocean Phoebus dips his wain,
>   A vast assembly moving to and fro;
> Then all at once in air dissolves the wondrous show.

---

[1] That famous, though rather eccentric, gentleman, whose family name was Frederick Augustus Hervey, was greatly interested in volcanic phenomena. He claimed to have been the first to draw attention to the geological formation of the Giant's Causeway, on the coast of Antrim, but there is a letter in the *Philosophical Transactions of the Royal Society*, dated 24th April 1693 — before the Bishop was born—and signed "R.B., S.R.S.," giving a brief description of the Causeway by a gentleman who had visited it with the then Bishop of Derry. Lord Bristol, the Bishop, has become famous for quite another reason. He was such a high authority on food and drink that more than 6,500 hotels have been named after him—Hotel Bristol.

In the Parochial Registers, VOLS. 544-1, for the parishes of Kilninian and Kilmore, in the County of Argyll (in MS. in the Register House, Edinburgh), there is a record under the date 6th January 1782 which states: " Archd. MacArthur in Staffa and Mary Lamont had their lawful daughter Christian baptised."

When Faujas, the French geologist, visited Staffa in September 1784, the population of the island consisted of sixteen persons, of whom he gives a very interesting account.

Fuajas's fellow-travellers left Oban three days before him, as Faujas wished to examine the rocks in that neighbourhood. They embarked from Torloisk, on the west coast of Mull, for Staffa at five a.m. on the morning of the day on which Faujas arrived at Torloisk about eleven p.m., rather than lose an opportunity of favourable weather, the first they had experienced since reaching Torloisk. When they were about half way to Staffa a storm arose suddenly, drove them towards the island and, together with the tide, prevented them from turning back. After considerable difficulties, and getting drenched thoroughly by the sea, the party was landed on Staffa, but the coast being too steep and rocky to allow hauling up the boats, the boatmen pushed off and sailed to Iona for shelter.

It was two days before the storm abated sufficiently to allow the boats to return to Staffa, and during that time the party stayed with the inhabitants of the island. They had quite an exciting time, as there were eight of them and only one day's provisions. Thus for two days Staffa had a population of twenty-four.

On arriving back at Torloisk they entreated Faujas and others who had come to the shore to welcome them not to disturb them with questions until they were a little refreshed and relieved of the multitude of lice which they had acquired in the huts of the Staffa inhabitants. "Fly! fly from us," they said, " we have brought some good specimens of mineralogy, but our collection of insects is numerous and horrible."

Relating their experiences, they said the islanders invited them to enter one of the huts, where they were ushered into the midst of six children, a woman, a cow, a pig, a dog and some fowls. There was laid out for them a remnant of oaten straw which had been used to litter the cow for several days before.

This served as their seat, table and bed.   They declared that the sea broke upon the island with such impetuosity, and rushed into the caves with such noise, that the hut shook to its foundations, and they could get no sleep.

Evidently they were scared thoroughly, for one of the Mull boatmen told a subsequent visitor that when the boats returned to Staffa from Iona, where they had been sheltering, the sea was still so rough that two of Faujas's companions had a violent quarrel about leaving the island.   Not only did they quarrel verbally, but they fought desperately on the stumps of columns near Fingal's Cave in order to decide whether they would leave the island and risk their lives in the stormy sea, or stay on Staffa and die of hunger, as the inhabitants had only some potatoes and a little milk.   Apparently the advocate of the first opinion triumphed, and fortunately they arrived at Torloisk safely.

The day after their return the sea had calmed sufficiently to allow Faujas himself and a friend who had accompanied him from Oban, also one member of the first party who was scarcely recovered from his fatigue, to visit Staffa.   They arrived safely on the island after an uneventful journey.

In his description of Staffa, Faujas says:

The total population at the time when I visited it consisted of two families, who lived apart in two huts, constructed of unhewn blocks of basalt roofed over with sods, and who amounted, men, women and children, to the number of sixteen persons.   Belonging to these were eight cows, one bull, twelve sheep, two horses, one pig, two dogs, one cock and eight hens.   These huts get no light except from the door, which was only three feet high, and from the chimney, which consisted of a pyramidical opening in the middle of the hut . . . .   Only on the highest part is there a flat piece of ground covered with a poor dry turf, alongside of which is a corner of ground newly broken up, where a little oats and a few potatoes are raised.   For firing, the inhabitants are obliged to make use of a bad turf, which they left in the summer season in order to dry it.   It is not a peat, since it consists simply of fibrous roots of common grasses, intermixed with earth.   Nothing worse in the way of fuel could be used, but here necessity reigns with absolute sway.[1]

The whole of the island belongs to Colonel Charles Camble of Cambletown, in Cantyre.   It is let at the rent of twelve pounds sterling on account probably of its fishery, for its territorial value ought to be considered as nothing.

[1] [Similar fuel was used by the natives of St Kilda up to the time of their evacuation in August 1930.]

Describing his reception on Staffa, Faujas says:

The women and children of the two families did not fail to come to us, and invited us to their habitations; but being already informed of their excessive dirt, we were inflexible; and preferred on good ground to receive their civilities and their compliments in the open air.

Finding that it was impossible to prevail with us by the most friendly gestures, they resolved to do us the honours on the small esplanade in front of their dwellings.

The men, women and children, with much gravity, first formed themselves into a large circle in which they placed us and our seamen.   Then one of the women, disgustingly ugly and dirty, brought out a large wooden bowl filled with milk, with which she placed herself in the centre of the circle. She viewed us all round with attention, and immediately came up to me, and pronouncing some words, presented the bowl with a sort of courtesy. I held out my hands to receive it, but she drank some of it before she gave it to me.   I followed her example and passed the vessel to my neighbour, William Thornton; he gave it to Mr MacDonald, and so on from hand to hand, or more properly from mouth to mouth, till every person had tasted of it.   Having made our acknowledgements for this kindness, they immediately appointed two guides to accompany us to Fingal's Cave and all the remarkable places of this small island.

After spending a busy and enjoyable day on Staffa, Faujas and his companions, well pleased with themselves, left at half past four in the afternoon and arrived safely at Torloisk in Mull, at nine o'clock in the evening.

There is no mention of inhabitants on Staffa in *An Account of the Hebrides, Etc.* (1785), by James Anderson, LL.D.   His account of Staffa, however, is so brief that it carries little weight on this point.   There is also no mention of inhabitants on Staffa in the Account of *A Voyage to the Hebrides* by a Committee of the British Fishery Society in the year 1787, published in *The Bee*, VOLS. VIII-IX.   This Committee visited Staffa from Torloisk, in Mull.

In one of two letters published in the *Philosophical Transactions of the Royal Society* (1790), giving " Some Account of the Strata and Volcanic Appearances in the North of Ireland and Western Isles of Scotland," Abraham Mills, a vulcanist, who visited Staffa in a boat from Iona, says:

There were [5th July 1788] three houses uninhabited, and barley, oats, flax and potatoes growing near the centre of the island, and good grass in several parts.   When the crops are ripe, labourers are sent to gather them in; after which thirty head of cattle are sent to winter on the island, which, with a solitary herdsman to attend them, continue till the seed time the ensuing spring.

In the old (Sinclair's) *Statistical Account of Scotland* (1795), the Rev. Arch. MacArthur states: " In the mouth of Lochnankell lie the islands. of Ulva, Gometra, Little Colonsay and Staffa, all of which are inhabited."

Thomas Campbell, the poet, who visited Staffa in 1795, mentions that in the centre of the island he saw " a lonely hut, in appearance very like the abode of a hermit or savage," but does not say anything about the occupant or occupants; while the Duke of Somerset, who also visited Staffa in 1795, says that there were two huts, but makes no mention of any inhabitants. This reference by the Duke appears in a book which was published privately in London in 1845, entitled *The Tour of the Duke of Somerset and the Rev J. H. Michell through parts of England, Wales and Scotland, in the year* 1795. Here are the actual words of the Duke:

After gratifying our surprise for some time at this prodigious sport of Nature [Fingal's Cave], we walked to the summit of the arches and found in the island some excellent verdure, with two rams feeding, and several patches of tillage forward and flourishing. Two huts, a spring of water and a few stony enclosures grace the surface of the island . . . . In one of the interstices of the shore we sat down to dinner and formed our furniture of the broken fragments of the basaltic cliff. Here we again contemplated this amazing scene. Near us was the wreck of a boat, which had been forced on shore in a storm, with three men who, by the providential assistance of a herdsman, fortunately left on the island, were saved. A cavern was pointed out to us where a boat and several men were driven and all perished. Indeed, the swell of the waves over the sunken rocks, which are everywhere scattered around the isle, make it generally dangerous to approach the shore. After remaining nearly two hours we sailed back.

Perhaps it is worth mentioning here that the only fatalities at Staffa, within living memory, occurred on 29th August 1884, when two tourists were washed off the narow causeway in Fingal's Cave and drowned by a heavy sea which caught them unawares. They happened to be at the lowest point of the causeway with their backs to the cave entrance when a large wave swept their feet from under them, and they slipped under the lower guide-rope and over the edge of the causeway. At that time there were no life-saving appliances in the cave, and the tourists had been landed from the paddle steamer *Chevalier* at the north end of Staffa. Consequently there was no boat at hand, otherwise they might have been rescued.

Professor T. Garnett, who was appointed to the first chair (Chemistry and Natural Philosophy) founded in the Anderson College, the forerunner of the Royal Technical College, Glasgow, when it was opened in 1796, and afterwards became Professor of Natural Philosophy in the Royal Institution, London, visited Staffa during the month of July 1798, and says in *A Tour through the Highlands of Scotland:*

Near the middle of the island we found two wretched huts, built with fragments of basaltic pillars and rude pieces of lava; one of these served as the habitation of a herd and his family, who take care of the cattle that feed on the island; the other is used as a barn or cow-house. Upon the side of a hillock near the hut we sat down and partook of our provisions, and the herd's wife presented us with some milk in a large wooden bowl so heavy that we could scarcely lift it to our mouths; they had no smaller vessels, nor spoons. Indeed, their manner of life is extremely simple, their food consisting chiefly of milk and potatoes with, now and then, a little fish. There being no wood on the island, the only fuel used by these poor people is the sods of earth which they carefully dry.

This family resided here both winter and summer for three years, but in winter their situation was frequently very unpleasant; for during storms the waves beat so violently against the island that the very house was shaken, though situated in the middle of it; indeed, the concussion was often so great that the pot which hung over the fire partook of it and was made to vibrate. This so much alarmed the poor inhabitants one very stormy winter that they determined to leave the island the first favourable opportunity, for they believed that nothing but an evil spirit could have rocked it in that manner. Since that time they have resided here only during the summer season and even at this time of the year (July) their situation is far from enviable, for it is impossible to keep a boat in the bay on account of the surf.

Staffa, therefore, seems to have ceased to be inhabited permanently a few years before 1798, though for about ten years afterwards it continued to be inhabited by herdsmen each year from early spring to late autumn.

John Stoddart, LL.B., who visited Staffa in 1799, says:

Landing on the east, we directed our steps towards the southern side; but first climbed a small eminence, on which is built the herdsman's hut. In this solitary abode remains the herdsman with his wife and family, during half the year, to attend twenty small cattle whose pasture is all the island produces, and in this hut, uninhabited during the other half of the year, must the unfortunate storm-stayed traveller take refuge without hope of any provision but what he brings with him.

Dr John Leyden, who visited Staffa in 1800, makes no mention of inhabitants, and the Hon. Mrs Murray of Kensington, who visited the island in 1800, and again in 1802, says: "There is not a hut upon the island." George L. A. Douglas, Advocate, who visited Staffa in August 1800, from Oban, *via* Ulva, corroborates this statement by saying: "The island is entirely uninhabited." If we are to believe M. Basset, Principal of the Lycée Charlemagne at Paris, who visited Staffa in 1802, there were inhabitants on the island during part of 1800 and 1801. This visitor gives a short description of Staffa in a notice published by him at the end of his translation of the Huttonian Theory. Regarding inhabitants, he says that until the year before his visit a whole family of poor cultivators of the soil were accustomed to come and settle here during the summer months and lived in a mean little hovel built near a little stream of fresh water. They lived on a little oats and a few potatoes which the poor soil hardly afforded them, and took care of the herd which had been brought to browse on the grass. Since then the island had remained deserted.

There is evidence, however, that herdsmen resided on Staffa from spring to autumn after Basset's visit. Necker de Saussure, the Swiss geologist, who visited Staffa during the month of August 1807, says:

On this shore [the point where he landed] are embarked and disembarked the herds which are brought every spring into the isle, and taken away at the commencement of autumn. The boatmen showed us the vestiges of a hut where there formerly lived for eight years a family appointed to care for the flocks; they were the sole inhabitants of the island. Sir Joseph Banks and Mr Faujas speak with horror of the wretchedness of this miserable abode. To-day the cottage is destroyed and the island completely deserted.

One of the sailors who were accompanying us had passed a part of his youth in this solitary habitation and the tales he told us of the life of anxiety and affliction which he led there touched us deeply. He himself recalled only with dismay those sad moments when his companions and he heard all around them only the roar of the wind and of the angry waves.

He told us that when the storm was reigning on the sea, which was for more than three-fourths of the year, the wind blew with such violence that one feared every minute to see the house blown away like a dead leaf. The sea rolled up in immense waves with such fury that, on breaking against the rocks, billows of foam spouted over the cliffs which encircled the island and inundated it. The waves, in running into Fingal's Cave and the other caverns, struck against the walls with a sound similar to the rolling of perpetual thunder. Staffa was disturbed by the tossing of that furious ocean as by an earthquake. In the evening, while these poor people seated in their weak cottage listened with fear to the terrible war of the elements, they often saw the very rock on which their peat fire stood stirring and vibrating with the ground under their feet at each toss of these mountains of water, which seemed to be bound to reduce the whole island to atoms. What a dreadful situation. One might wish to witness one moment of such a scene to judge of the entire powers of the boundless ocean. But to live there for eight long years—what an existence of fear and horror.

As evidence of the height to which the waves reach at Staffa during the storms of winter: when we landed on the island, before the tourist season commenced, we found the guide-rope stanchion at the entrance to Fingal's Cave bent inward to an angle of about thirty degrees from the vertical (the wire guide-ropes are removed at the end of summer). This stanchion is made of wrought iron about two inches in diameter and is set into the rock at the highest point of the Causeway inside or outside the cave. If the stanchion was bent solely by the force of the waves they must have been of solid water at this height, therefore their crest must have been still higher. If the stanchion was bent by a blow from a log of driftwood or other floatsam, the waves must have carried it to this height. It is therefore apparent that during winter gales the sea sweeps over the whole Causeway inside and outside Fingal's Cave, and probably reaches higher. This statement may surprise visitors who view the island only in fine weather during summer, and walk over the Causeway in calm conditions.

The herdsmen, mentioned by Necker, who lived on Staffa from spring to autumn in 1807, seem to have been the last long-period residents on the island.

There were no inhabitants on Staffa during the visits of Dr John MacCulloch, the geologist, in the years 1811 and 1821. But though there were no permanent inhabitants on Staffa at that time, apparently some of the islanders in the vicinity were, occasionally, temporary residents. Dr S. H. Spiker, who was Librarian to His Majesty the King of Prussia, and who visited Staffa from Ulva during the month of August 1816, says that his party found five men, who belonged to Little Colonsay, marooned on Staffa. These men had visited the island for a few days for the purpose of burning kelp, and while engaged on this work their boat, which apparently had not been moored securely, was carried away by the tide. Owing to the weather being misty, their signals of distress could not be seen from any of the neighbouring islands. As there were no regular visitations to Staffa at that time, their plight might have been dire had not Dr Spiker and his friends rescued them.

A statement in W. L. Manson's book *Highland Bagpipe* suggests that Staffa may have had permanent inhabitants about the year 1822, but the evidence, in my opinion, is not convincing. He says:

> When the King visited Edinburgh in 1822 this MacArthur [Archibald] followed in the train of his chief from whom he held a cottage with a small portion of land. That part of the Island of Staffa on which the croft was situated was sold but MacArthur, though no longer employed in his former capacity, was allowed by the new proprietor to remain in his old home.

I think the words " That part of the Island of Staffa " should read, " That part of Staffa's estate," as Ranald MacDonald, to whom MacArthur was piper, retained the territorial title, " Staffa," though he no longer possessed the island.

A Yorkshire gentleman who visited Staffa during the month of July 1826 does not mention inhabitants in his unpublished manuscript.

M. Ducos, who also visited Staffa in 1826, one week after the Yorkshire gentleman, says in his book, when describing the plateau of the island:

> Two horses, three cows and some sheep browse there without a guardian and without shelter. Ruins of a hut and of a stable testify to the sojourn at one time of a few human beings on that solitary and almost sterile ground. Indeed, a household had been set up there once but cold and storm ultimately defeated them. Since that time, no other has resigned himself to such a miserable and sad existence.

Beriah Botfield, F.R.S., who visited Staffa during the month of August 1829, describes the island as being uninhabited, in his book *Journal of a Tour through the Highlands of Scotland during the Summer of 1829.*

C. L. F. Panckoucke, who visited Staffa in 1830, says in his *L'Ile de Staffa et sa grotte basaltique:*

> Near the middle of the island the walls of a cottage were still to be seen, though the roof had disappeared: further on, some herdsmen were watching a herd of horses and cows, all of very small breed, and all black. These herdsmen approached us and offered us milk which we willingly accepted. With the help of our interpreter we entered into conversation with these

shepherds, who speak neither English nor Scottish: their language is perhaps ancient Celtic or Gaelic.

The eldest of the herdsmen told us that he had lived there for a long time: his sad expression was a reflection of the weariness which he had felt in this cheerless home when he and his companions heard, during the winter nights, so long in this climate, only the moan of the winds which dashed the waves against the island with such violence that they often swept over the highest parts; the hut shook, and it seemed that the winds would carry it away and hurl it into the sea. "The storms last here for about nine months in the year," he said, " and we have abandoned so gloomy and unhealthy a habitation."

These herdsmen lived on the island of Iona and told us that they came to Staffa with their animals when the weather made it possible, which, they added, is very seldom, and only in the summer season which, in this climate, cannot be called the fine season. . . .

We were served with a meal according to the custom of the country; this meal consisted of milk and a few herrings: our sailors and the herdsmen had torn from the rocks a few plants of a kind of seaweed and these, unprepared in any way, they ate with apparent relish.

That seaweed was probably dulse, which is still torn from the rocks of Staffa and eaten by visitors who know its value as a tonic, owing to the natural salts which it contains.

In one of his drawings of Staffa, Panckoucke shows horses being towed in the sea by a rowing boat, which suggests that this was the method of conveying from Iona to Staffa the horses which he mentions. Although this method is still adopted when bringing horses across the Sound of Iona from Mull, the swim from Mull to Iona is only about one mile, whereas it is about six miles from Iona to Staffa, and there is always a swell on the sea even in calm weather. From Iona to Staffa would be a long and dangerous swim for a horse, yet Panckoucke is not likely to have portrayed this method of conveying the horses unless he had seen it in operation or had been told of it.

In the description of Staffa given in *Anderson's Guidebook to the Highlands and Islands of Scotland*, published in 1834, it is stated: " At present there is not a hut of any description [on Staffa] to take shelter in during a storm."

Sir George Head, who landed on Staffa from the steamboat *Highlander* in 1835, says, in *A Home Tour through various Parts of the United Kingdom*, published in 1837, that he saw " a bed of black peat from which a considerable quantity had already been dug." He adds:

About a dozen head of small horned cattle as wild and active as deer, remarkable for their beauty, and smaller than the Alderney breed, seemed by bounding and leaping away at the approach of strangers, to enjoy by right of inheritance, and unmolested, the free pasture of the soil.   These cattle were, however, as we perceived afterwards, together with as many sheep and a goat, under the guardianship of an old woman and a young girl, both of whom, by the way, were in appearance as wild and timorous as themselves. If not inhabitants of a cave in some concealed nook within the territory, these native shepherdesses were probably ferried across daily from the island of Mull in a boat.   On this point I endeavoured to get information, but was unable to obtain a reply from either.   At any rate, neither house, cabin nor tenement of any description was to be seen on this island.

S. van Baalen, a Dutchman, who visited Staffa in 1837, says there was no sign of habitation during his visit.

James Wilson, who visited Staffa in 1841, says:

We then visited the more central summit of the island, passing by the side of a pretty large unroofed, and therefore desolate-looking, building of modern structure.   It was intended as a place of refuge and refreshment for visitors who might desire to prolong their stay, but the proprietor seems to have reckoned without his host, as the latter never made his appearance, and the traveller who now expects to find shelter here must rest satisfied with his share of what Shakespeare calls "the canopy of kites and crows."   The northern portion of the island bears marks of agricultural ridges and the grass is beautifully verdant.

The Rev. D. MacArthur, writing in the *New Statistical Account of Scotland*, in September 1843, says: " Staffa is uninhabited "; and this statement is repeated by W. Maxwell when describing Staffa in his *Iona and the Ionians*, 1857.

Jules Verne, the famous French author, who visited Staffa in 1859, says: " A few Highland ponies and black cows were grazing on the meagre pastureland of the plateau . . . neither was there a house to be seen, only the ruins of a hut destroyed by the storms."

Professor MacLean, in his *Report on Fingal's Cave*, 1887, states:

A few years ago a shepherd and his family were persuaded to go on the isle, but they soon beseeched to be removed, because the hollow roar made by the sea through the caverns during times of storms sounded so dismally that they became terrified.   To a superstitious people there would be something more than natural forces in the fetch of the ocean which bursts through these pillared portals with a sound as of artillery.

This "few years ago" of Professor MacLean, however, is probably a vague reference to the more than ninety years that had elapsed since Staffa had been inhabited permanently, as there have been no permanent inhabitants on the island within living memory. Professor MacLean may have been told by some of the neighbouring islanders that there had been inhabitants on Staffa at one time and he coined the phrase "a few years ago," merely to include mention of inhabitants in his *Report*.

At the present time the only sign of habitation on Staffa is one sadly-decayed pile of ruins, situated in a hollow near the centre of the island, which until the Second World War retained a comparatively well-built Gothic, or pointed-arch, window. These ruins were thirty-one feet long by thirteen feet broad (internal), by eighteen inches thick. The highest part of these ruins, as far back as 1922, was about eight feet high from ground level. The arched window was four feet six inches, from sill to apex of arch, by two feet six inches broad, with a six-inch splay in the wall broadening inward. The back window was four feet six inches high by two feet broad with a similar splay and lintel over. At ground level in the north-east wall there was a recess—three feet by three feet by seven inches—which used to have a lintel over it, and appeared to have been a fireplace. The stone lintel over this recess was of a very porous nature and did not possess the compact texture of the other blocks of the building; probably a piece of *scoriae*, the outer part of a lava flow, which, being full of steam bubbles, hardens into a cindery mass. The front wall of the ruins was built of rough-dressed basalt coursed rubble with bonder sneck stones, while the end walls and back wall were of undressed basalt random rubble built to courses. The mortar was produced from the shells of molluscs. Each wall had a central core composed of a mixture of rubble and mortar. The threshold stone of the doorway consists of a micaceous sandstone obtained, probably, in Mull or Inchkenneth as there is no sandstone on Staffa. During the Second World War, when Staffa was visited only by the men who rented the grazing, the greater part of the walls collapsed, leaving only parts of the back wall which are now crumbling.

These ruins are situated near the little bay of Port an Fhasgaidh, where the gradient is of easy access and where there are plenty of loose boulders, large and small. The building stones may therefore have been obtained from this natural quarry, though considerable labour would require to be expended on them to trim square, even roughly, the stones of the front wall: these front wall stones are more than twice the length of the largest stones in the other walls.

The pointed-arch window in the ruins appeared to be rather elaborate workmanship for a shepherd's house. It was also noticeable that the wall was recessed in way of this window, the recess being five feet wide and six inches deep. There was also a similar recess in this wall to the north-east of the doorway, and in this recess there appeared to be the sill of another window, although it had stones piled upon it, probably by some well-meaning visitor who wished to retard the decay of these walls. The building was compared to St Oran's Chapel, in the neighbouring island of Iona, which is twenty-nine feet long by fifteen feet broad, but the arched window of the Staffa building was plain and without any decoration, unlike the ornamented Norman doorway in St Oran's Chapel, Iona.

These ruins were first brought to the notice of the public by the late Lord Guthrie and the late Mr Alex. Ritchie, Iona, who visited Staffa and examined them during the summer of 1914. But they must have been examined previously, though perhaps not in a detailed manner, by the Officers of H.M. Government Ordnance Survey, when this part of the island was surveyed in 1875, as they are indicated clearly on the Scottish Survey map, Sheet 93 (scale six inches to one mile).

From a photograph, these were judged by the Royal Commission for the Preservation of Ancient Monuments to be the remains of an ancient chapel, probably of thirteenth or fourteenth-century date. Two writers, at least, expressed and enlarged upon somewhat similar opinions in contributions to the press, and suggested that Staffa with its lofty cliffs was a more secure place of retreat than Iona for religious devotees during troublous times in the past history of western Scotland. Neither of those writers mentioned the apparent fireplace opening which would be incongruous in a chapel.

While the appearance of the structure suggested that it was once a religious building, it is surprising that no mention is made

(*Above*) Puffins on Staffa; (*below*) the ruin, photographed in 1922, during the author's stay on Staffa. The right hand end has been used to provide improvised shelter. In the centre is Mr Archie MacCulloch, the author's father, at that time Second Officer of the Macbrayne passenger steamer

Fusilier

The ruin on Staffa showing (*left*) the recess in the north-east wall and (*below*) the arched window, before they finally collapsed

by keen observers like Banks and Faujas of a pointed-arch window or recessed walls in any building which they saw on Staffa. These features would attract anyone's attention on a lonely little island, such as Staffa, and would prevent the building from deserving the descriptions of " a wretched hut " (*vide* Garnett) and "a hovel" (*vide* Basset).

I was informed by the late John McCormick, F.S.A. SCOT., an authority on Mull and the surrounding islands, that arched windows had been built in houses in Mull when no stones of sufficient length for lintels were available. This would not appear to have been the reason for the arched window on Staffa, however, for although the voussoirs, or arch stones, were only rough-dressed, there were two lintels fitted in other parts of the building which were of sufficient length to span this window-opening. Some years after discussing with Mr McCormick the subject of arch window-openings in old Mull cottages, I located one of them but found it was not the pointed-arch style as in the Staffa ruin but was an angle arch. This type is primitive and simple, consisting merely of two long stones inclined towards one another to meet at the apex. The window in the Staffa ruin was a genuine, though rudely-constructed, pointed, or Gothic, arch with keystone and voussoirs, or arch stones.

It is noticeable that the building on Staffa is not oriented like the other religious buildings in this region. It is built according to the contours of the ground, that is, from south-west to north-east with the doorway facing south-east.

If these ruins are not a relic of mediaeval Christianity, and as they appeared too elaborate and too large to have been a herdsman's hut, how then did they come into existence? After searching diligently in descriptions of ancient visits to Staffa and making enquiries, both by correspondence and verbally, I have come to the conclusion that the description given by James Wilson is correct, that is, that the building was partly erected, but never completed, by the proprietor of Staffa, who intended it to be a hostel for visitors to the island, and dates from about 1815. This belief would account for visitors previous to that time—Banks, Faujas, Necker de Saussure, etc.—not mentioning any building on the island other than crude huts. According to this reasoning, these walls were built before Dr MacCulloch ceased his visits to Staffa, but as he would know that they were of modern construction, at that time, and as they were never completed, apparently he did not think them worthy of mention, or perhaps Dr MacCulloch did not traverse the surface of Staffa during his later visits to the island. Being a geologist, he could view the structure of the island best from a boat, landing at suitable points of interest.

My father was told by Mr John MacDonald, a native of Gometra, who died in 1896, at the age of ninety-three years, that his (Mr MacDonald's) father remembered when this building was erected. He said that it was built by the proprietor of Staffa, whose name was also MacDonald, but known locally as *Fear Staffa*, Gaelic for "man of Staffa"—meaning that he was *the* person of Staffa. My father's friend said that the building had never been completed and no roof had been laid, owing to the financial failure of the laird. On making enquiries in 1933 I learned that this information was still recognised as correct by the inhabitants of Ulva and Gometra, the nearest inhabited islands to Staffa.

Although Mr MacDonald (my father's informant) and the present inhabitants of these islands could not say in what year the building was erected, we can arrive at a reasonable conclusion, if we remember that this *Fear Staffa* was evidently Ranald MacDonald, friend of Sir Walter Scott and Necker de Saussure, and who was obliged to dispose of Staffa owing to financial difficulties in the year 1816. It is quite likely that this generous laird would endeavour to erect some shelter on Staffa for storm-stayed travellers or those desiring to spend more than one day on the island. The majority of visitors to Staffa at that time passed through his island residence of Ulva on their journey. We have already learned that he fitted supports in Fingal's Cave. As he was a professional and cultured gentleman, he would be likely to introduce some design into the building and what more appropriate than that it should be, to some extent, in harmony with the religious buildings on the islands nearby? The rough-dressed stones of the front wall may have been shaped on Ulva and ferried to Staffa (a boat large enough for ferrying cattle would be capable of carrying a fair cargo of building stones) as this method would save men residing on Staffa to carry out this work: Ulva is also formed of basaltic rock. It is noticeable that the rough-dressed blocks of the ruin are much larger than the unhewn blocks. For the back and end walls of undressed blocks of basalt he may have made use of the stones that had been used for the huts of Staffa's early inhabitants.

That is my own opinion regarding these ruins on Staffa. It is based upon ascertained evidence and personal reasoning rather than on sentimental considerations, but I possess suffi- cient sentiment to welcome any reliable evidence which will support the claim that the ruins on Staffa are the remains of an ancient chapel, as it would add still more interest to this famous little island. It would be very interesting if some society could be induced to undertake a reasonable amount of excavation here which might throw light on the history, and if necessary preserve what some people believe to be a relic of mediaeval Christianity in the Hebrides.

In one of the plates in Panckoucke's folio, which shows a view of the surface of Staffa in 1830, there is only one small building indicated on the island, and it is shown with walls entire but with no roof. It appears facing south-east, that is, in the same direction as the ruins existing on Staffa now, but not on the same site as the present ruins. It is shown situated on a small eminence to the south of the little valley which crosses the island obliquely. Panckoucke shows a semicircular-arch, or Norman- arch, doorway in the south-west gable and two pointed-arch windows in the longitudinal wall facing south-east. Under the drawing there is a note: " Sketched on the spot by C. L. F. Panckoucke." The site of the present ruins on the island ap- pears on his drawing without any indication of a building. It is noticeable, however, that the building shown on his drawing is almost on the line of sight of the ruins existing at the present time, from the point from which he sketched his view, but he shows it on an eminence about half the distance away. That may have been an error on his part, and in fact he probably was sketching the building which is now in ruins on Staffa. His published drawing was probably made from a hurried sketch done on the site. If so, the mistake is quite reasonable.

In corroboration of this assumption, Pankcoucke says in his description of Staffa, "Near the middle of the island the walls of a cottage were still to be seen, though the roof had disappeared."

During the summer of 1889 my father and his companion erected a substantial wooden bothy within these walls for their own use while spending their annual sojourn, which they did for many years, also for the use of anyone requiring shelter while on the island. This bothy, with annual repairs, withstood the storms of summer and winter for about twenty years, till some thoughtless traveller left the door unlatched. The result of this act was that the next gale of wind tore off the roof; the remaining parts were gradually blown down, and now can be found scattered widely over the island.

A few yards to the south-west of these ruins are the remains of what was probably a small house, or hut, perhaps one of those mentioned by early writers, or perhaps even a monastic cell. Decay has advanced so far that it is now a mere low ring of undressed rubble and it is therefore difficult to know how the stones were built. There does not appear to be any mortar. It seems to have been a more or less circular building about ten feet in internal diameter, almost similar in size and shape to the old Hebridean sheiling bothies.

A short distance east of these two ruins there are remains of what appear to have been three sheep or cattle fanks, as their size is in excess of any dwelling house ever likely to have been built on Staffa. They have now crumbled to mere outlines of stones among the grass, approximately forty feet by thirty feet. Some of the stones used for the building of these fanks may, however, have been taken from the stone dwelling huts referred to by Faujas.

The last occasion on which Staffa was occupied by a single inhabitant was, probably, during the summer of 1897, when my father was forced to spend two days and nights alone on the island. This isolation was caused by his companion, who had sailed to Gometra, being unable to return owing to a gale arising suddenly.

The nearest human beings to Staffa at the present time are those on the island of Gometra, about four miles to the north-east, where there are nine permanent inhabitants, and three occupied and four unoccupied houses.

CHAPTER XI

FAMOUS VISITORS TO STAFFA
AND THEIR COMMENTS

SINCE it was first brought to the notice of the public in 1772, Staffa has been visited by celebrities in every walk of life. As aesthetic values are as real as scientific facts, though more elusive—they can be sensed rather than defined— it is fortunate that, in addition to the eminent men of science already mentioned, the island has been visited by many renowned votaries of the Muses. Their tributes reveal how deeply the emotions can be stirred by magnificent colonnades and caves, not built, but hewn out of the living rock by the mighty shaping tools of Nature. There is an additional appeal and value in all the works of Nature when we ponder and appreciate as well as observe and investigate. Even the ordinary visitor to Staffa, with no literary claims, feels inclined to express himself in terms worthy of the subject, but modesty and lack of appropriate words usually restrain him to a moderate, though sincere, expression of admiration. Of course, there are always the "irrepressibles" who must " let themselves go." Of such was the ebullient pilgrim in the early days of Staffa's fame who recorded for posterity his enthusiastic expectations, as he set out on the steamboat bound for the island, commencing his effort thus:

> Away! Away! O'er the bounding waves
> To Staffa's celebrated caves.

Perhaps he was the prototype of McGonagall. Then there was the modern American tourist—one of the "Macmillions"— who was heard to exclaim when he first viewed Fingal's Cave, " Gee! What a cute hole."

The earliest literary lions to visit the vicinity of Staffa were, apparently, Dr Johnson and his biographer, Boswell. During their famous tour of the Hebrides they passed by the island but were unable to land on it owing to the heavy swell on the sea.

In *A Tour to the Hebrides with Samuel Johnson, LL.D., in 1773,* Boswell says: " We saw the island of Staffa at no very great distance, but could not land upon it, the surge was so high on its rocky coast."

It would have been interesting to learn the great lexicographer's opinion of Fingal's Cave, for he became quite enthusiastic over MacKinnon's Cave in the coast of Mull opposite Staffa. This cave in Mull is uninteresting except for its spaciousness, and a large square stone within called Fingal's table; it is described by another traveller as " an abyss of vacancy."

The first eminent personage whose recorded visit to Staffa I have been able to locate, in addition to the men of science already mentioned in previous chapters, is Thomas Campbell, the poet, who landed on the island in 1795. During the summer and autumn months of that year, Campbell resided as a domestic tutor to a laird's son at Sunipol on the west coast of Mull, about twelve miles north of Staffa. It is a very outlandish place and Campbell felt the loneliness of his situation keenly. One indication of his feelings is the title of his letter from Sunipol, in which he describes his visit to Staffa. The letter is headed: " Thule's Wildest Shore, 15th day of the Harvest Storm, Sept. 16th, 1795." He visited Staffa and Iona "with enthusiasm" in an open boat from Sunipol, manned by sturdy Mull boatmen and accompanied by a piper, who played his pipes as they entered Fingal's Cave, " which made a most tremendous echo."

In his description of that outing Campbell says:

I have no reason to be disappointed with my short voyage, having visited the famous Staffa and Icolmkill [Iona]; I had formed, as usual, very sanguine ideas of the happiness I should enjoy on beholding these wonders so new to me and I was not in the least disappointed. The grand regularity of Staffa and the venerable ruins of Iona, filled me with emotions of pleasure to which I had been hitherto a stranger.

Staffa he describes as " the most admirable of all the Hebrides."

At that time Campbell was only eighteen years of age and is described as having " read much but written little," his poetic talent not yet being developed fully, which would account, no doubt, for his not having voiced his impressions of Staffa in poetic vein. His brief stay in Mull and his visits to the surrounding islands at that time impressed him deeply, however, and acquainted him with sea and mountain, Highland legends and Highland characteristics which he incorporated in many of his later poems. As his biography says: " The early impressive scenery in Mull and the classic islands of Staffa and Iona retained their influence when those of a much later date were enfeebled and forgotten."

Loch na Keal, in western Mull, opposite Staffa, is generally regarded as the Lochgyle of Campbell's well-known poem, *Lord Ullin's Daughter:*

> Now who be ye would cross Lochgyle,
> This dark and stormy water?
> O, I'm the chief of Ulva's Isle,
> And this Lord Ullin's daughter.

According to Alasdair Alpin MacGregor, in his recent book *Skye and the Inner Hebrides*, p. 302, the above belief regarding Loch na Keal is incorrect. He states that Campbell himself when questioned on this subject said that the loch he had in mind when he wrote the poem was Loch Goil, in the Firth of Clyde. The first line of the poem, " A chieftain to the Highlands bound," would seem to corroborate this opinion.

Mr MacGregor's statement may be correct as far as it goes, but there is reason for believing that Campbell based his poem upon a story he heard when residing in Mull.

In an interesting series of articles on " The Parish of Kilfinichen and Kilviceon " (of which Loch na Keal forms a boundary), published in the *Oban Times*, January 1954, the writer, Duncan Cameron, says that a tragedy similar to the one described in *Lord Ullin's Daughter* did in fact happen in Loch na Keal. He says a young chief of the Clan MacQuarrie, who owned the Island of Ulva, abducted the daughter of the gentleman who at that time owned Grulin Estate, which borders Loch na Keal. As Grulin is not a very poetic word, the poet, using poetic licence, softened it by dropping the first two letters *Gr*, thus making it Ulin, or Ullin, and made it more impressive by adding the title "Lord." Mr Cameron says that the boatman was a Gribun fisherman: Gribun is on the south shore of Loch na Keal, about seven miles west of Grulin, and is the nearest point of embarkation from this side of the loch to Ulva. This route, of fully two miles, is wholly exposed to the Atlantic billows and in stormy weather could be very dangerous, especially in a " lugsail."

The next person worthy of note to land on Staffa was apparently James Hogg, the Ettrick Shepherd, who visited the island during one of his wanderings in the Highlands. He gave poetic expression to his appreciation of Fingal's Cave in an album kept at the Sound of Ulva Inn for visitors to Staffa and Iona.

I have been unable to locate the present whereabouts of this album, which is likely to contain many interesting and valuable contributions owing to the famous people who visited Staffa from Ulva before the advent of the steamboat. My information about Hogg's visit to Staffa has been obtained from a small book entitled *A historical Account of Iona from the earliest Period*, by L. MacLean, Honorary Member of the Glasgow Ossianic Society, and published in 1833. This little book, which is now very scarce, has the distinction of being the first book devoted wholly to Iona. It is surprising that diligent search and enquiries have failed to reveal any other reference to this visit of Hogg to Staffa. There does not appear to be any record in his poems, tales or letters. Neither is there any reference in Wilson's *Noctes ambrosianae* nor in Edith C. Batho's *The Ettrick Shepherd*, which has a very good bibliography. Presumably he visited the island in 1803, for, though he does not mention this region in his letters describing his 1803 tour (the collection is incomplete), he says in one of his letters describing his 1804 tour in the West Highlands that he landed at Tobermory, in Mull, for an hour while northward-bound, in a sailing smack via the Sound of Mull, and continues: " Although I did not tarry above two hours at this place last year . . . I was surprised at being told that the whole village knew me." In a previous paragraph on the same page, describing his sail up the Firth of Lorn, he says: " We kept nearly the same road by which I came last summer " (*The Scots Magazine*, October 1808).

Here is his poetic description of Staffa which he wrote in the Visitors' Album at Ulva:

> Dark Staffa! in thy grotto wild,
> How my wrapt soul is taught to feel!
> Oh! well becomes it Nature's child
> Now in her stateliest shrine to kneel!
> Thou art no fiends' nor giants' home—
> Thy piles of dark and dismal grain,
> Bespeak thee, dread and sacred dome,
> Great temple of the Western Main!
> The airy harp is heard in thee
> Sounding its holiest lullaby,
> For in thy vaults the mermaid sings,
> And the sea-birds' note responsive rings,
> As the hymn of the wind and the ocean's roar
> Are heard in thee for evermore.
> Tho' other wonders meet my eye,
> Yet never from my mind shall fly
> Thy arches, cavern'd, green and torn,
> On Nature's gifted columns borne—
> Rude as they be, yet firm and sure,
> They prop the wild entablature,
> And round each copse and architrave,
> In awful murmurs weep and rave,
> The whole of Nature's grand turmoil,
> When billows burst and cauldrons boil,
> Thro' portals stern of pavements riven,
> Unmoved by architect of heaven,
> Thro' darken'd domes and dens of wonder,
> And caverns of eternal thunder!

Apparently the Shepherd "changed his tune" after he had settled with the local boatmen, for he added this verse:

> I have sail'd round the creeks and the headlands of Mull;
> Her vales are uncultur'd, unhallow'd and weedy;
> Her mountains are barren—her haven is dull;
> Her sons may be brave, but they're cursedly greedy.

A visitor, signing himself " A Son of Morven," who happened to see these lines the day after Hogg wrote them, added the following rebuke underneath:

> Ah! Shepherd of Ettrick! why sorely complain,
> Tho' the boatmen were greedy for grog?
> The beauties of Staffa, by this you proclaim,
> Were pearls cast away on a *Hog*.

There is a note in MacLean's *Historical Account of Iona from the earliest Period* mentioning a visit to Staffa by William II, King of the Netherlands, when Prince of Orange, in the year 1810. It is probably quite correct though I have failed to find any other reference to that visit.

Sir Walter Scott, whose novels and poems have done so much to proclaim far and wide the grandeur and romance of Scotland, visited Staffa on two occasions and did not hesitate to voice his appreciation, in glowing terms.

Previous to the publication of the works of Ossian and Scott, the Highlands and Islands of Scotland had been regarded by strangers as a kind of *terra incognita* somewhere in the North; the Thule of the ancients, populated by half-naked, ferocious free-booters, who raided the Lowlands periodically and who would not stop at any crime to obtain their object. It was said that usually when any Lowlander or Englishman found it necessary to travel on business in any part of the Highlands at that time he thought it best to commence the preparations for his journey by making his will, and, if he returned safely, related tales of a dolorous desolation, of rain-swept mountains and gloomy glens under a sullen sky. Although the odes of Ossian modified those opinions to some extent, they were so mystic in character and their origin became so controversial that they did not convey definitely or fully a new conception of the Highlands to the out-side world. Dr Johnson and Boswell took little notice of scenery. It required the works of Scott, with their vivid scenes and characters throbbing with life, and standing out with stereoscopic clarity, to impress a new conception of the High-lands and Islands of Scotland upon strangers. His readers were made to realise that these parts of Scotland were regions of scenic grandeur, history and romance, and the inhabitants a proud, sturdy race of warriors, excelling in many sports, whose code of ethics, if rough and ready, had at least the virtues of valour, loyalty, natural courtesy, and a pride born of self-respect. Their life was primitive, hard, and frugal, but this is the lot of all tribes who dwell in lonely mountainous lands, and it breeds endurance and ingenious adaptations to a harsh environment. As one of the characters in Shakespeare's *Cymbeline* remarks:

> 'Tis wonder
> That an invis'ble instinct should frame them
> To loyalty unlearned; honour untaught;
> Civility not seen from others; valour
> That wildly grows in them, but yields a crop
> As if it had been sow'd.

Not having the temperament of the Gael, Scott wisely did not assume the mystic mood and hazy phraseology of the Celtic Twilight writers but sent forth his romances clear as a trumpet call.

Some of Scott's critics say that he vulgarised the Highlands and the Highlanders, but this accusation seems unfair. His works certainly aroused the interest of strangers in this hitherto comparatively unknown territory, but if he did not present the Highlands and their inhabitants in the way that a native Highlander would have done there was an excuse. He visited the Highlands as a very observant, enquiring and enthusiastic traveller and described them accordingly. Surely that was not a fault. If we bear this point in mind we should give him credit for revealing to strangers that there was grandeur and romance rather than gloom in the Highlands and Islands of Scotland. It must be admitted, however, that Scott's Highland scenes, though remarkably clear and true-to-life, are less spontaneous than those of Ossian. Although faithful and graphic, they are composed of many laboured touches, while those of Ossian are produced by a few masterstrokes, but it is a matter of opinion whether one prefers the representation of an impression to be well-defined or merely suggestive.

The present age of materialism is inclined to depreciate the works of Scott but this view can be accounted for when we consider how greatly human ideals have changed since his time. If Scott did not delineate the Highland crofter, fisherman or farmer, as the modern ideas of democracy desire, it was probably because he had little acquaintance with the subject. He dealt with those aspects of Highland life of which he had knowledge, and which appealed most to him, namely the scenery, romance and chivalry, and he dealt with them worthily. Any subject that the " Wizard of the North " touched with his pen became imbued with an atmosphere of romance; he could even gild the gallows. That was his forte, so it is unfair to criticise him on this point. It was left to others to portray the domestic aspect of the common Highlander—the polite, shy and peaceful crofter and fisherman type who go about their daily tasks without fuss; but it is doubtful if anyone, even the true-born Highlander, has dealt with this subject adequately.

Scott paid his first visit to Staffa during the month of July 1810, accompanied by Lady and Miss Scott and several distinguished personages, from the neighbouring island of Ulva. He was the guest of Ranald MacDonald, laird of " Ulva's Isle," who was also owner of Staffa at that time, and who resided with his mother and three sisters on Ulva.

The warm Highland hospitality of this young laird evoked tributes of admiration from all who had occasion to come under his roof, and they were many. During the early part of the nineteenth century, before the advent of the steamboat, the island of Ulva was the usual starting place for the short sea trip to Staffa by the numerous pilgrims who came to worship at this little shrine of Nature lying out in the Atlantic. The fame of Staffa had by that time begun to spread far and wide and it had now become a focal point for visitors from "a' the airts" who possessed sufficient means to travel in the Highlands, and sufficient intelligence to appreciate the works of Nature.

Every laird had his own piper in those days, and it was part of the piper's duty to accompany the laird when he went on short journeys, such as when Ranald MacDonald conducted guests to Staffa. He also played in front of the house every morning, but apparently all the visitors to Ulva did not appreciate this music. Sir John Carr, who resided here for a few days in 1807, during which he visited Staffa, describes this piper in his *Caledonian Sketches* as "this barbarous musician" and relates that he was informed that one of the pipers in this district " attempting, in a fit of enthusiasm, to pipe over eighteen miles, blew his breath out of his body." Sir John adds: " it would have been well if he had been the last of his race."

Ranald MacDonald's piper was Archibald MacArthur, a member of the family who founded and conducted the famous College of Pipers in Ulva which supplied the piper to the lairds of Ulva for many years; the first of that race of pipers was

taught by the famous MacCrimmons of Skye.   It is related of
MacArthur that during the sojourn at Ulva of a titled English
gentleman, he asked the visitor what was the age of his piper.
On the Englishman replying that he had no piper, this "worthy"
said, " Then you are not a real gentlemen," and looked upon
him with disdain during the remainder of his stay.

It was the custom at Ulva, in those days, for every party of
visitors to Staffa to engage a piper to accompany them, if they
were unaccompanied by the laird and his piper.

Sir Walter Scott was greatly charmed with Ranald Mac-
Donald, with whom he had been acquainted in Edinburgh for
some time previous to his visit to Ulva.   In prose he describes
him as " a young gentleman possessed of a large estate in the
Western Isles, which he improves with the prudence and wisdom
of a Scottish farmer, combined with that love of his people, and
desire to render them happy, which was the finest feature in the
character of an ancient Celtic Chief."   Later, Scott says:
" Staffa's achievements, we doubt not, will be sung to the oars
by the men of Ulva when those of Fingal shall have faded from
the memory."

During his stay in Ulva, in July 1810, Scott inscribed a
spirited poetic address to Ranald MacDonald.   There is a
manuscript of this poem in the National Library of Scotland
with the date 1810, but the whereabouts of the Ulva manuscript
are unknown.   As it was an impromptu composition, Scott did
not include this poem in any edition of his collected poetical
works, and thus several versions of it appeared, varying slightly
in wording, in magazines and newspapers.   Dr James C.
Corson, assistant librarian in the University of Edinburgh and
an authority on Scott's works, after examining the various versions, considers the correct text of the poem to be:

> Staffa, sprung from high Macdonald,
> Worthy branch of old Clan Ranald!
> Staffa, king of all kind fellows,
> Well befall thy hills and valleys,
> Lakes and inlets, deeps and shallows,
> Cliffs of darkness, caves of wonder,
> Echoing the Atlantic's thunder;
> Mountains which the grey mist covers
> Where the chieftain spirit hovers,

> Pausing while his pinions quiver,
> Stretch'd to quit our land for ever.
> Each kind influence reign above thee!
> All thou lov'st and all that love thee!
> Warmer heart, 'twixt this and Jaffa,
> Beats not, than in breast of Staffa.

Scott and his party were ferried from Mull to Ulva in the boats belonging to the laird, with " colours flying and pipes playing." In a letter to Lady Abercorn, dated 30th September 1810, he describes his reception thus: " In the Isle of Ulva, where the Laird of Staffa has his house, we were treated with something like feudal splendour. His people received us under arms, and with a discharge of musketry and artillery. His piper was a constant attendant on our parties, and wakened us in the morning with his music."

In connection with the friendship between MacDonald of Staffa and Scott, it is interesting to learn from *A Book of Scottish Anecdote* that: " Highland Honours were given for the first time (and it astonished the party) at one of the early meetings of the Celtic Society, by the late accomplished Ranald MacDonald of Staffa, then Sheriff of Stirlingshire, who was an enthusiastic Highlander. It was on the occasion of drinking Sir Walter Scott's health, who, on returning thanks said:

> There is not 'twixt this and Jaffa,
> A warmer heart than beats in Staffa."

Describing his first impressions of Staffa, in a letter to Joanna Baillie, the Scottish dramatist and poet, Scott says:

It [Staffa] is one of the most extraordinary places I ever beheld. It exceeded, in my mind, every description I had heard of it; or rather, the appearance of the cavern [Fingal's Cave] composed entirely of basaltic pillars as high as the roof of a cathedral, and running deep into the rock, eternally swept by a deep and swelling sea, and paved, as it were, with ruddy marble, baffles all description. You can walk along the broken pillars with a little danger, as far as the furthest extremity. Boats also can come in below when the sea is placid, which is seldom the case.

In honour of Scott's visit the boatmen on that occasion

took the whim of solemnly christening a great stone seat at the mouth of the cavern, Clachan an Bairdh, or the Poets' Stone. It was consecrated with a pibroch, which the echoes rendered tremendous, and a glass of whisky, not poured forth in the ancient mode of libation, but turned over the throats of the assistants . . . . The head boatman [Scott continues], whose father had been himself a bard, made me a speech on the occasion; but as it was in Gaelic, I could only receive it as a silly beauty does a fine-spun compliment—bow and say nothing.

Scott also mentions this incident in his letter to Lady Abercorn, where he describes the head boatman's speech as containing

a great deal of compliment on account of my being "the great bard of the Lowland border," and "burnishing the shields of ancient chieftains," with much more figurative eulogy, of which I regretted I could not get an accurate translation. It concluded with acquainting me with their determination to have a remarkable pillar of the cavern called after me, "Clachan an Bairdh Sassenach Mohr,"[1] or the stone of the great Lowland bard.

Scott visited Staffa again during the month of August 1814, while on a tour of the Scottish lighthouses in the yacht of the Commissioners of Northern Lights. He describes this tour briefly in his Introduction to *The Pirate*. During that visit the mist became so thick while on Staffa that Scott and Stevenson, the Superintendent Engineer to the Commissioners, got separated from the other members of the party. They lost their bearings, and instead of arriving at Fingal's Cave, wandered to the opposite side of the island, where, " after a clamber of great toil and danger," they came upon " the ' Cannon-ball' [as Scott calls the Gunna Mor], a round granite stone moved by the sea up and down in a groove of rock, which it has worn for itself, with a noise resembling thunder." According to the Hon. Mrs Murray of Kensington, the stone had been removed before 1800, and Scott's term "groove" is not an apt description of the bore. He may have meant that though he was told of its position he did not view it personally. There is no granite here, but it would be hypercritical to question him on this point.

Shortly after that visit Scott wrote his well-known poem, *The Lord of the Isles*, in which he gives the following fine description of Staffa and Fingal's Cave:

> The shores of Mull on the eastward lay
> And Ulva dark and Colonsay,
> And all the group of islets gay
> That guard famed Staffa round.

---

[1] [Should be " *Clach a' Bhaird Shasunnach Mhoir*."]

Then all unknown its columns rose,
Where dark and undisturb'd repose
The cormorant had found,
And the shy seal had quiet home,
And welter'd in that wondrous dome
Where, as to shame the temples deck'd
By skill of earthly architect,
Nature herself, it seem'd would raise
A Minster to her Maker's praise;
Not for a meaner use ascend
Her columns, or her arches bend;
Nor of a theme less solemn tells
That mighty surge that ebbs and swells.
And still, between each awful pause,
From the high vault an answer draws,
In varied tone prolong'd and high,
That mocks the organ's melody.
Nor doth its entrance front in vain
To old Iona's holy fane,[1]
That Nature's voice might seem to say,
Well hast thou done, frail child of clay,
Thy humble powers that stately shrine
Task'd high and hard—but witness mine!

During the month of July 1818, John Keats, the poet, visited Staffa in a boat from Iona. In a letter to his brother Tom, he says:

I am puzzled how to give you an idea of Staffa. It can only be represented by a first-rate drawing. One may compare the surface of the island to a roof; this roof is supported by grand pillars of basalt standing together as thick as honeycomb. The finest thing is Fingal's Cave. It is entirely a hollowing out of basalt pillars. Suppose now the giants who rebelled against Jove, had taken a whole mass of black columns and bound them together like bunches of matches and then, with immense axes, had made a cavern in the body of these columns. Of course the roof and floor must be composed of the ends of these columns. Such is Fingal's Cave, except that the sea has done the work of excavation and is continually dashing there, so that we walk along the sides of the cave, on the pillars which are left as if for convenient stairs. The roof is arched somewhat Gothic-wise, and the length of some of the entire side pillars is fifty feet. About the island you might seat an army of men, each on a pillar. The length of the cave is 120 feet [!] and from its extremity, the view into the sea, through the large arch at the entrance, is sublime. The colour of the columns is black with a lurking gloom of purple therein. For solemnity and grandeur it far surpasses the finest cathedrals. At the extremity of the cave there is a small perforation into

[1] [Iona Abbey can be seen from Fingal's Cave.]

(*Above*) A westward headland with the Treshnish Islands visible in the background and, just discernible on the skyline, the island of Coll; (*below*) until 1968, visitors to Staffa were landed by launch from *King George V*; from 1969 to 1974, although not landing passengers, *King George V* did pause off the island to show passengers the caves but the vessel has now been withdrawn from service

(*Left*) The arms of Alastair de Watteville of Staffa were granted posthumously to his father by the Court of the Lord Lyon in 1973; the shield contains the stag's attires of the Mackenzie Arms and the wings of the de Watteville Arms. The celtic cross associates Staffa with the nearby island of Iona; (*below*) a late evening view of the cliffs either side of MacKinnon's Cave at the south-west extremity: the island's owner, Alastair de Watteville, is seen in his inflatable dinghy

another cave, at which the waters meeting and buffeting each other, there is sometimes produced a report as if a cannon, heard as far as Iona, which must be twelve [!] miles. As we approached in the boat there was such a fine swell on the sea that the pillars appeared immediately rising from the crystal sea. But it is impossible to describe it:

> Not Aladdin magian
> Ever such a work began;
> Not the Wizard of the Dee
> Ever such a dream could see:
> Not St John on Patmos' Isle,
> In the passion of his toil,
> When he saw the churches seven,
> Golden-aisled, built up in heaven,
> Gaz'd at such a rugged wonder,
> As I stood its roofing under.

In an imaginary talk with the Spirit of the Sea, Keats is told:

> This was architectur'd thus
> By the great Oceanus—
> Here his mighty waters play
> Hollow organs all the day;
> Here, by turns, his dolphins all,
> Finny palmers, great and small,
> Come to pay devotion due,
> Each a mouth of pearls must strew.
> Many a mortal of these days
> Dares to pass our sacred ways:
> Dares to touch audaciously
> This cathedral of the sea: . . .
> So for ever will I leave
> Such a taint, and soon unweave
> All the magic of the place!
> So saying with a spirit's glance
>   He dived!

In the original poem there are six lines which Keats omitted, judiciously, when copying these verses later. These lines occur between the third and fourth last lines given above and are as follows:

> 'Tis now free to stupid face,
> To cutters and to fashion boats,
> To cravats and to petticoats;
> The great sea shall war it down,
> For its fame shall not be blown
> At every farthing quadrille dance.

Because of Ossian's odes and Sir Walter Scott's poems and novels, Scotland became a land of romance at the beginning of the nineteenth century. Everyone who had read these works felt the mountains, islands, and mists of the north to be full of inspiration. Even so massive and serious a mind as that of Mendelssohn, the great composer, was influenced to such an extent that, having finished his first London season (1829) of concerts, balls, and parties, he and his friend Klingemann set out to spend the rest of the summer touring Scotland. Mendelssohn was at that time a young man twenty years of age, highly cultured and with charming manners which endeared him everywhere he went. Naturally, they visited the Hebrides, and Mendelssohn was so impressed with Staffa, which they visited during the month of August, that he was inspired with the theme of his well-known Overture, *Fingal's Cave*, sometimes called *The Hebrides* Overture. In Fingal's Cave the first two bars of the Overture came into Mendelssohn's mind. There is a letter of his from Tobermory which contains the first twenty bars of the Overture. It was not composed, however, until the following year during his stay in Italy,[1] when he called it the Overture to *The Solitary Island*. But he was dissatisfied with his first version of the work, and two years afterwards said that part of it did not smell enough of "seagulls and salt fish, and must be altered." His new version has remained one of the most popular works in the concert programme.

A musical critic has described this wonderful work as " one of the most ideal pieces of tone pointing in the musical art." The atmosphere is unmistakable. One can note the restless theme with which the Overture opens, reminiscent of the surging waves. The effective writing for the wood wind is described by Wagner as " rising above the other instruments, wailing like sea winds through the cave."

An account of a conversation with Mendelssohn at Leipzig in 1840 is given in *A Day with Mendelssohn-Bartholdy*, by George Sampson. The author says that on mentioning the Hebrides to

---

[1] During this stay in Italy, Mendelssohn visited another little island of caves which has become world-famous because of its principal grotto; the island of Capri, at the entrance to the bay of Naples—another famous volcanic region. Mendelssohn's account of the beautiful Blue Grotto, given in a letter to his sisters, was the first description ever published of this natural wonder.

Mendelssohn the latter exclaimed, " What a wonder is Fingal's Cave, that vast cathedral of the sea, with its dark lapping waters within, and the brightness of the gleaming waves outside!" Sampson continues:

This Overture of his is made of the sounds of the sea. There is first a theme that suggests the monotonous wash of the waters and the crying of sea-birds within the vast spaces of the cavern. Then follows a noble rising passage, as if the spirit of the place were ascending from the depths of the sea, and pervading with his presence the immensity of his ocean fane. This, in its turn, is succeeded by a movement that seems to carry us into the brightness outside, though still the plaint of crying birds pursues us in haunting monotony.

Mendelssohn and his companion had a very rough voyage from Oban to Staffa, on the steamboat, and both were very sea-sick. Klingemann writes of Mendelssohn: "He was on better terms with the sea as a musician than as an individual. . . . As we proceeded, the pleasure increased in gravity; where yesterday nice conversation went on, to-day silence was indulged in." He mentions a fellow-traveller, or rather a sister-traveller, an old woman of eighty-two, who, on being landed at Staffa, " scrambled about Fingal's Cave laboriously; she wanted to see the cave of Staffa before her end, and she saw it. . . . A greener roar of waves surely never rushed into a stranger cavern—its many pillars making it look like the inside of an immense organ, black and resounding."

Those two Germans, it appears, had always confused the Hebrides with the Hesperides—" and if we did not find the oranges on the trees, they lay at least in the whisky toddy."

It would have been very interesting if Mendelssohn's contemporary and fellow-countryman, Wagner, had visited Fingal's Cave in the stormy conditions that Mendelssohn experienced, because the sound and setting are then truly Wagnerian.

During the year 1830, J. M. W. Turner, the famous artist, was commissioned by Cadell, the publisher, to make twenty-four drawings to illustrate a new edition of Scott's poetical works. The contract necessitated Turner viewing personally the principal scenes of Scott's poems, and included a visit to Staffa during that year. The result of that visit was a water-colour vignette of Fingal's Cave painted in the following year (1831) from sketches made on the site. In was engraved in

1833 by E. Goodall and used to illustrate *The Lord of the Isles*. The painting passed into the Novar collection but was disposed of before 1865. It was sold at Christie's about 1880 to a Mr Hugh Munro, but its subsequent history I have been unable to discover.

Great artist though Turner was, he does not appear to have been a happy choice for Cadell's commission. As an artist he was too original to re-tell in paint what had already been told in print and, although he excelled in expressing through his pictures the elusive qualities of light and colour in a scene, he seemed to be impatient with form and structure. As he himself said: " My business is to paint what I see, not what I know is there." When working to commission, even if under no restraint, it is a moot point whether the artist should express himself or the subject with greater emphasis.

Even allowing artist's licence, it is difficult to understand how Turner could see a setting sun from the inner end of Fingal's Cave, as shown on his painting for Cadell, when the cave faces south and its western side projects as a colonnade to a considerable distance beyond the cave entrance. He also shows the cave formed of curved columns, but there are no curved columns in the precincts of Fingal's Cave. Indeed, it is the straightness of the vertical columns forming the cave which gives it so much serene dignity and concentration of effect.

It is surprising that a year after painting the inaccurate water-colour picture of Fingal's Cave, Turner painted a large and, as far as can be seen through a dense atmosphere of luminous mist, a scenically correct oil-colour painting of the cave viewed from without, which was exhibited in the Royal Academy in 1832. This picture was the first of the great artist's work to go to America, and was chosen from his collection by C. R. Leslie, R.A., for Mr James Lenox of New York, U.S.A., in August, 1845. It was purchased by Messrs Thomas Agnew & Sons of London for £16,785 and brought back to Britain in October, 1956. It is now in the possession of Lord Astor of Hever. It possesses the typical misty atmosphere of a " Turner," so much so that Mr Lenox, when acknowledging receipt of the picture after a first hasty glance, said he could almost fancy it had sustained some damage on the voyage, it appeared so indistinct throughout. Turner, on hearing this, said to Leslie, " Tell him that indistinctness is my forte." Later on, Lenox wrote saying that every time he looked at the picture it gained in his estimation and ultimately delighted him, but he admitted that it was a picture which was not likely to become popular with the multitude. I possess a photographic reproduction of this oil painting of Fingal's Cave by Turner, which I received by the courtesy of the Assistant Director of the New York Public Library, and would have included it in this book had it been suitable. Unfortunately, though the technical quality of the photograph is all that could be desired, the original painting is very indistinct, and as a second reproduction would render it still more so, it would puzzle the reader to know what it represented, were it reproduced here. Again, the colour effect is lost in monochrome, and it is the colour effect rather than the subject that is the principal attraction of Turner's paintings. Only a very faint image of the cliffs and cave appear, and in some parts they are imperceptible, being lost in an atmosphere of luminous mist. The only recognisable features, and they are very hazy, are a stormy sea and sky and small paddle steamer with a tall thin funnel in the offing; a good example of Turner's inherent liking for melodramatic effects. Until I had studied the photograph minutely, I thought the title had been given to a wrong reproduction.

In a letter to Lenox, dated 16th August 1856, reproduced in an early edition of the *Guide* to the Lenox Library (now long out of print), Turner describes his visit to Staffa which inspired the paintings of Fingal's Cave. He says:

We left the Sound of Mull, in the *Maid of Morven*, to visit Staffa, and reach Iona in due time; but a strong wind and head sea prevented us making Staffa until too late to go on to Iona. After scrambling over the rocks on the lee side of the island, some got into Fingal's Cave, others would not. It is not very pleasant or safe when the waves roll right in. One hour was given to meet on the rock we landed on. When on board, the Captain declared it doubtful about Iona. Such a rainy and bad-looking night coming on, a vote was proposed to the passengers: " Iona at all hazards, or back to Tobermory?" Majority against proceeding. To allay the displeased, the Captain promised to steam thrice round the island. The sun getting towards the horizon, burst through the rain cloud, angry, and for wind; and so it proved, for we were driven for shelter into Loch Ulver, and did not get back to Tobermory before midnight.

William Wordsworth visited Staffa by steamboat in 1833, but the crowd of noisy tourists prevented the silent meditation which this poet of Nature desired here.   After viewing Fingal's Cave, in their company, he wrote:

> We saw, but surely, in that motley crowd,
> Not one of us has felt the far-famed sight;
> How *could* we feel it? each the other's blight,
> Hurried and hurrying, volatile and loud.
> O, for those motions only that invite
> The Ghost of Fingal to his tuneful cave
> By the breeze entered, and wave after wave
> Softly embosoming the timid light!
> And by *one* votary who at will might stand
> Gazing, and take into his mind and heart,
> With undistracted reverence, the effect
> Of those proportions where the Almighty Hand
> That made the worlds, the Sovereign Architect,
> Has deigned to work as if with human Art!

In a footnote Wordsworth says: " At the risk of incurring the reasonable displeasure of the master of the steamboat, I returned to the cave [after the crowd had departed] and explored it under circumstances more favourable to those imaginative impressions which it is so wonderfully fitted to make upon the mind."   After that second visit he voiced his sentiments thus:

> Thanks for the lessons of this spot—fit school
> For the presumptuous thought that would assign
> Mechanic laws to agency divine;
> And, measuring heaven by earth, would over-rule
> Infinite Power.   The pillared vestibule,
> Expanding yet precise, the roof embowed,
> Might seem designed to humble man, when proud
> Of his best workmanship by plan and tool.
> Down-bearing with his whole Atlantic weight
> Of tide and tempest on the structure's base,
> And flashing to that structure's topmost height,
> Ocean has proved its strength, and of its grace
> In calm is conscious, finding for his freight
> Of softest music some responsive place.

Sir Robert Peel, in a speech delivered at the public dinner given in Glasgow on 13th January 1837, on the occasion of his being elected Lord Rector of the University, said of Fingal's Cave: " I have stood on the shores of Staffa; I have seen the 'temple not made with hands'; I have seen the majestic swell of the ocean, the pulsations of the great Atlantic beating in its inmost sanctuary, and swelling a note of praise nobler far than any that ever pealed from human organ."

During the month of July 1844, the King of Saxony and his physician, Dr C. G. Carus, visited Staffa from Oban on the small paddle steamer *Brenda*. Although they had viewed the scenic beauties of Germany, Belgium, England, and the Lowlands of Scotland on their tour, Dr Carus describes the day on which they visited Mull, Staffa and Iona as "the most considerable, magnificent and beautiful excursion of our whole journey." He says of Fingal's Cave: " The singularity of the view from this dark pillared Church, filled with the ocean, out upon the blue horizon of the sea, may, perhaps, *in some measure*, be imagined." While His Majesty and Dr Carus were on Staffa another steamboat arrived and anchored off the island. It proved to be the vessel on which the Lighthouse Commissioners were making their annual inspection of the Scottish lighthouses. They had heard that the King of Saxony was visiting Staffa and had come to pay their respects to him.

Queen Victoria and Prince Albert, accompanied by the youthful Prince of Wales and the Princess Royal, visited Staffa on the 19th August 1847, on the Royal yacht *Victoria and Albert*, during their first visit to the Highlands of Scotland. William Keddie, who was Lecturer in Natural Science in the Free Church College, Glasgow, and who was present on the occasion of the Royal visit to Staffa, being one of a party on board one of the ships that formed the attendant squadron accompanying the Royal yacht, describes the scene:

The *Victoria and Albert*[1] having cast anchor at 3.30 p.m., preparations were made for Her Majesty's landing. The blue barge was lowered, the seats covered with cushions, the yacht's gangway let down to the barge and laid with a carpet. The barge was manned by sixteen sailors, fourteen of whom stood with oars erect, as their manner is on such occasions; and fine fellows they were, prompt and regular in all their movements. The Royal Standard was placed at the bow of the vessel, two sailors stood in front with boat hooks, and a naval officer took his place at the rudder, accompanied by Captain McKillop of the *Dolphin*, who had the honour to be selected for the

---

[1] [That was the first of the two paddle-propelled Royal yachts of that name, and not the third Royal yacht of the same name, which was a screw steamer.]

guidance of Her Majesty's yacht throughout its voyage in the western waters. Her Majesty having been handed down the steps, took her seat in the barge, and was followed by Prince Albert and the Royal children, when the oars were lowered and the vessel shot forward towards Fingal's Cave. The weather being unusually favourable, the tide low and the water as quiet as could be expected in that turbulent region, Her Majesty visited the island in the most advantageous manner.

After Her Majesty's barge had left the Great Cave two others of the yacht's boats entered, filled with members of the suite, and the officers of the vessels. After lingering for a short time in view of the cliffs, the barge put back to the yacht and the Queen went aboard. Prince Albert, however, returned to the cave, and spent a considerable time in it, along with one of the naval officers. His Royal Highness afterwards ascended to the summit of the island, followed by several of the suite, while others examined the basaltic columns below.

In *Leaves from the Journal of our Life in the Highlands*, Queen Victoria, who was known to the Highlanders as the *Ban-righ* (literally, " She-King," as there is no Gaelic feminine term for Sovereign), records her impressions of Staffa:

At three we anchored close before Staffa and immediately got into the barge with Charles, the children and the rest of our people, and rowed towards the cave. As we rounded the point the wonderful basaltic formation came in sight. The appearance it presented was most extraordinary: and when we turned the corner to go into the renowned Fingal's Cave the effect was splendid, like a great entrance into a vaulted hall, it looked almost awful as we entered and the barge heaved up and down in the swell of the sea.

There appears to be a conflict of evidence as to whether or not Lord Tennyson and Francis Turner Palgrave visited Staffa during their brief stay in the West Highlands in 1853. On that occasion they travelled direct from Edinburgh to Oban and thence to Ardtornish, in Morvern, on the Sound of Mull, where they were the guests of Professor Sellar for a few days. After their stay they returned to Edinburgh via Oban, crossing in an open boat from Ardtornish to Oban.

In the article on Tennyson which appears in *Chambers' Encyclopaedia*, it is stated: "These [journeys of Tennyson] include the Western Highlands, Staffa and Iona, 1853." On making enquiries I learned that this article was written by Palgrave for an early edition of the *Encyclopaedia*, which would seem to make the statement unquestionable. Again, in a letter written by Palgrave to his father, from Ardtornish, dated August 3rd, 1853, he says: " I reached this wild place to-day

. . . to-morrow is vowed to Iona and Staffa"; but there does not appear to be any other letter referring to the subject.

In opposition to those statements is the evidence of Mrs William Sellar, the hostess, who writes in her *Recollections and Impressions:* " They [Tennyson and Palgrave] arrived on a Saturday, in August, and stayed till the following Wednesday afternoon." She describes the outings for each day, but does not mention a trip, or even the suggestion of a trip, to Staffa and Iona, which would require a full day at least from Ardtornish, and at that time the Sellars had no yacht. She mentions that they went to church on the day after arrival, which means that that day was a Sunday, though the date of arrival given in Palgrave's letter is that of a Wednesday, making the day after arrival a Thursday and not a Sunday.

It is difficult to understand how two reliable writers should give such conflicting statements. I have made many enquiries, and communicated with members of the three families concerned, to solve this inconsistency, but without success. To me, the most reasonable evidence that Tennyson and Palgrave did not visit Staffa or Iona is that diligent search has failed to reveal any mention of these famous islands in the works of either writer. One can hardly credit persons like Tennyson and Palgrave visiting Fingal's Cave without making some remarks worth preserving. I would not have raised this subject had not Palgrave been responsible for the statement in *Chambers' Encyclopaedia* that Tennyson visited Staffa.

Jules Verne, the famous French writer of imaginary voyages and romances of a scientific nature, visited the Hebrides, including Staffa, in 1859. Staffa impressed him so much that in his book *The Green Ray*, published in 1885, he set the climax of that romance on the island. From its western cliffs the characters of his story witnessed that rare phenomenon, the green ray, or flash, which appears when atmospheric conditions are suitable at the moment the sun shoots its last rays as it sinks into the sea. An old legend says that anyone who has seen this ray is endowed with the mental powers of penetrating all falsehood and deceit.

Jules Verne visited Scotland again in 1880, but there is no record of his having been near Staffa on that occasion. He seems to have spent his time touring the mining districts of the industrial area.

When referring to his visit to the Western Isles of Scotland in 1859, Jules Verne says:

I know nothing comparable to the Hebrides. We have here another Archipelago. Perhaps the sky is not so intensely blue as among the Grecian Isles, but the rugged rocks and hazy horizons make it much more romantic. The Greek Archipelago gave birth to a whole society of Gods and Goddesses. That may be so! But these are very ordinary divinities, positive and endowed with material existence, a little too closely resembling the human beings whose weaknesses they share. It is not like that in the Hebrides. These islands are the retreat of supernatural beings. They are Ossian, Fingal and all the shadowy crowd escaped from the Sagas. I would not exchange this group of two hundred islands and islets washed by the Gulf Stream, these tumultuous seas, and skies loaded with mist, for all the archipelagos of eastern seas.

Writing of Fingal's Cave, he says:

From this point in the cave there is an admirable vista broadening out to the open sky, and the water, filled with clear light, allows one to see every detail of the sea bed. On the side walls one sees an astonishing play of light and shadows. When a cloud covers the entrance to the cave, everything grows dark, as when a gauze curtain is dropped over the theatre proscenium. But everything sparkles and glints gaily with the seven colours of the rainbow whenever the sun breaks through again, reflected off the crystal of the cave bottom and glancing upwards in long luminous streaks to the threshold of the central nave. Beyond that, the waves break at the foot of the gigantic arch which forms the opening to the cave: and this frame, black as ebony, throws all the foreground features into full relief. Further out still, the horizon between sea and sky stretches out in all its splendour, with the dim height of Iona two miles out in the open sea, and the pale silhouette of its ruined monastery.

What an enchanted place this Fingal's Cave is! Who could be so dull of soul as not to believe that it was created by a god for sylphs and waternymphs! And for whom do the wandering winds strike music from this vast aeolian harp? Surely this was the unearthly music that Waverley heard in his dreams?

I am indebted to a descendant of Jules Verne, namely Madame Allotte de la Fuÿe, for these and some other interesting notes regarding his visit to Staffa and his enthusiasm for the island. Being a literary person, she has examined minutely his unpublished manuscripts and diaries, including the account of his visit to Staffa, which are in the possession of one of her relatives who has not her qualifications for doing so.

Before setting out on his third, and last, journey to Africa, Dr David Livingstone, the famous missionary and explorer, visited Staffa by steamer from Oban in 1864. The only mention which I have been able to locate is given in *Personal Life of David Livingstone*, by W. G. Blaikie, but the author makes no mention of any remarks made by Dr Livingstone on that occasion, which is unfortunate because the doctor had a personal interest in this region. From Staffa he could see the island of Ulva, where his paternal grandparents had their home, and where his father was born.

When a student at Edinburgh University, Robert Louis Stevenson landed on Staffa while on his way by steamer from Oban to spend three weeks on the nearby island of Erraid where the stones were being quarried and shaped for the building of Dubh Hirteach lighthouse, of which his father and uncle were the engineers. It was on Erraid that he laid the shipwreck scene of *Kidnapped*. He sailed from Oban to Iona, via Staffa. At Iona he disembarked and hired a small boat to ferry him to Erraid. In a letter to his mother from Erraid, dated 5th August 1870, he describes his journey from Oban to Iona, but he seems to have been much more interested in a pretty girl he met on board the steamer than in the scenery. His only mention of Staffa is that he had the pleasure of conducting this young lady into Fingal's Cave. His other companion on the steamer was Sam Bough, the artist, who was on his way to spend a painting holiday on Iona, which has always been a favourite haunt of artists.

That doughty Scotsman, Professor John Stuart Blackie, was well acquainted with this region and in *A Psalm of Ben More* [Mull], describes Staffa thus:

> World-famous Staffa, by the daedal hand
> Of Titan Nature piled in rhythmic state,
> A fane for gods, and with the memory wreathed
> Of Fingal, and the ancient hero-kings
> Whom Ossian sang to the wild ringing notes
> Of his old Celtic harp, when Celtic songs
> Were mighty in the land.

William Black, the novelist, was a regular visitor to Staffa and other parts of the West Highlands and Islands for many years.

He laid the principal scenes of his novel *MacLeod of Dare*, one of the most widely read and discussed novels of the seventies, in the region surrounding Staffa. The ruins of Burg Castle, which are situated on a cliff in the coast of Mull opposite Staffa, figure in the story as Castle Dare.

While engaged on the writing of this novel Black spent two days and nights on Staffa along with my father and his companion, which enabled him to obtain a bird's-eye view of the principal scenes of his story. He described Staffa as " an author's Utopia with nothing to disturb me but the sound of the waves." *MacLeod of Dare* is dedicated to twelve eminent Scottish artists who were friends of Black and also frequent visitors to the West Highlands and Islands. Each of them presented Black with a drawing to give pictorial expression to some scene or character of his story. These illustrations form a unique collection and the artists who contributed them were: J. Pettie, R.A.; T. Graham; G. H. Boughton; W. Q. Orchardson, R.A.; Colin Hunter; J. MacWhirter; C. E. Johnson; J. A. Aitken; T. Faed, R.A.; J. E. Millais; F. Powell; P. Graham, A.R.A. In his youth Black himself was an art student, when he gained the friendship of these artists.

James Aitken, one of the artists mentioned above, made Fingal's Cave the subject of two fine murals on the walls of one of the public rooms in the Argyll Hotel, Iona. These pictures are painted in oils directly on to the wall surface; one view, six feet by three feet, showing the exterior of the cave, and the other, three feet by two feet six inches, showing a view looking out of the cave. Although painted about seventy years ago, they still are in a wonderful state of preservation.

Mary Anderson (later Madame de Navarro), the famous Shakespearian actress, whose remarkable beauty and acting took America and Britain by storm during the 'seventies and 'eighties, visited Staffa on several occasions while at the height of her fame. The immense success of her tour of America as leading lady with Johnston (later Sir) Forbes-Robertson is still recalled when Shakespearian successes are discussed. In addition to her histrionic talent she was regarded by competent opinion as one of the most beautiful women of her day, and it was an age of beautiful women; a modern encyclopaedia says,

" Her beauty was proverbial." Her retiral from the stage when at the zenith of her career surprised many people but, as she wrote later, " The extreme publicity of the life had already begun to be distasteful to me."

Mary Anderson and William Black were personal friends, and she figures as a principal character in several of his books. In his well-known novel, *MacLeod of Dare*, many people have sought to identify the heroine, the beautiful actress who bewitched MacLeod, and in the end drove him to madness and death, with Mary Anderson. Black maintained, however, that in this story the heroine was a creature of his own imagination. He and Mary Anderson had never met when he wrote *MacLeod of Dare*, though later in life they became close personal friends. It was as the guest of Black and his wife that Mary Anderson first visited the West Highlands and Islands of Scotland and they appealed so strongly that she continued to visit this region, including Staffa, even after her marriage to Antonio de Navarro.

My family acquaintance with Mme de Navarro originated before I was born and was renewed when I was writing the first edition of this book. From that time onward until her death I had the pleasure of her charming friendship. During the writing of that first edition, and when re-writing and enlarging it for the second edition, she kindly sent me letters and books containing much helpful information and also guided me to other interesting sources regarding famous visitors to Staffa. She was very earnest that I should complete a book on Staffa at times when I was doubtful about doing so. Indeed, her enthusiasm was quite an inspiration to me, as that was my first venture as an author, apart from magazine and newspaper articles. During that indecisive stage in my literary and photographic work she wrote: " Do not hesitate, please persevere and if I personally or through friends can assist you in any way it will give me great pleasure to do so." Incidentally, she mentioned that the first qualified person to give her encouragement at the outset of her career as an actress was John McCullough, the Shakespearian actor. So what was given to her by one McCullough was received from her by another MacCulloch. Her death, in 1940, evoked tributes in the press from many who had known her not only as a famous actress and a beautiful woman but as a friend who joyed in doing good deeds, and she was a lady of strong character as well as of charm. I cherish the memory of her friendship and encouragement which remained undiminished to the end.

Ellen Terry, in a published collection of her letters, says of Mme de Navarro (at that time, Mary Anderson): " Hearing her praises sung on all sides, I was particularly struck by her modest evasion of publicity off the stage. I personally know her only as a beautiful woman and as kind as beautiful. Certainly she took England by storm." Bernard Shaw wrote, " The world which once sent Mrs Siddons back to the provinces as a failure prostrated itself like a doormat to kiss the feet of Mary Anderson." Ellaline Terriss, in her autobiography, says, " When Irving's company and my father returned to London in the summer of 1884, a very lovely American actress appeared at the Lyceum in *Romeo and Juliet*. Her name was Mary Anderson, one of the most beautiful women who ever graced the stage and a most sensitive actress as well. She was the rage of London."

Mary Anderson was a great admirer of the West Highlands and Islands. In one of her letters, which she wrote to me when I was writing the second edition of this book, she says:

I shall never forget my first visit to Staffa, on the *Grenadier*. It was a beautiful summer day—a day of azure sky and sun-kissed sea. As the small boat entered Fingal's Cave I was quite breathless at seeing such loveliness; nothing else like it in the world. Such an array of rich colours, as the sunlight sparkled on the sea and lichened rock of this pillared cavern, I never saw before and have never seen since. It is a beautiful fairyland and seems almost too beautiful for reality; it makes one feel one is having a glorious dream. In my memory and in my dreams—when specially good ones—this wonderful scene lives as clear as when I first viewed it.

Bret Harte, the American novelist, visited Staffa during his term of office as U.S. Consul in Glasgow (1880-5), and described it as the only sight in Europe that quite fulfilled his expectations.

Another American literary visitor to Staffa on several occasions during the eighties was William Winter, poet and writer, who was a contemporary and friend of Longfellow and Emerson. Winter's books are not nearly so widely known in Britain as they should be. He toured our country several times and was impressed deeply with its scenery and associations, and has given us his beautiful sentiments in language which is both rich and seemly. In his *Over the Border*, he says of Fingal's Cave: " It is a solemn and awful place, and you behold it without words and leave it in silence, but your backward look remains long fixed upon it, and its living picture of gloom and glory will never fade out of your mind."

William Sharp ("Fiona MacLeod") the last of the Celtic Twlight romancers, was well acquainted with Staffa and its surrounding islands. In his book, *Earth's Voices*, appear the following lines:

THE CAVES OF STAFFA

(Gale from the South-West)

The green Atlantic seas wash past
The mighty pillars of basalt;
A vast sea-echo through the vault
Swells like a captive thunder-blast;
The wind fierce show'rs of spray doth sweep
Through the cave's gulf, and loud the deep.
Resistless billows in their course
Thunder within in tumult hoarse.

Lest any reader should think that the foregoing eulogies on Staffa were confined to an age of sentimentality, it may be worth giving the opinions of three hard-headed modern writers. Neil Gunn, the Scottish author, who visited Staffa in his motor boat while on a cruise of the west coast, says in his book, *Off in a Boat:* " Usually, the show places of a country are disappointing, but I must say Staffa was arresting. . . . It certainly did not look like a piece of haphazard nature. The economy, the precision, and the regularity seemed altogether too human. . . . Staffa is not at all spectacular in the grand manner. It comes upon one with an air of surprise and wonder like a work of genius in a picture frame." William Power, another modern Scots author, says: " Fingal's Cave is, I suppose, the unique marvel of Scotland, as Stonehenge is of England. It has no compeer in Scotland or in Europe." Stephen Bone says of Staffa: "It has to be seen to be believed. . . . The most blasé tourist will be startled by Staffa."

Although Staffa has received many glowing tributes, the description given in a small pamphlet, first published in London 1791 and again published in Dublin 1792, Glasgow 1798, 1802,

and Belfast 1820, would be difficult to beat for an attempt to
" gild the lily." The person who wrote it appears to have
searched his imagination instead of his memory.

This quaint little brochure is entitled *A Description of the
Curious Monuments and Antiquities in the Island of Icolmkill, or the
Island of St Colman-kill [Iona]; also an account of the Island of Staffa,
where the rural throne of the late King Fingal is extant; being the
Chief of the Heroes, so much admired by the Poets. By a Gentleman
who made the Tour of Europe, prior to this Description, in a letter to a
Friend. It is now published by the desire of several Gentlemen of
Distinction who reside in the Country; and given to the bearer, John
McCormick, upon account of his misfortunes, to help him to support a
small family.* Here is the account of Staffa:

Three leagues north from Icolmkill is the famous island of Staffa. It is
supported upon pillars in the middle of the ocean; the pillars are of a mixed
marble, and no marble containing such a variety of brilliant colours was ever
discovered in Britain. The island is square, and extends about three-
quarters of a mile; the subterraneous part thereof is so naturally arched and
decorated, that it exceeds the most exquisite performance of the greatest
artists in the world. There is a melodious cave in the island; any music
played or sung therein will in reality have a sound more melodious than an
organ. The rocks towards the sea seem as if they were polished by artists of
great taste; the pebbles on the shore have every appearance of beautiful
pearls. There is only one family in the island; in stormy weather the house
not only shakes, but even the very kettles on the fire. There is further a
greater curiosity, a barge under sails and at low water will, with ease, proceed sixty yards into the said cave; and at the distance of a league, when
passing the same in dark nights, a visible sparkling like diamonds will cast a
lustre at a great distance. On the top of the island there is a beautiful
natural seat of marble, resembling an easy chair, which is said to be King
Fingal's throne, and contiguous thereto there are three pyramids resembling
a sugar loaf, which beautifies the royal seat.

Even Hollywood's publicity experts could hardly add anything to this description of Staffa.

CHAPTER XII

CONCLUSION

PERHAPS it will not be out of place to conclude this book with a few personal memories of Staffa.

As mentioned in Chapter I and also in the preface to the first edition, this book owes its origin to a fortnight which I spent on Staffa along with my father and a friend during the early summer of 1922. Previous to that time I had paid many brief visits to the island and have continued to visit it at intervals since then, but one requires to reside on the island for a few days at least to explore it and appreciate it fully.

During our sojourn on Staffa we made our home in the north-east end of the ruins mentioned in Chapter X. Our beds were insulated from the ground by a waterproof sheet spread across a few weather-worn planks of wood which we found in the island. For a roof, we first laid a wooden pole stretching from the front wall to the back wall of the ruin and about eight feet from its north-eastern wall. We then laid two planks of wood from the end wall to rest on the pole, several feet apart, and fastened them with rope. On this framework we laid a heavy tarpaulin, carrying the inner end over the pole and down to ground level, thus forming a fourth wall. On top of the tarpaulin we laid two planks at intervals and at right angles to those underneath, to lessen its flapping in the wind. The whole structure was fastened securely with ropes weighted down at their lower ends by being tied to large stones which we buried among the fallen rubble outside the ruin.

Although situated in a hollow, our shelter was exposed to the south and south-west Atlantic winds, and they can blow very strong. When these winds blew, our roof required frequent inspections and adjustment, and in rain or during night time this task was rather unpleasant as we clambered over the heaps of large stones which surround these crumbling ruins. Fortuntely, during our stay on the island the only dark nights were during a brief spell of stormy weather and when the sky was overcast. On cloudless nights there was no real darkness, merely a form of half-light, or twilight, and June nights are quite short in this region.

Although we were favoured with a beautiful day for landing on Staffa, which was followed by two of similar nature, the weather broke on the fourth day and developed into a severe gale of wind and rain. About mid-day the atmosphere became calm and sultry and the sun shone brassy through a haze. Gradually the sky became overcast with an ominous gloom and clouds banked quickly and menacingly in the south. Later, a southerly wind arose which by evening was blowing strong, with dark, low-flying clouds sweeping across an angry sky. The Atlantic swell became very heavy. Its huge, heaving undulations were whipped by the wind into white-crested combers that hurled themselves against the cliffs and boomed as they burst in a smother of foam, throwing spray and spindrift high into the air. A deeper-toned cannonade echoed from the caves.

During the night, the wind veered to the south-west and increased to gale force, carrying with it torrential rain that rattled like hailstones. As we lay in our beds talking and reading in flickering candlelight while the elements raved, we could see our tarpaulin roof straining and flapping with thuds that threatened to bring down the loose stones of the ruin walls on which it rested, especially when the more violent gusts struck our shelter and moaned in the chinks. Fortunately, everything held, though we had several alarms.

For four days we experienced fierce southerly and south-westerly winds driving drenching mist and rain in from the Atlantic and over the island in serried, grey curtains, screening off completely all the neighbouring islands. Although visibility under those conditions was, naturally, very limited, at times it was sufficient to reveal all around a wild waste of raging seas frothing white and marbled with streaks of foam.

We thus early encountered weather conditions which are often regarded as typical of the Western Isles of Scotland but are really not so prevalent as the exaggerated reports of some occasional visitors would lead strangers to believe, much to the detriment of these islands as a holiday haunt. Fortunately, there are other aspects of the Hebrides, and eventually the gale blew itself out, though the swell on the sea was slow in subsiding and, surprisingly, it continued to heave in from the south-west though the wind had veered round. Fine weather, however, had now set in. The wind veered and backed in varying strength between west and north with occasional rain-squalls from the gleaming cumulus that had replaced the sombre scene of storm. It then settled to blow as a stiff, fresh breeze from the north which brought brilliant sunshine from an azure sky flecked with a few small tufts of snow-white cloud. We had occasional spells of strong and cold north wind but visibility was of crystal clarity and the sea an intense blue of racing waves scattered with white crests. As if to compensate for the previous wild weather, these favourable conditions continued throughout the remainder of our stay on the island.

On the night the gale began to abate we had some thrilling glimpses of Staffa as the moon gleamed fitfully through rifts in the hurrying storm wrack. It seemed in the darkness as if an aerial searchlight were sweeping over the island at intervals, flashing its features into sharp silhouette, silver on one side and sable on the other. Later, during our sojourn, we had the pleasure, after midnight, of viewing Staffa in clear moonlight with an almost cloudless sky, a scene never likely to be forgotten by anyone fortunate enough to witness it. In the pale, cold light the dark and massive southern headlands thrust out into a glittering moon-silvered sea. Eastward rose the faint blue and purple outlines of the mountains of Mull, while to the south lay the small, dim form of Iona as if asleep on the sea. Slightly west of Iona, but much further off, appeared the welcome blinks of the Dubh Hirteach lighthouse. All around was silence save for the rumbling of the waves on the rocks and the occasional cry of a lone sea-bird. Surprising as it may seem, the isolation of our island home was impressed upon us more strongly by clear moonlight than on nights of darkness.

During our first week on Staffa the Atlantic swell was so heavy that the *Fusilier* was able to approach and land tourists only on two occasions—the day we landed and one other day. During the second week, however, the swell had worked round to a more westerly approach and had lessened sufficiently to allow her landing her passengers on the three alternate days scheduled (the regular daily service does not commence until the third week of the summer season). With the exception of those five hours or so of visitation to a fringe of the island, our only companions for the fortnight were the sea-birds and sheep, and perhaps the ghosts of the old inhabitants who may return to view the scenes of their lonely island home.

To be awakened in the morning by the sound of the sea and the gulls screaming overhead; to go out and kindle the morning fire in bright sunshine with white clouds drifting slowly across an azure sky, and see the waves breaking against the rocks in showers of flashing spray; to inhale ozone-laden winds that had swept many miles over the broad Atlantic without obstruction, and unsullied by smoke or dust, was an experience that made life feel good. The view in all directions helped to increase the feeling of invigoration. There was a sense of isolation, but not of loneliness, in our situation. To the true lover of the Wide Open Spaces there is no loneliness in wild nature. There are voices and companionship in the heaving billows, the drifting clouds, and the singing sea winds, in addition to the wild bird and animal life. This feeling or influence of untamed nature is not sentimental but elemental.

Owing to lack of light in our shelter, and as our cooking was done outdoors, we took our meals in the open air when weather permitted, attended usually by numerous seagulls squawking and squabbling loudly as they swooped overhead or perched on the walls of our ruin on the lookout for scraps of food. At all other times we ate in our shelter by candlelight.

The scenery surrounding Staffa is both grand and interesting, presenting a wonderful panorama of mountain, loch, sea and island, each with its storied past. Some of these stories tell of the advancement of the Cross of Christianity when the early Celtic saints risked life and limb in their arduous and perilous travels to spread the Gospel. These saints were not indolent dreamers or weaklings but men imbued with inspiration, active in body and mind and having the hardihood and zeal of true pioneers and servants of the Master. Other stories of Staffa's surrounding scenery tell of the advancement of that sinister symbol, the Fiery Cross, which summoned the clans to battle in days of old, when internecine feuds caused the heather to be drenched frequently with the blood of Highland warriors.

On a calm summer day the heat haze sheds an opalescent light which softens the outlines of the scenery, while a stiff breeze, especially from the north, and clear sky, causes each scenic object to stand out clearly in sharp relief.

Northward appears the long, low north-west projection of Mull, called Treshnish Point, and, much further off, the high jagged profiles of Skye, Rum, Eigg and other islands of the Inner Hebrides, also the higher peaks of the Moidart district of the mainland.

These northern islands and mountains recall many stirring events of the Jacobite Rising of 1745, when Prince Charles Edward Stuart—Bonnie Prince Charlie—made his daring and romantic attempt to win back the crown of his forefathers; a campaign of triumphs and tragedy and the turning-point of Highland history.

In the coast of Mull on the north side of Treshnish Point is the lovely little sandy bay of Calgary, open to the Atlantic, where there are only a few lonely dwellings. Indeed, Calgary is more of a placename than a place, thought there is evidence of a former larger settlement in the *laraich*, or crumbling ruins of humble cottages, now fading into the bracken; those inhabitants emigrated to America at the beginning of last century, during the time of the Highland Clearances. Although so insignificant and isolated, it is from this little settlement that the thriving City of Calgary, Alberta, Canada, derives its name. The name was given to the present site of Calgary, Canada, by Colonel J. F. MacLeod, a Skyeman, and one of the first Commissioners of the famous North-West Mounted Police (now the Royal Canadian Mounted Police)—the " Mounties." During a period of leave in Scotland, Colonel MacLeod spent some time at Calgary House, Mull, as the guest of Mr John Munro MacKenzie, who had bought the Calgary estate in Mull after being unable to obtain the estate of Letterewe in Ross-shire. Colonel MacLeod enjoyed his stay in Mull so much that he commemorated it after returning to Canada by giving the name Fort Calgary to the next most western outpost established by the North-West Mounted Police in Red Indian territory.

It is on the site of that fort that the city of Calgary, Canada, is built.

About four miles to the north-east of Staffa lies the Island of Gometra, which is separated by an almost imperceptible channel from the larger Island of Ulva. In this vicinity also are the small islands of Inchkenneth, Little Colonsay, and Eorsa. These islands lie at the entrance to a bight in the coast of Mull, called Loch na Keal. Each one has its own particular charm and interest. Ulva was the home of the paternal grandparents and birthplace of the father of Dr Livingstone, the African missionary and explorer. It was also the birthplace of Major General Lachlan Macquarie, an early Governor of Australia, who did much towards the development of that vast continent. Inchkenneth was, in the past, one of Iona's dependent islands and still retains the ruins of an ancient chapel and interesting burial ground. During Dr Johnson's famous tour of the Hebrides, he spent on Inchkenneth what he described as " the most agreeable Sunday he had ever passed," with Sir Alan MacLean and his family. Inchkenneth was for some time the property of Sir Harold Boulton, the well-known writer of Scottish songs, while Gometra was owned for several years by Mr Hugh Ruttledge, leader of the Mount Everest (climbing) Expedition, 1933.

To the east of Staffa, beyond a seven-mile stretch of sea, the coast of Mull projects in the peninsula of Gribun and Ardmeanach to the headland of Burg. Here the land rises in one vast sweep of precipice and terraced slope from sea level to a height of over one thousand six hundred feet, consisting of superimposed horizontal beds of lava and intervening beds of tuff.

Beyond this peninsula the mountains of Mull rise in grandeur, Ben More, the highest peak, towering to a height of 3,169 feet. On their lonely slopes and crags dwell the red deer and golden eagle. Set in the sea between Staffa and Gribun is the islet of Enisgeir, which, though of insignificant size, enters into the legends of Mull. On the south side of the peninsula the sea penetrates into Mull for about nine miles to form Loch Scridain. The name Scridain is derived from the Norse word *skrida*, meaning a land-slip, and the peninsula of Ardmeanach, which bounds Loch Scridain on the north, presents many huge landslips in its talus slopes. The outermost headland of Ardmeanach is called Burg, a name which is also Norse, derived from the word *borg*, meaning an eminence.

Although now sparsely populated, the island of Mull is famed in Highland history for its traditions, legends and superstitions; tales of clan feuds, love and romance and eerie supernatural happenings. There is an expression well known among West Highlanders and Islanders: "As superstitious as a Muileach" (Mull-man). Our present age of materialism and mechanism may scoff at these old Highland tales of the supernatural, but the minds of people dwelling in lonely places are undoubtedly more sensitive than ours to influences and happenings which would perhaps be better described as supernormal rather than supernatural. There are too many stories of these occurrences to allow us to attribute them all to mere imagination and coincidence: perhaps there is a sense, or faculty, highly developed in certain persons, that knows what can neither be seen nor heard.

Mull presents a striking landscape, which is repeated in the larger of its attendant isles, of long level lines of terraces rising one above the other, their upper parts composed of brown weathered basaltic crags and their base hidden by grass-covered talus slopes scarred by the bare grey channels of winter torrents. The loose boulders which lie scattered on the lower slopes and glens were believed by past generations to have been thrown out from the riddle of God when He made the world.

To the south-east of Staffa the nearest land is the low-lying peninsula of the Ross of Mull, about six miles distant, stretching in a westerly direction, bounded by the Atlantic on the south and Loch Scridain on the north. The deep-red granite coast-line of this projection of Mull contrasts strongly with its surface covering of green and golden bracken, varying shades of heather, and the cobalt sea washing its base. In the glow of a setting sun these colours become very vivid. Topping the low ridge of the Ross, but much further off, appear the hazy blue hills of the islands of Colonsay, Scarba, Jura and Islay.

About six miles to the south of Staffa, and lying off the western extremity of the Ross of Mull, is the green isle of Iona, sacred with the memory of St Columba and his followers who made it a centre from which to radiate religion and knowledge throughout heathen Scotland and to regions far beyond: " You never tread upon it but you set your feet upon some reverend history." Within its Royal burial ground lie sixty Scottish, Irish, and Norwegian kings, as well as many Lords of the Isles, clan chiefs, and other notable personages, while St Oran's Chapel, the Abbey, Nunnery, and Crosses, though of a much later period than that of St Columba, are relics of religious zeal and skilled craftsmanship. According to a prophecy attributed to St Columba, Iona shall once again attain her pristine pre-eminence in religious life:

> I-mo-chree, my heart's own isle,
> Where monks intone, shall cattle low:
> Yet ere the hills shall pass away,
> Thine altar lights again shall glow.

Although the distance separating Staffa from its illustrious neighbouring island of Iona is only six miles, the scenic difference between the two islands is remarkable. Staffa presents stern grandeur and impresses more by form than by colour, while Iona displays pastoral, or idyllic, beauty and is more a pattern of limpid colour than of form. The predominant colours of Staffa are the strong tones of viridian turf, umber cliffs, and ultramarine or prussian-blue sea, owing to the reflection from its dark, rocky bed; colours in keeping with a rich oil painting. The principal colours of Iona are the pastel shades of lime-green turf, creamy-white sands, emerald and cobalt sea, colours usually associated with a water-colour painting. Staffa may be described as the brunette and Iona as the blonde. Iona, with its low and broad fringe of gently sloping machair land, lies placid and verdant, set in the vivid green and blue Atlantic, whose foaming rollers sweep over and break on beaches of sheen white sand, to spend themselves in lacy foam. Its colourful and peaceful atmosphere is appreciated most in radiant sunshine or in the mellow glow of a clear evening. By contrast, Staffa suggests latent power as its dark mass rises sheer in stern grandeur from the deep, presenting a solemn sphinx-like mien. It appears most impressive in times of storm, when wind and sea roar in their riotous rampage and fragments of scud race across a leaden sky like the weird ride of the Valkyries; when the waves crash and climb high in a welter of white foam and spray on the dark frowning cliffs.

In one vast sweep from south to west stretches the unbroken horizon line of the Atlantic where Staffa is exposed to the full fury of the sea, and southerly and south-westerly winds are the most prevalent in this region.

Slightly north of due west, and about fifteen miles distant, stretch the long low-lying islands of Tiree and Coll, like thin streaks on the horizon. About ten miles south-west of Tiree stands Scotland's finest lighthouse, namely the Skerryvore, first lighted in 1844, which is world-famous in the realm of lighthouse engineering. The tower, to the underside of the lantern, is one hundred and thirty-eight feet high, and the small rock on which it stands is only about ten feet above sea level at high tide. This rock is situated in the centre of a small cluster of low, sea-swept rocks where the furious onslaughts of the Atlantic beat against the tower of the lighthouse; Tiree is the nearest land.

South of Iona stands another magnificent and lonely lighthouse, namely, Dubh Hirteach, first lighted in 1872. The tower to the underside of the lantern rises to a height of one hundred and six feet from a small rock about two hundred and fifty feet long and about thirty-five feet above sea level at high tide. This rock lies out in the Atlantic about fifteen miles south-west of the Island of Mull—the nearest land—and rises abruptly from deep water with no fringing rocks like those at Skerryvore, therefore it is struck by heavier seas than the Skerryvore. In rough weather, the solid seas sweep right over the rock and crash against the lighthouse tower, sometimes licking up in feathery tongues to near the gallery at the base of the lantern.

The rock of Dubh Hirteach forms the outpost of a dangerous reef stretching south-west from Mull, called the Torran Rocks, from the Gaelic word *torunn*, meaning " a loud murmuring noise, or growl," like distant thunder, because of the sound heard on Mull of the ceaseless seas breaking on these rocks. This reef should be familiar to readers of R. L. Stevenson's *Kidnapped*, as it was the scene of the wreck of the brig *Covenant* of Dysart. The Torran Rocks were also a favourite haunt of a famous West Highland witch called *Cailleach Bheur*.

Skerryvore lighthouse was designed by Alan Stevenson, uncle of R. L. S., while Dubh Hirteach lighthouse was designed by Thomas and David Stevenson, father and another uncle of R. L. S.

The far-off flashes of Dubh Hirteach lighthouse can be seen from Staffa on a clear night with the unaided eye, but the Skerryvore lies below the horizon. On two very clear nights during our stay on Staffa, we thought we saw above the horizon the loom of the flashes of the Skerryvore lighthouse. Since then, I have been informed by the Secretary of the Northern Lighthouse Board that our surmise was quite probable. I regret that in the last edition of this book I stated that we saw the flashes of the Skerryvore lighthouse from Staffa when I should have said the flashes of the Dubh Hirteach lighthouse.

About five miles to the north-west of Staffa, there is a chain of small uninhabited islands, stretching for about six miles in the shape of an arc, called the Treshnish Isles. They form one of the very few breeding places of the large grey, or Atlantic, seal, which brings forth its young during the stormy months of October and November. These islands are also the haunt of innumerable seabirds. They are really very seldom visited owing to their few available landing places and also to the miles of open sea which separate them from Mull and Iona, yet on the several occasions I have explored them I have found many subjects for my camera.

On one of the Treshnish Isles, called Cairnburg Mor, there are remains of a fort said to have been built on the site of a still older fort dating back to the time of the Norse possession of the Hebrides. The present ruins are believed to be those of a fort which originally belonged to the chief of clan MacDougall, Lord of Lorn. In 1354 he ceded it to the Lord of the Isles, who made his vassal MacLean of Duart hereditary keeper. It is said that during religious persecution on Iona the records and books of the Iona monastery were sent to this fort for safe keeping, but they were lost when Cromwell's forces besieged and captured it about 1651. John of Fordun, writing about 1380, says: "Out at sea, at a distance of four miles from Mull, is Carneborg, an exceeding strong castle."

On the small nearby island, called Cairnburg Beag, are the

ruins of a small fort or barrack with crenellated walls. The Cairnburg forts were garrisoned as recently as the Jacobite Rising of 1715. In the narrow channel separating these two islands, seals' heads keep bobbing up and down almost continually.

Another of the Treshnish Isles, which has a broad, flat brim and a rounded hill in the centre, is called the "Dutchman's Cap," but it is not known how it received this name, as it bears little resemblance to the cap of a typical Dutchman: it appears more like a large sombrero. It may be that the name Dutchman's Cap was given to this peculiar-shaped islet owing to a confusion between the Gaelic *ceap an Dutchaich* (" Dutchman's cap ") and *ceap an Doideag* (" Doideag's cap "). The pronunciation of these two Gaelic names is very similar. The *Doideag*, or *Doideag Mhuileach*, was a famous Mull witch about whom there are many tales in this region. The island, with its broad flat brim and high crown, is a very good representation of the typical witch's hat (in Gaelic it would be called " cap," as there is no Gaelic word for hat). The old legends ascribed to witches the power to change their form at will. Sometimes they assumed the form of an animal and sometimes the form of a giantess. The *Cailleach Bheur*, another famous Mull witch (Lewis Spence says she was an ancient Celtic goddess), is reputed to have been able to wade across the Sound of Mull knee-deep. The island would thus be appropriate as a hat for the Doideag when she was in the form of a giantess. This derivation is in keeping with the old custom of ascribing peculiar features of nature to witches and giants. The shape of this island has also been compared to that of a large targe, or shield (Gaelic, *sgiath mhor*), as used by Highland warriors in days of old, the little hill representing the *umbo*, or boss, in the centre of the targe. The correct, though less often used, name for this island is Baca (on Blaeu's *Atlas* of 1662 it is named " Back"), derived from the Norse words *bak*, meaning a back, or hump, and *ey*, meaning island; hence, *bak-ey*, hump island, the letter *a* being substituted for *ey*, as in the name Staffa. The Gaels have added the adjective *mor* (Gaelic for great, or big), thus making the name Baca Mor—the " big hump island "—to distinguish it from an islet nearby which they have named Baca Beag—the " small hump island." The latter name indicates that the

Gaels did not know the meaning of the word *Baca*, as the small island has no hump.   Baca Mor owes its peculiar form to pre-Glacial marine erosion; the brim marks the level formerly reached by the waves, and the hill, or crown, is the island that then stood alone above the sea.   At that time almost the whole of Staffa must have been submerged.

In addition to these four islands, the Treshnish group in-cludes Fladda and Lunga.   The latter island has a large colony of seabirds of many types, and at its northern end, in the shelter of the only hill, or hillock, called the Cruachan, are the ruins of about half a dozen old-type cottages with thick walls and rounded corners, deserted for about one hundred years and now peopled by nothing more than vague and shadowy memories. Towards the centre of this island and south of the hollow, called the Dorlinn, which almost cuts it in two, there is a deep circular hollow about twenty yards in diameter and about twenty feet deep, with sheer sides, except at one part where a stepped slope gives access.   Few persons who visit Lunga are aware that there is a dark tunnel exit from this hollow leading to the western cliffs of the island, from which point one can return to the Dor-linn by clambering along the rocky coast.

Far beyond the Treshnish Isles, on a clear day, appear the faint outlines of Barra and Uist, two of the Outer Hebrides famed in song and story.

The only claim which Staffa can make to treasure is vague references in the traditions of the neighbouring islanders.   They refer to the island having been used in the past as a rendezvous by the Vikings, those roving barbarians, both Danes and Nor-wegians, who terrorised and devastated the western seaboard and islands of Scotland and Ireland with their raids during the eighth and ninth centuries; the first of several brutal raids on Iona was in 795.   Their chiefs were really coastal kinglets with limited jurisdiction who owed no allegiance to their national king.   They adopted piracy as the easiest means of gaining wealth.   Ultimately some of the Norwegian Vikings settled in these regions of Scotland and refused to submit to the rule of Norway, so, about the year 890, a punitive expedition was sent out against them, which resulted in the annexation of the Western Isles of Scotland by Norway;   the Scottish king seems to have had too much trouble on hand elsewhere to allow him to interfere against the Norwegians. Even after that date Norway found it necessary to pursue with further raids in order to quell the rebellious islanders, including the Viking settlers.

The early Viking pirates and, later, the Norwegian sea forces sallied forth from their lairs in the Scandinavian coasts on their marauding expeditions against the western islands of Scotland during the summer months, and are believed to have secured their plunder and hoarded it at favourable places, Later on, they visited these caches, collected the loot and sailed home. I heard this belief regarding Staffa expressed in a rather ambiguous form. When I asked some of the neighbouring islanders if they knew how Fingal's Cave received its name they replied, " Oh yes, it is called after a great pirate named Fingal, who used to plunder the west coast and islands of Scotland and who hoarded his spoil on Staffa and kept his galley in the big cave." There is evidently a confusion here between the name of an individual Fingal and the Gaelic plural *Fionn-ghoill*, meaning the fair foreigners, or Norsemen. It was this answer which suggested to me the derivation of the name Fingal, as applied to Fingal's Cave, which I have given in Chapter VIII, namely, that it is a perpetuation of the memory of the Norsemen who possessed the island at one time. Staffa would form an excellent place for the Vikings to cache their loot temporarily as a small number of men could defend its few available landing places and sheer cliffs would prevent access to the island elsewhere. It is also on the direct route which they would follow when homeward bound.

If Staffa was one of the places where those seawolves hoarded their loot temporarily, some remnant may still remain on the island. Loss in battle or storm would sometimes mean a hurried retreat homeward, and that flight might result in some of their plunder remaining uncollected. Treasure, consisting of over three hundred tenth-century coins, a gold and silver brooch, and a piece of thick gold wire, was unearthed on the neighbouring island of Iona, in August 1950, by members of the Iona Community while excavating a drain in connection with the restoration of the Abbey. It was found at a depth of about two feet. Several guesses have been made as to the origin of this hoard. Authoritative opinion, based upon the discovery of similar hoards elsewhere, tends to the belief that this treasure was collected and hidden by Norse raiders who failed to recover it, perhaps during the raid on Iona in 986.

Under the varying weather conditions of this region, magnificent seascapes can be seen from Staffa, but the most impressive, certainly the most dramatic, is sunset in the Atlantic. The deep-blue ocean swell comes heaving inward in stately rhythm with, here and there, a foaming roller, the sky dappled and streaked with feathery cirrus or gleaming with billowing masses of snowy cumulus, while etched on the skyline, and about five miles off are the russet Treshnish Isles of Lunga and the Dutchman's Cap, long, low and level, except for a rounded knoll on each of them. As the sun sinks like a ball of fire into the sea, its glowing radiance sweeps over the whole scene; the sky becomes a luminous pale green; the clouds blaze with a flaming opalescence shot with beams of amber light; Lunga and the Dutchman's Cap become deep purple silhouettes, while the sea is splashed and flecked with a gorgeous gold and coppery lustre, presenting a kaleidoscopic spectacle which even the most prosaic could not help admiring.

Every evening, after tea and a wash-up, when the weather was favourable, our company of three climbed over the island to its western cliffs and there enjoyed our smoke viewing the sunset, and, when the sun sank below the horizon, watching for the first friendly blinks of the far-off Dubh Hirteach lighthouse beginning to flash their night-long warning to mariners. Adding life to the scene were the seabirds and seals disporting themselves until the afterglow deepening into twilight caused them to disperse. We then returned to our shelter and had supper alfresco in the pungent fragrance of our driftwood fire before turning in for the night.

The lines applied to Iona by William Winter, the American poet, apply equally well to Staffa:

> Gone the isle and distant far
> All its loves and glories are:
> Yet for ever, in my mind,
> Still will sigh the wand'ring wind,
> And the music of the seas,
> 'Mid the lonely Hebrides.

APPENDIX I

The following poem on Staffa was awarded the Newdigate Prize for Poetry at Oxford in 1832. It was written by Roundell Palmer, who capped a brilliant academic and legal career by attaining the position of Lord Chancellor in 1872. A few days after his appointment he was raised to the Peerage and became the first Earl of Selborne. The conditions required the poem to be written in the metre of Pope, though, occasionally, the influence of Wordsworth is apparent. The footnotes given here appear in the original publication.

STAFFA

The shades are gathering on the mountain's breast,
Where lone Ben Nevis rears his giant crest,
The stars are faintly glimmering into light
Round the pale chariot of the queen of night.
No curling foam, no ripping gales betray
The smooth swift currents on their noiseless way,
But calm is brooding on the tranquil deep
As though some spirit watched o'er Nature's sleep,
And tower, and cape, and crested island seem
To bask reclining in the mellow beam.
Charmed by the loveliness of that sweet hour,
Pride melts to reverence, Gloom forgets to low'r;
And there is peace to sorrow and to care,
Peace in the sapphire wave and star-lit air,
Peace in those orbs that whisper as they move,
Comfort and Hope and Holiness and Love.
And now 'tis sweet to soar on Rapture's wings
Beyond the narrow sphere of mortal things
To read the mystic characters of flame,
Which God's eternal majesty proclaim,
Stamped on his glorious works:—'tis sweet to glide
O'er the calm bosom of the Western tide,
Musing in silent thought on that fair scene,
Those clustering isles, and glassy waves between.
Bright is each jewel of the circling main,
Bleak Ulva's cliffs, and green Iona's plain.
But not bleak Ulva's promontoried steep,
Nor that green isle where Lochlin's heroes sleep.[1]

[1] Iona—where the ancient kings of Scotland and Scandinavia are buried.

Not the blue hills in Eastern distance lost,
Not the white range of Mull's retiring coast,
Can breathe a charm, or move a soul like thee,
Fair Staffa, peerless daughter of the sea.
Fair Staffa! Proudly on her crystal throne
She sits with marble crown and pillar'd zone,
And for the homage of obsequious slaves
Lists the rough music of the foamy waves—
Stern flatterers they! Full oft her shatter'd side
Has felt the shock of many a warring tide,
Though lifting their broad summits to the skies
Buttress on buttress, arch on arch arise,
Column on column piled! Projecting here,
Like some grey castle the tall rocks appear,
In stern commanding majesty severe:
There, swelling on the sight with gentler change,
Slope the long vista and descending range,
Till the dark surges and the curling spray
Close on the secrets of their onward way.
Yet oft the fisher, when the waters lie
All calm beneath some bright and summer sky,
Bending in curious gaze his eye profane
Through the clear azure of th' unruffled plain,
Follows their course, and many a fathom deep
Sees their light pillar'd forms around him sweep,
Bound the dark caves of Ocean to explore
And join their brethren on Ierne's shore.[1]
Oh! well in days of old might Fancy's child
With shadowy beings and creations wild
People that land of beauty—well might hear
Sounds of weird music bursting on his ear,
And deem that Morven's tutelary God
Held joyance proud in Staffa's lone abode!
For gorgeous as the dreams of heav'nly light
Which cheer some lovelorn poet's tranced sight,
Strange as the tales of Runic minstrels told
Of sea-girt domes and palaces of gold,
She smiles in rugged grace, and charms from rest
The last warm beam that gilds the crimson west.
Sweet are the voices of her cavern'd cells,
Where the grey bittern and the seabirds dwells,
Fair is each islet rock around her side
Darkening the gleamy surface of the tide,
Like the pale star which veils its humble rays
Beneath some neighbouring planet's prouder blaze.

---

[1] Alluding to the submarine connection which was supposed to exist between Staffa and the Giant's Causeway.

— But whither wanders the transported glance,
Breathless, and fixed in mute amazement's trance?
Oh! 'tis some wondrous pile of fairy birth,
Born but to fade, too beautiful for earth!
So tenderly the glittering moonbeams fall
Through the deep shadows of the vaulted hall,
Tracing each niche, each column silvering o'er,
And streaming full upon the wave-beat floor!—
Haply pavilioned on his pearly throne,
Beneath that arching canopy of stone,
Old Ocean sits; or at some sorcerer's will
Rose yon proud fabric of mysterious skill,
From the dark bosom of the rock profound,
To pensive lute, or timbrel's gentle sound.
For never did the work of mortal hand
Vie with that natural temple, or command
Such reverence and deep awe.   The brooding air
Breathes holiness around, and whispers prayer;
The pillar'd rocks their silent voices raise,
The deep sea murmurs her Creator's praise.
Nor wants there blazon'd roof or sculptur'd dome,
O'er which the worshipper's rapt eye may roam—
What though no vain device, no tinsel glare,
No monument of human pride be there,—
The moulded rock is nobler far than they,
The spangled crystal shames their flaunting ray:
And that unchiselled fretwork might not yield
To gilded tracery, or storied shield.
Yet thence, in transport gazing, till his heart
Thrill'd with the rapturous hopes of dawning art,
The unlettered architect of Morven drew
Science more noble than the Grecian knew,
And bade yon shadow Minster's vaulted pile
Frown on the waves which guard Iona's isle.[1]
Alas, Iona!—sternly o'er thy brow
Long years have past, and laid thine honours low!—
For hands may raise the column and the shrine,
And bid the trophied arch and cornice shine,—
But that high privilege to vanquish fate
Hands cannot give, nor will of man create.
They cannot give the wonder and the fear
Inspired by giant rock and mountain drear,
The solitude, the stern magnificence,
The willing thraldom of the awe-struck sense,

[1] The Cathedral of Iona is visible from Staffa.   May not the idea of such a
building be supposed to have been derived from such a source?

And that mysterious sanctity sublime,
And those dread memories of primeval time.
— 'Twere sweet at dead of night to muse alone
On yon grey beach with matted seaweed strown,
Nor heed the passing hours' swift flight, nor give
One thought to this vain world in which we live.
Alone, but not companionless:—the shore,
The battlemented cliffs and columns hoar,
And yon pale orb with melancholy smile
Gilding each headland of the desert isle.
These have their language to the feeling mind
Deep, still, and eloquent,—in these we find
A charm, a sympathy, a sacred tie,
A link of fellowship to worlds on high!
Nor here does Silence reign:—the seamew's yell
Complaining from her airy citadel,
The hoarse loud murmur of the chafing waves,
The sleepless echoes of a thousand caves,
Swell in wild chorus;—though the busy strife,
The stirring energy of human life,
Intrudes not there—though no proud cities shine,
Though no tall vessel stems the boisterous brine,—
Nor glade nor forest of luxuriant green
Disturbs the barren grandeur of the scene.
From those rude clefts no mountain flow'ret springs,
No clustering shrub to those lone pillars clings,
The glossy saxifrage of purple hue,
The golden samphire, or the tufted yew.
All, all is desolate.   The eagle there
Has fixed her place of refuge high in air,
Queen of the feathered tribes which love to dwell
In the scarr'd bosom of the rifted fell.
There, when contending winds are loud and high,
When waves on waves are mounting to the sky,
Poised on sure wings above the rolling flood,
In mazy circles round her callow brood
She wheels exulting, and with clamorous voice
Bids the dark spirits of the storm rejoice,—
Or, gorged with carnage, from her grim repast
Rides on her homeward flight the wintry blast.
Above—around—in wild confusion hurl'd
The shatter'd remnants of a former world,—
The broken shaft, the shelving colonnade,
The deep rock rifted from its marble bed—
All tell of God's great vengeance—when the sky
Yawned on the land—when Heav'n's whole armoury

Whelm'd the wide earth. The fountains of the sea
Broke from their central caverns fierce and free,
Wave upon mountain wave! While worlds survive,
That day's wild memory still unchanged shall live,
Graved on the summits of the cloudcapt hills,—
Traced in the channels of a thousand rills,—
Stamped on the relics of a mightier birth,—
Recorded in the marble womb of earth!
Yet in that hour of bitterness and dread
Sweet Mercy did her dovelike wings outspread,
And order smiled again; her sovereign will
Bade the fierce ministers of wrath be still,
Chased the rude Ocean from her realm profound,
And marshalled all her elements around,
Each in his several station, kind on kind
Harmonious ranged, and hue and hue combined.
She clothed the mountain in his craggy vest,
And stored with secret wealth his teeming breast;
She paved with marble Moray's shelving bed,
She crowned with adamant Ben Nevis' Head,
And bade yon clustering range of pillars sweep
From Staffa's cave to Antrim's haunted steep.
And what though vainly man's presumptuous sight
Would pierce the gloom of unrecording night,
Trace the deep steps of Earthquake and of Flame,
And ask the voiceless stone from whence it came?
It was not Chance, it was not Fortune blind
Which rear'd the pile, and yon proud arch design'd,—
Nor that vain phantom Fate:—but One was there
Whom the Flame worships and the Earthquakes fear.
For there the Warrior of the Northern sea
Curbed the strong arm and bowed the stubborn knee,
There the rude fisher of the isles adored
The wand'ring shade of Morven's fabled lord,
There in high joy the Child of Wisdom[1] trod,
And poured the rapture of his soul to God.
And still, while Staffa gems the Western wave,
While the winds murmur in the pillar'd cave,
Still on that holy ground the stranger's prayer
Shall seek the maker of a scene so fair,
And rise in fervent thankfulness to bless
The Great, the Merciful, whom these confess.

ROUNDELL PALMER,
Trinity College.

[1] Sir Joseph Banks.

APPENDIX II

This poem on Staffa was published anonymously in the *Metropolitan Magazine* at the beginning of last century. It is believed to have been written by a nobleman. In 1834 it was reproduced in a book entitled *The Recess, or Autumnal Relaxation in the Highlands and Lowlands*, by James Johnson, an Irish doctor, who also wrote under the *nom-de-plume* of Frederick Fag, from which source I derived it. As Johnson's book is long since out of print, I think it worth while preserving the poem here.

The footnotes given here appear in the original publication.

STAFFA

I've gazed on Nature in the sleeping lake,
The vine-clad hill, the wildly-tangled brake—
I've heard her whisper in the flutt'ring trees,
Sing in the brook, and murmur in the breeze,
Until her quiet music to my heart
Would peace, and love, and happiness impart;
And every fretful feeling die away,
Like lover's frowns before his loved One's lay.
And then I've turned on wilder scenes to brood,
And court thee, Nature, in thy sterner mood.
Helvetia's cliffs—the glacier high and hoar—
The moaning cavern, and the cataract's roar—
The cloud-envelop'd mountain's tranquil pride—
The gloomy forest sleeping on its side—
Do not such scenes of liveliness control
With majesty—with beauty win the soul?
Nor need the breast which glows at sights like these
Thirst for the climes beyond our native seas;
Not Mont Blanc's brow or Jungfrau piled on high,
Or glacier glittering in the clear blue sky,
Such solemn awe—such pleasing fear impart—
As Staffa's isle, where Nature scoffs at Art!
There, on the bosom of the wildest sea,
That longs to trespass on earth's boundary,
'Neath low'ring skies, amid whose twilight grey
The joyous sunbeams seem afraid to play—
Serenely calm, in solitary pride,
A glorious pile reposes on the tide.

From Ocean's depths the giant columns rise,
And lift the self-born structure to the skies.
Firm on its rocky base each pillar stands—
No chisell'd shaft, no work of mortal hands.
Ere man had ceased in savage woods to dwell,
Roots for his food, his drink the crystal well;
Ere yet he knew the joys of social life,
And scarcely sought his fellow but in strife;
Ere cities grew, or Parian marble shone,
Yon columns stood—and stand while they are gone.
Yet many a broken pillar strew'd around,
And many a vista levell'd to the ground,
Proclaim that not e'en Nature's works are free,
All-conquering Time, from thy sure mastery!
Much hast thou spared, yet still the eye can trace
A thousand relics of colossal grace;
Which, mouldering in magnificent decay,
Tell of the wonders of a former day—
Of many a lofty palace now no more,
When Staffa stretch'd her arms to Antrim's shore;
And her huge walls could other tenants vaunt
Than the sad wind, or screaming cormorant;
Though now the wild wave washes over all,
And sports the kraken[1] in the giant's hall![2]
Then, mortal, blush to own the selfish grief
Which prompts a murmur if thy days be brief;
When Nature's brightest glories disappear,
Shall thy mortality demand a tear?
Mark where the portal, yawning o'er the wave,
Reveals to view the beauties of the cave;
Majestic columns raise on either side
The arched canopy above the tide,
Which, mildly glittering with a starry light,
Shines like the spangled firmament of night.
Deep to the island's heart recedes the dome,
Till fade its lengthening vistas in the gloom.
'Tis Nature's palace! scorning to abide
In temples less in reverence rear'd than pride;
The surges roar more grateful to the ear,
And tempest-hymn, than voice of hollow prayer;
She fled, disdainful of a Doric fane,
And built her minster on th' Atlantic main.

---

1 The Kraken, largest of living animals, is a native, or rather is supposed to be a native, of northern seas. 2 It is still the fond belief of many an Antrim peasant, that Staffa was united to the Giant's Causeway by a colonnade of basalt pillars, and that the immense city was tenanted by a gigantic race, whose wondrous actions are still the theme of many an interesting legend.

Still, as we gaze, a feeling more intense
Grows with each look, and steals on every sense;
The frowning arch above, the sea below,
The time-cemented pillars' serried row;
The sea-mews flitting from their rocky nest,
Like sullen broodings from a gloomy breast—
The ocean wrestling with the pile in vain,
That hurls its breakers back in calm disdain—
Blend in a scene so solemn, yet so fair,
That man seems almost an intruder there!
Each hollow blast, that slowly dies away,
Sounds like some spirit's melancholy lay;
And, as th' harmonious cave sends forth its song
You scarce would start to see an airy throng
Of mermaids, flitting o'er th' unruffled wave,
And breathing low, soft dirges through the cave!
Here, too, 'tis said, when storms convulse the day,
And ruddy lightnings gild the glistening spray,
Loud o'er the tempests noisy revelry,
Fingal's pale ghost shrieks out his battle-cry!
Or, when the trembling moonbeams meekly fall
In timid reverence on the haunted hall,
Hold sweet communion with each passing cloud,
Perchance some once-loved warrior's sable shroud![1]
Let Reason coldly smile; I blame them not
Who with such spirits people such a spot.
There is a stillness—but not of the grave—
A breathless life within that wondrous cave—
A deep contentment—a mute harmony—
A holy presence that we cannot see,
But yet can feel; for Ocean murmurs on,
As if in prayer, his deep-toned orison;
And winds without, that rage in lawless din,
Are hush'd to music as they enter in.
Oh! let the sceptic, on whose doubting eyes
In vain the beauties of creation rise;
Who, while he views the loveliness of earth,
Can yet disown the power that gave it birth—
Here let him gaze, and say 'twas chance alone,
That rear'd the pile and nicely carved the stone,
That lent each shaft such noble symmetry—
Alas! it mocks his poor philosophy,
Suggests a truth he little dreamt before—
Man was not made to question, but adore!

[1] It was one of the doctrines of Runic mythology, that the soul of the brave who had died in battle, wandered among the heavens in light fleecy clouds for some time after death.

INDEX